COLLINS

HOW TO IDENTIFY

TREES

HarperCollins*Publishers*
77–85 Fulham Palace Road
London W6 8JB

98 00 02 01 99

2 4 6 8 10 9 7 5 3 1

First published 1998

Patrick Harding dedicates this book to his wife Jean and children Martin and Bryony.
Gill Tomblin dedicates this book to Alfie's memory.

Patrick Harding has taught biology and natural history to adults for over 20 years. Author, freelance lecturer and study tour leader, he is based in Sheffield. His other titles include Collins Gem Photoguide *Mushrooms & Toadstools*, and (with Tony Lyon) Collins *How to Identify Edible Mushrooms*.

Artist Gill Tomblin trained at Bath Academy of Art and the Central School of Art in London. She has illustrated many books on natural history, gardening and children's fiction and non-fiction.

ISBN 0 00 220067 8

Designed by Wilderness design, Rochester, Kent
Colour reproduction by United Graphic Pte., Singapore and Saxon Photolitho
Printed and bound by Rotolito Lombarda SpA, Milan, Italy

COLLINS

HOW TO IDENTIFY

TREES

PATRICK HARDING • GILL TOMBLIN

HarperCollins*Publishers*

CONTENTS

CONTENTS

What is a Tree?

A TREE IS A SELF-SUPPORTING, PERENNIAL PLANT capable of reaching at least 6m in height, normally with a single woody stem (trunk) from which branches grow to form a crown.

A woody stem (see next page) is also a feature of shrubs (also termed bushes) – these are usually less than 6m high and have many stems arising from near ground level. See fig. 1.

Woody-stemmed climbers such as Ivy and Honeysuckle require a wall, fence or tree for support if they are to reach above 6m so are not classed as trees.

Trees do not form a distinct group of plants as, for example, ferns do, but are defined by their growth form. This is influenced by many factors including soil conditions, wind damage, available space and above all, management. A parkland Hawthorn can exceed 6m with a single trunk: it is a tree. The same species in a hedge forms a low growing, multi-stemmed, shrub.

As with other examples in biology, attempts to pigeon-hole species into different categories are problematical. Boundaries are rarely distinct. Purists would classify Hazel, Elder, Juniper and Wayfaring Tree as shrubs but they are all native species which can reach tree height (though usually with many stems), so I have included them in this book along with a number of dwarf garden cultivars (varieties) of trees such as Box.

Species of tree are found in both major groups of the Flowering Plants; Broad-leaved trees are Angiosperms (flowering plants with seeds hidden in an ovary). Gymnosperms (plants with naked seeds) include Conifers (cone bearing trees) which are mostly evergreen with needle or scale-like leaves and a more symmetrical growth pattern.

Angiosperms with two seed-leaves are classed as Dicotyledons; those with one as Monocotyledons. Families in the former group include Primulaceae with only non-woody, herbaceous plants (herbs); Fagaceae with only trees and Rosaceae with herbs, shrubs and trees. Palm trees are Monocotyledons and have unbranched stems covered with old leaf bases.

Casual observation can lead to mistaken identification; Alder has tiny cone-like fruit but its protected seeds, broad leaves and other characters place it among the Broad-leaved Angiosperm trees. Maidenhair Tree has a broad leaf but is a primitive Gymnosperm, more closely related to the Conifers than the Broad-leaved trees.

Most books on tree identification order species under Broad-leaved or Conifers and within these major sections trees are grouped within their families. This book concentrates on leaf shape (and configuration) so related species which differ greatly in leaf shape are described in different sections. Tree classification is outlined on pp.179–82.

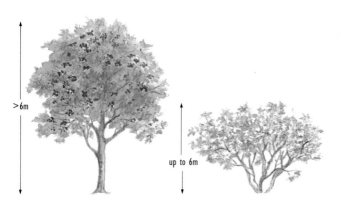

>6m

up to 6m

Fig. 1: Tree, shrub, climber

What is Wood?

ONE OF THE DEFINING CHARACTERISTICS OF A TREE is the presence of a woody stem. Some trees are grown for aesthetic reasons, others for their edible fruits, but most are harvested for their woody stems.

Trees have an extensive root system which absorbs water and dissolved minerals from the soil as well as providing anchorage. Tree leaves manufacture soluble sugars from the water and atmospheric carbon dioxide, using the power of sunlight (photosynthesis). These sugars provide the whole tree with food and become incorporated into more complex substances such as cellulose, fats and proteins.

Just as blood vessels in an animal form a transport system in which oxygen, dissolved food and other substances can reach all parts of the body so flowering plants have developed a vascular system. Veins in leaf blades contain vascular tissue of two kinds, xylem which transports water and dissolved minerals (root-sap) into the leaf where photosynthesis occurs and phloem which transports the sugar-laden leaf-sap to other parts of the plant. In the petiole (leaf stalk) and in young stems transport occurs in the xylem and phloem of the vascular bundles.

In herbaceous perennials most of the above-ground part dies down each winter (in annuals the whole plant dies) and the narrow stem is made up of soft cells (pith) interspersed with vascular bundles. Tree stems do not die back but increase in diameter from new tissue added each year.

From its second year a tree shoot changes from one of discrete vascular bundles in pith to a pattern where a thin ring of actively dividing cambium cells produces new xylem (wood) on its inner surface and new phloem (bast) on its outer surface. The wood volume increases every year but the bast remains a thin layer just below the bark cambium. As the circumference of the stem grows the original outer layer splits and is replaced by bark which forms a waterproof barrier and limits entry by fungi and insects. Breathing pores (lenticels) allow the passage of air and these and other characteristics of the bark are a useful aid to identification.

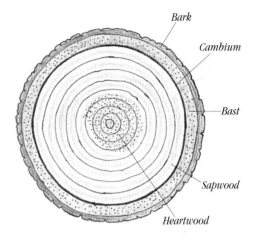

Fig. 2: Cross-section of woody stem

Water continues to be transported up the xylem in what is known as sapwood which also provides strength and acts as a storage tissue. In most trees after some 10–20 years, the older vessels (nearer the stem centre) become filled with a hard, insoluble chemical (lignin), and their function alters from transport to support. This heavier heartwood is typically darker and often contains chemicals such as tannins (Broad-leaved trees) or resins (Conifers) which help prevent insect and fungal attack.

Both heartwood and sapwood are used as timber. The latter is not always undesirable; a high proportion of sapwood in a young Scots pine would make a better telegraph pole as sapwood soaks up more timber preservative than does heartwood.

Timber from Broad-leaved trees is referred to as hardwood and that from Conifers as softwood. Anatomically the Conifers and other woody Gymnosperms are not as highly evolved as the Broad-leaved Angiosperm trees and the xylem con-

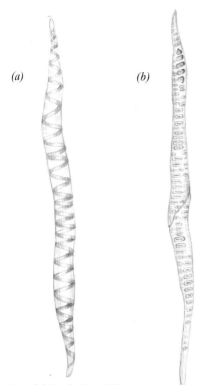

(a)   *(b)*

growth results in a series of annual rings from which the age of a tree can be determined. (See fig. 4.) In sub-tropical regions there may be more than one limiting season and more than one growth ring per year while in tropical rain forests there may be no annual growth check and hence no annual rings.

Water and its dissolved contents are not only conducted up and down the stem but also laterally as materials go into and out of storage and this takes place in ray tissue which runs across the rings. Large rays are a feature of hardwoods such as Oak; softwoods have only small rays and thus a less pronounced grain.

Every species of tree has a different arrangement of cells making up its wood and this produces a characteristic colour (or colours), pattern, grain, texture and even smell which enable experts to determine the species from which a wood sample has come. Differences in hardness, toughness, elasticity and durability help explain why timber from different species has been used for a wide range of purposes (see pp.19–21).

Fig. 3: (a) Tracheid and (b) vessel

sists only of tracheids which are very narrow cells running vertically up the stem. The Broad-leaved trees have wider vessels in addition to tracheids, allowing a faster flow of liquid and greater physical support. (See fig. 3). Even so some Gymnosperm trees such as Yew have very hard wood and the soft-wooded Balsa tree is Broad-leaved!

New wood is laid down on the inner side of the cambium every year. Broad-leaved Ring-porous species such as Oak and Ash produce large, pale-coloured, thin-walled tracheids and vessels (pores) in spring but during the summer these are smaller, darker and with much thicker walls. Diffuse-porous species such as Beech and Birch show less difference between spring and summer wood but as with all northern temperate species there is no wood growth during late autumn or winter. For most temperate trees this pattern of

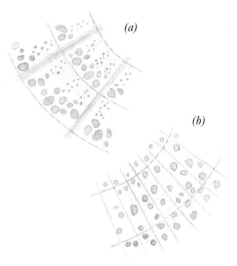

(a)

(b)

Fig. 4: Sections showing (a) ring-porous and (b) diffuse porous growth

Tree Longevity

TREE HEIGHT AND SPREAD INCREASE WITH AGE but in old trees growth may stop and size can be reduced by loss of branches. As a result tree size is not an accurate predictor of age.

As new wood is added each year so the circumference (girth) of the trunk (or bole) increases. Although the increase per year is greatest in young trees and the thickness of new rings declines with age, the average girth increase for most mature native trees is about 1in (2.5cm) per year. Bole girth is now measured at 1.3m from the ground and must not include swelling due to burrs (caused by abnormal proliferation of bud growth) or side branches. A girth of some 12.5ft (3.8m) indicates about 150 years for a spaced tree but trees from dense woodland grow much slower and take 250–300 years to reach the same girth.

London Plane and many introduced species including some of the Redwoods, Firs, Cedars and Gum Trees have a much faster growth rate and the above formula will over-estimate their age. Mature Scots Pine, Yew and Horse Chestnut have a slower rate and the formula under-estimates their age.

Counting the annual rings in felled trees or in core samples from living trees is a much more precise estimate of age. Unfortunately many ancient trees are hollow; decay of inner wood does not affect transport of water which takes place in young tissue near the periphery but it does make accurate dating difficult. Historical records of large or important trees may help to date them.

As with animals different species of tree have differing lifespans. The oldest known trees are Bristlecone Pines in California where individuals can live for 5,000 years.

Yews in Britain can live for at least 2,000 years but their slow growth rate and tendency to go hollow makes exact dating difficult. Oak can exceed 500 but Beech rarely lives more than 250 years.

Few Birches in Southern England reach 100 but in the climate of northern Scotland many reach 200. Some introduced species have not yet reached maturity in Britain but we cannot assume their lifespan will be the same as in their native lands. Climate, soil and disease (especially fungi) all affect longevity.

Windthrow (when a tree blows over or the bole snaps) and fungal attack are the most common natural causes of tree death. In many cases coppicing a tree (see p.17) not only reduces wind damage and delays fungal attack but results in a tree where the stump is considerably older than the current trunk (or trunks). Previously coppiced trees may be much older than their girth measurements suggest.

Hazel has a natural lifespan of about 150 years but some coppiced individuals have been found to be over 1,500 years old.

Fig. 5: Ancient hollow Yew in churchyard

Tree Biology

IT IS POSSIBLE TO IDENTIFY TREES without knowing how they grow and reproduce but a knowledge of tree biology not only aids identification, it makes the subject much more interesting.

Seed size, shape and weight differ enormously between species. Several thousand of the tiny, winged seeds of Birch represent a fraction of the weight of the large, heavy seeds of Horse Chestnut. Willow seeds are only viable for a few hours after being dispersed and will die if they don't quickly come to rest in suitable conditions. Seeds often fail to germinate immediately even in suitable conditions; the seed is dormant.

Seed dormancy may be physical (eg. an impermeable seed coat) or chemical. The action of frost, rain or an animal's digestive juices may be needed to break down a thick seed coat or remove a chemical inhibitor. When the seeds of Handkerchief Tree were first brought into this country from China they did not germinate until thrown onto a compost heap where fungal activity and alternating temperature broke the dormancy.

Seeds from a tree do not all germinate at the same time thus reducing the risk of the entire stock being killed by one event eg. fire or frost. A staggered pattern of germination increases the likelihood that some will develop into young trees (saplings). Seeds need water, air (so will not readily germinate under water) and an adequate temperature for germination. Many will only germinate in the dark (the action of mammals and birds burying seeds can be beneficial) but others such as Scots Pine and Silver Birch germinate better in the light. Both are pioneer species often growing in open ground where light intensity is high.

The root emerges first and under the influence of gravity grows down into the soil. Tiny root hairs develop which actively absorb water and dissolved minerals to supply the young seedling. The roots also anchor the plant. By this time the shoot has emerged and grows towards the light.

The first or seed-leaves are known as cotyledons and are often of a different size and shape to subsequent leaves. Broad-leaved trees are Dicotyledons: they have two cotyledons. Palm trees belong to the Monocotyledons and typically have only one seed leaf. A few Conifers (gymnosperms) have two cotyledons; most have many more (see fig.6) but are all included in the Dicotyledons.

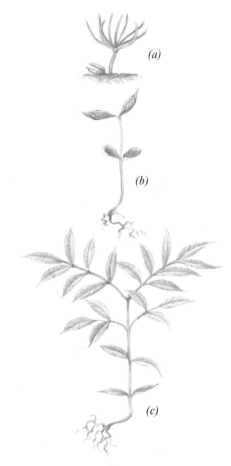

Fig. 6: a) Norway Spruce seedling (conifer)
b) Beech seedling
c) Ash seedling

Some trees (eg. species of Juniper and Gum Tree) produce juvenile leaves in the first year or two of growth which differ in shape from subsequently produced adult leaves.

Leaves from the upper canopy of a tree are typically smaller and thicker than those from the more shaded lower regions; colour and shape can also vary. In many Conifers the leaf arrangement on young and old growth differs. Juvenile needles of Scots Pine are borne singly, adult needles are borne in pairs. When collecting leaves for identification try not to gather them from the youngest growth; they may be atypical.

Most Broad-leaved trees in north temperate regions are deciduous – that is they drop their leaves in autumn (having first withdrawn valuable nutrients, a process which often produces colour changes) and grow new ones the following Spring. This prevents the soft tissues from being damaged by frost but also significantly reduces the amount of water loss as large amounts evaporate from leaves. The ability of roots to absorb water from frozen soil is severely limited so those trees that retain their leaves (evergreens) have water retaining features such as a waxy covering eg. Holly and Holm Oak.

Most Conifers are evergreen and have leaves of reduced size (needle-like in Pines and scale-like in Cypresses) which helps to reduce water loss. Individual leaves live for up to four or five years most being shed in autumn. Deciduous Conifers include the Larches and Dawn Redwood.

In temperate regions shoot growth stops in autumn. A terminal bud continues the main shoot growth in the following Spring. Side-buds develop into branches. Introduced Gum Trees continue to grow in Winter and have only minute buds; this latter feature is also found in some introduced Conifers. Bud position, size and shape, plus the number of protective scales, are all important criteria for the identification of trees in winter.

The regularity of branching and the angle which the branches make with the main trunk, together with the length of unbranched bole, all vary with different species. Many Conifers have a very regular, whorled branch pattern contrasting with the more random branching in Broad-leaved trees. When the main bud in Ash is damaged the next pair of buds take over, producing a forked habit. The outline shape of the branches is called the crown and is a useful diagnostic feature for spaced trees (see fig. 7 below).

Fig. 7: Branching pattern in Ash, Oak, Norway Spruce and Lombardy Poplar

Sexual Reproduction

HERBACEOUS ANNUALS PRODUCE FLOWERS AND SEEDS within a few months of germinating but long-lived perennials such as trees take much longer. Pines and Larches produce seed after as little as 10 years but Beech remains fruitless for about 30 years. Modern fruit trees have been bred to flower young and many result from the grafting of sexually mature material.

Once trees reach sexual maturity some, including Sycamore and Maple, produce a seed crop most years. In contrast Ash tends to produce seeds every other year. Beech and Oak show a less regular pattern with good (mast) years often synchronized over the country. A mast year usually follows one with a hot, sunny summer when trees build up large food reserves. Masting also occurs in conifers such as Spruce and Scots Pine. The seeds of all these species are vulnerable to predation from mammals (eg. Squirrels) and birds (eg. Jays) and the irregular production of bumper crops is regarded as a mechanism to ensure that in those years the seed supply outstrips the predatory demands and some seeds survive.

Flowering season, flower structure and the shape of the flowerhead (inflorescence) differ even between closely related species. Some Broad-leaved species such as Lime and Horse Chestnut flower in summer and have perfect flowers with an outer whorl of sepals (often green), an inner whorl of petals surrounding the male anther-bearing stamens which produce pollen and the central female pistil composed of a basal ovary with a stalk-like style ending in a stigma.

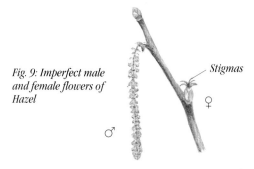

Fig. 9: Imperfect male and female flowers of Hazel

Stigmas

♂ ♀

flowers lack sepals and petals. Showy petals are unnecessary and would, like leaves, get in the way of pollen wafting in the wind.

Conifers are wind pollinated and have separate male and female flowers, usually in different parts of the same tree. This monoecious condition is also found in many Broad-leaved species but a few including Holly and the Willows are dioecious, having separate male and female individuals. No male holly tree will bear berries. Some Ash trees bear both male and female flowers, others are all male or all female and are not always the same sex from one year to another!

Following fertilisation seeds develop while other parts of the flower fall away or become parts of the fruit. Fruits play an important role in seed dispersal. Birds and mammals disperse the seeds of Cherry and Yew having eaten the fleshy fruit. Wind wafts the winged fruits of Sycamore and the feathery plumes of Willow. Most Conifers have a woody cone fruit containing winged seeds. Fruits may ripen quickly as in Ash where they develop as the new leaves emerge or take 4–5 months as in Oak or over two years as in Juniper. The shape, size, colour and texture of fruits are definitive for different tree species.

Stamen
Petal
Sepal
Pistil

Fig. 8: Perfect flower of Lime

Trees with perfect flowers are usually insect pollinated and in addition to the visual attraction of the flowers may, like Lime, produce nectar to attract bees. In contrast trees such as Hazel and Elm are wind pollinated and flower early, before the leaves emerge. Their imperfect, separate sex

Origins of the Wildwood

TREES HAVE BEEN A PART OF THE BRITISH FLORA for millions of years and prior to the Pleistocene period (nearly two million years ago) included species now native only in warmer climates and the New World.

Areas of deep snow and ice coupled with low temperatures during the Ice Ages severely reduced the number of plant species in Britain. The last of a series of glaciations began about 110,000 B.C. and this Devensian period ended about 12,000 B.C.

Some authors state that no trees survived in Britain during the colder parts of the Devensian period but others present evidence for survivors in the tundra-like conditions. These include Arctic (or Dwarf) Birch – *Betula nana*, still frequent in highland Scotland and Arctic (or Dwarf) Willow – *Salix herbacea*, still found in upland N. Britain. Another contender is the prostrate form of Juniper – *Juniperus communis* ssp. *alpina*.

None of the above species fits the strict definition of a tree (see p.6); all are low-growing shrubs. Some trees may have survived but not where there is land today. During the Ice Age so much water was locked up in snow and ice that sea levels were considerably lower than they are today. Land south of Ireland and west of Cornwall (away from the extreme cold), is thought to have harboured the Strawberry Tree. As temperatures rose, it spread into S.W. Ireland before the increased sea level submerged its previous habitat.

Lower sea levels at the end of the Devensian period uncovered land in southern parts of the Irish Sea, in the North Sea and in the English Channel. Land bridges linked Britain with Ireland, Brittany, and the Netherlands. Trees which had not been able to endure the intense cold in the north survived in southern parts of mainland Europe. When conditions improved the land bridges enabled them to recolonise Britain and Ireland.

Rising sea levels submerged the South-western bridge and southern Ireland was separated by the Irish Sea as early as 10,000 B.C. but there may have been a bridge between Northern Ireland and Scotland as late as 8,200 B.C. The link between England and mainland Europe was cut later, prob-

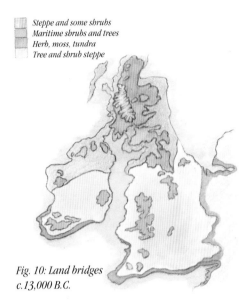

Steppe and some shrubs
Maritime shrubs and trees
Herb, moss, tundra
Tree and shrub steppe

Fig. 10: Land bridges c.13,000 B.C.

ably between 6,300 and 5,500 B.C. There was a much shorter period for trees to recolonise Ireland which is one reason why it has fewer native trees (warm-loving species such as Beech came north too late to be able to cross to Ireland and are not native there). Snakes also never made it to Ireland – St Patrick had nothing to banish!

The story of the overland return of tree species to form the native Wildwood of Britain and Ireland is still being deciphered. Wood, as with other plant material, does not decompose if kept permanently wet and the stumps of 'bog-oaks' (and Pines) have been found in fenland and peat-bog sites. Features of the wood (see p.8) enable samples to be identified while several methods are used for dating.

When carbon (from atmospheric CO_2) is incorporated into plant tissues it includes a tiny amount of naturally radioactive C-14. This slowly reverts to normal C-12 at a regular rate. Carbon-dating of wood relates to its percentage of C-14 content.

A much more accurate method of dating tree samples is that of dendrochronology. As previously explained (see p.8) seasonal variation in the size of new wood cells produces ring-like bands and counts of these annual rings from the trunk centre to the outer edge indicate the tree's age (see fig. 11). Initially the method was used only to estimate the age of living trees (using a bore sample) or complete trunk cross-sections. The realisation that the particular pattern of thick and thin rings in any geographic area resulted from a unique sequence of climatic conditions (eg. from 1820–45) enabled accurate dating of small samples and non-trunk material (see fig.12).

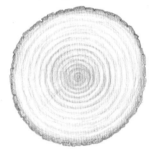

Fig. 11: Trunk showing 12 annual rings

Using overlapping sources including building timbers, wooden picture frames, archaeological artefacts and bog-trees a British tree-ring sequence has been assembled for certain species (fig. 12). That for Oak reaches back over 7,000 years.

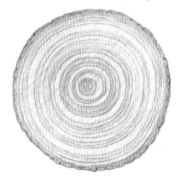

Fig. 12: Sequence of annual ring thickness in Oak

Evidence for the timing of recolonisation by certain tree species and the composition of the post-glacial Wildwood comes from Palynology – the study of pollen grains. Most species of plant can be identified by microscopic observation of the size, shape and pattern of their pollen grains. Waterlogged conditions prevent the growth of fungi and bacteria which normally cause pollen to decay. Analysis of pollen from carbon dated peat or mud deposits indicates which trees were present and when. The relative abundance of each species is estimated from the amounts of pollen found.

The picture is clouded by several factors. There is however a paucity of suitable sites in central and S. England. Species (Alder and Willow) which frequent wet sites, will be over-represented; those from dry habitats or which produce less pollen (eg. Small-leaved Lime) will be under-recorded.

Despite the shortcomings of the various dating methods we can form some idea of how our woods developed before the English Channel reformed. Early colonisers of the wet, disturbed ground (as the ice retreated) included both Downy Birch and Silver Birch, Aspen and species of Willow. These pioneer species have wind-dispersed seeds which germinate under high light conditions. They probably spread by land bridges. (See figs. 10 and 13.)

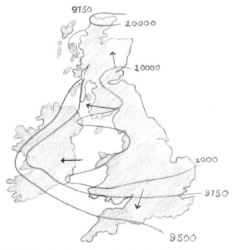

Fig. 13: Early colonisation by species of Birch (figures refer to number of years ago)

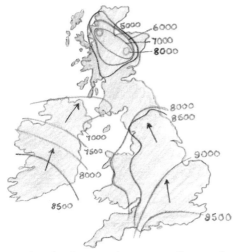

Fig. 14: Early colonisation by Scots Pine (figures refer to number of years ago)

Scots Pine appears to have entered S. England and N. Scotland as two separate populations and, like Hazel, was present at least 9,000 years ago (see fig. 14). Other early colonisers include Alder, Mountain Ash, Holly, Yew, Wych Elm and the Oaks.

Species arriving a little later included Field Maple, which appears in pollen records from about 5,000 B.C., as does Small-leaved Lime. The last species to arrive before Britain once more became an island included those such as Hornbeam, Whitebeam, Beech and Box which require warm conditions for successful fruiting and survival. Unlike their predecessors these species did not rapidly colonise the colder north. Fig. 15 lists those species which can claim to be native in that they arrived before the English Channel. Natural seed dispersal after this time by wind, bird and even water cannot be ruled out.

The composition of the Wildwood changed as new species arrived; it varied in different regions, affected by local soil and climatic conditions. Birch is short-lived and its shade makes conditions more suitable for other tree species to become established. Successions of different species developed and by 4,500 B.C. there was a more stable 'climax' woodland covering much of Britain except for some coastal areas, mountain tops and possibly natural moorland in parts of Scotland.

Rackham (1986) argues that by 4,500 B.C. there were five different woodland provinces. Each area contained many different species, but the **commonest** species varied; eg. Small-leaved Lime in 'lowland' England, Oak and Hazel in much of Wales, N. England and S. Scotland. (See fig. 16.)

Species of tree native to Britain	
Alder	Lime, Large-leaved
Ash	Lime, Small-leaved
Aspen	Maple, Field
Beech	Oak, English
Birch, Hairy	Oak, Sessile
Birch, Silver	Pine, Scots
Box	Poplar, Black
Cherry, Bird	Rowan
Cherry, Wild	Service Tree, Wild
Elm, Wych	Strawberry Tree (Ireland)
Hawthorn	Whitebeam
Hawthorn, Midland	Willow, Bay
Hazel	Willow, Crack
Holly	Willow, Goat
Hornbeam	Willow, White
Juniper	Yew

Fig. 15: Species of tree native to Britain

Hazel, Elm
Birch
Pine
Oak, Hazel
Lime

Fig. 16: Woodland provinces c.4,500 B.C.

The Early Influence of Man on the Wildwood

NOT LONG AFTER THE CHANNEL FORMATION had restricted the natural entry of new tree species Neolithic people began to colonise Britain. They felled woodland to build shelter and fed their animals on tree foliage. Later cereals were introduced and cleared areas became grassland which replaced tree foliage as fodder. Much of the evidence for this again comes from pollen records, this time of grass and weed species.

Clearing the Wildwood was not simply a case of chopping down the trees, difficult enough with only primitive tools, but removing the large trunks and also grubbing out the stumps. This last procedure is necessary because most native British trees don't readily burn green and they send up new shoots – aptly named 'spring wood', from the cut stump or stool. Between 3,000 and 4,000 B.C. there was a sudden drop in Elm numbers as indicated by pollen records. It is now thought that this was not due to the selective use of Elm by our ancestors but to the ravages of the Dutch Elm fungus. Future researchers may detect a similar picture towards the end of the 20th Century; we have lost over 25 million elms to the fungus since 1965.

Despite lacking sophisticated tools the effect of Neolithic and Bronze Age people on the Wildwood was enormous and it is now thought that up to 50% had already been cleared by the end of the Bronze Age (750 B.C.). The clearance continued under the Romans and the Anglo-Saxons. The first definitive estimate of the amount of woodland cover in England can be calculated from the Domesday survey of 1086. This gives a figure of only about 15%.

The fate of woodlands in the last 900 years is discussed on pp.27–29 but it is important to realise that most of the clearance was carried out much earlier. It is also evident that in many places uncleared Wildwood was not left untouched (see Woodland Management pp.17–18).

Fig 17: Men chopping down a tree

Woodland Management

THE PREVIOUS SECTION CONCLUDED with figures showing the early impact of mankind in the clearance of woodland. What of the remaining Wildwood – was it simply a source for timber and an unkempt hiding place for robbers and outlaws? Over the last 20 years this fairytale picture has been redrawn with the help of archaeology.

Most of our native trees (Pine is an exception) do not die when they are felled. New shoots from the stump (stool) grow into a multi-stemmed, shrub-like tree. (See fig. 18.) This produces easily-gathered foliage which prior to the expansion of grassland and cereals was used for feeding and bedding stock. The many uses of the small shoots or **wood** (as distinct from **timber** from a large trunk) led to the development of woodmanship.

Early evidence of woodland management for both wood and timber comes from excavations of ancient wooden trackways preserved in peat on the Somerset Levels near Glastonbury. The Sweet Track consists of a walkway of Oak timber supported by numerous stakes and poles. The Oak has been ring-dated (see p.14) to 3,806 B.C. Other, broader trackways date from about 3,000 B.C. They consist of thousands of interwoven rods of Ash, Hazel and Lime; such wood could not have been collected from unmanaged woodland.

Coppicing (from the French 'couper', to cut) involves the periodic cutting down of tree shoots to ground or just above ground level allowing regrowth from the stool. Native species most amenable to coppicing include Hazel, Willow, Wych Elm, Small-leaved Lime, Ash, Birch, Field Maple, Oak and Alder. The introduced Sweet Chestnut also coppices well.

Historically cutting was done in late autumn and winter – away from busy times for agricultural work. Regrowth or spring wood was rapid: many species grow 2m in the first year after coppicing; willows up to 4m. The new growth is easily damaged by browsing animals so managed woods were surrounded by ditches, walls or fences.

Managed woods contained both coppiced trees (underwood) and some larger trees (standards); the latter grown for timber, the former for wood. Standards were grown from seedlings (maidens) or by removing all but one shoot from a coppice stool (staddles). Oak and Ash were the most common species grown as standards.

The interval between coppice cuts varied with the species, the intended product and growing

Fig. 18: Coppiced stool with new growth

Fig. 19: Woodland with standards interdispersed with coppiced trees

conditions. Hazel typically had a short rotation, being cut every 7–10 years: Birch for broom handles was cut every 10–15 years; Oak every 20–35 years. Standards were felled as required.

Coppicing increases the life span of a tree. Death from fungal and insect attack or windthrow is more prevalent in trees with large trunks. Repeated coppicing is now known to have produced individuals of over 1,000 years among species which naturally only live to 400.

Usually only small sections of a wood (called panels, cants or hags) were coppiced in any one year. This maintained both a regular annual supply of wood and continuity of work. It also created a mosaic of different-aged growths within one wood. As we shall see on p.30 this resulted in a very diverse flora and fauna.

While coppicing was apparently started by Neolithic settlers it is difficult to assess how widespread it was by Roman times. It is likely to have been a common practice near their iron, pottery and brick works – all of which required a ready supply of wood for fuel. By the Domesday survey of 1086 it is apparent that coppicing was the norm in lowland England and most English medieval woods are thought to have been mixed coppice-with-standards. Parts of northern and western Britain were much later converts to the system with many Oak woods in Scotland only being coppiced for the first time in the early 18th Century.

Woods were not the only place where trees were grown. The Domesday Book records a category of Wood Pasture which consisted of pasture or grazing land with only occasional trees. Later the royal Forests and noblemen's Chases contained large areas with no trees, areas of coppice woodland and also park-like areas which consisted of well-spaced mature trees in grassland.

The conflict between grazing animals and the production of wood in pasture and park was solved by the process of **pollarding** (from 'poll', meaning 'head'). Trees were cut, not to a basal stool but to a trunk (bolling) some 2–5m high where the new growth was out of reach of browsing animals (see fig. 20). Species regularly pollarded included

Crack and White Willow, Hornbeam, Oak, Beech and Ash. Willows beside streams and rivers were pollarded to provide stems for rough basket work. Trees were often pollarded in hedges and on woodland margins where these formed a boundary such as that between parishes.

Fig. 20: Pollarded Willow

Coppice management started to decline in the late 19th Century. Wood and charcoal fuels (major products from coppiced trees) gave way to coal and coke distributed by the expanding rail network. Other woodland products were replaced by iron and steel. The loss of manpower as a result of the two 20th Century world wars hastened the demise of the labour-intensive coppice system. The decline started in the north and by the 1960s most active coppicing was limited to Kent and Sussex.

In recent years a small amount of coppicing has been reinstated, mostly in woods owned by conservation bodies, and the Somerset coppiced osier (Willow) beds still provide material for basket weavers. Currently a new role for coppiced wood is being trialled in the form of annual cuts of Willows (and non-native Alders and Poplars) to supply renewable fuel for electricity generation as a possible replacement for coal, gas and oil supplies.

Trees and their Uses

In 1991 A WELL PRESERVED 5,000 YEAR OLD CORPSE WAS DISCOVERED near an Alpine glacier. The 'Ice Man' carried a backpack constructed of Hazel and Larch, two Birch bark containers, a Yew bow with arrows of Wayfaring Tree and a dagger with a handle of Ash, the blade bound with 'rope' from Lime bark.

Timber from different species differs in strength, texture, weight and durability as do features of their coppiced wood and bark chemicals. Some species bear edible fruits others have leaves with medicinal properties. Most uses required particular qualities found in only one species of tree; hence the importance of woodland diversity.

Surnames such as Wright, Cooper, Sawyer, Turner and Tanner are reminders of the large number of craftsmen who worked with tree products. In addition occupations such as building, farming, shipbuilding, iron making, glass smelting, mining, spinning and weaving were all heavily dependent on wood, whether for structural support, fuel or in the form of specialist tools.

Trees have long supplied essential material for buildings, from the primitive hut made with little else to the modern house with wooden rafters, skirting boards and floors. Before the use of softwood and concrete, Oak was much used for structural support, both as huge beams in larger houses and barns (with posts 'upside down' to reduce rising damp via the wood vessels) and as smaller pieces in ordinary houses. It took some 300 trees for the timber and wood needed for a large farm-

house. Oak was also the main timber support in stone and brick built churches and cathedrals. Oak supplies strength and durability – as evident by the existence of the original Oak roof to the vaults of Lincoln cathedral.

Oak is also used as roofing tiles (shingles); Birch bark does the same job in Scotland. Birch twigs occasionally replace reed for roofing while ordinary thatch is held in place by cleft Hazel pegs (spars). Oak and Elm timber make good weather boarding. Poles of coppiced Hazel are 'woven' to make wattle hurdles which in the past were covered with daub (a mud plaster) for wall construction where today brick and plasterboard are used.

Oak is also much used for high class furniture including carved cabinets, tables and ecclesiastical pews. Ash and Pine provide timber for dressers and kitchen tables while Ash, Beech and Elm are used, often steam bent, for chair making. Bodgers turn chair legs from unseasoned wood using simple pole-lathes. The legs and back need to be attached to the chair seat without splitting it – the cross grain of Elm is thus ideal for the seat.

Oak was favoured for animal stalls and gates; often replaced today by Larch and other treated softwoods. Hollowed Elm trunks provided feeding troughs. Woven Hazel hurdles made both permanent and temporary fencing. Today we use barbed wire or palings of wire and cleft Sweet Chestnut wood. Coppiced Sweet Chestnut also makes good hop poles. Gardeners also need fences too, today made mostly of interwoven or overlapping softwood such as Larch. Ash makes the best wooden wheelbarrows. The traditional carrying trug is of cleft Willow on a frame of Ash or Sweet Chestnut.

Transport, before the developments of metals, rubber and plastics, was a large consumer of trees. Three species were required for a cart wheel: a rim of Ash – renowned for its ability to absorb shock;

Fig. 21: Oak-framed house

strong spokes of Oak and a hub of non-splitting Elm. Carts used a number of different timbers and some were lined with Willow which absorbs heavy loading pressures without splitting. Train carriage body-work used Oak which was also used for sleepers in the pre-concrete era. Cars, buses and even aircraft made much use of Ash in their framework.

Early settlers came by boat. Tiny coracles of hide stretched over a Willow frame, wooden warships and many modern boats, all need wood. The warships used a lot of Oak, often cobbled from small pieces; many were destroyed by dry rot fungus. Keels made of Elm do not rot if kept permanently waterlogged. Wooden masts are typically of Scots pine or Norway Spruce.

Wood provides a source of fuel either directly or as charcoal. Extracts from an old poem neatly explain the burning characteristics of different species:

Birch logs will burn too fast
Alder scarce at all.
Chestnut logs are good to last
If cut in the fall.

Oak logs will warm you well
If they're old and dry.
Larch logs of pinewood smell
But the sparks will fly.

But ash logs, all smooth and grey
Burn them green or old;
Buy up all that come your way
They're worth their weight in gold.

Oak and Birch were most widely used for domestic fires but a faggot (bundle of sticks) of Hazel or, if available, Hornbeam was preferred for bread ovens. Wood from coppice or pollarded trees (easy for small pieces) provided fuel for brick and earthenware manufacture and to heat limekilns making slaked lime for mortar.

Charcoal has a hotter flame than wood and is lighter to transport. For centuries thousands of charcoal burners made a living producing it from coppiced wood. It fuelled processes such as iron smelting, steel making and glass production (the latter also used wood ash as a source of potash). The 19th Century railways brought cheaper coal and coke, replacing charcoal. Today thousands of tons of charcoal, much from tropical hardwoods, are imported for barbecues and this has stimulated the rebirth of our own charcoal trade at a time when coppicing is being restarted.

Charcoal is also used in industrial filters, for treating gastric upsets and by artists; that for the latter coming from Willow coppice. Together with sulphur and saltpetre it makes gunpowder. The best charcoal for this comes from Alder Buckthorn and Alder. Ordnance factories were originally sited near wet ground for this reason.

Different industries had their own requirements. Pit props for coal mining used local trees – Oak, Sweet Chestnut, Pine and Larch were among the preferred ones. The cotton mills required millions of spools, reels and bobbins, many of which were turned from Birch, while Sycamore rollers were used to dry cloth or treated hides. Cogs, pulleys and wooden screws used the hardest wood, preferably Hornbeam – also a favourite for butchers' chopping blocks.

Fig. 22: Charcoal burning

Tannin from Oak bark (and the Oak Marble Gall) was mixed with iron salts in the manufacture of ink. Bark, preferably from young or coppiced Oak, was peeled off in huge quantities to supply the leather tanning trade. In the first half of the 19th Century tanning consumed more acreage of Oak than the naval dockyards but in the 1850s foreign imports and chemical substitutes virtually killed off the trade. Trees such as Alder and Elder supplied important dyestuffs; predating synthetic dyes.

Before the emergence of Staffordshire crockery, kitchen ware included wooden platters, bowls and mugs turned from Maple, Sycamore and Elm. Sycamore and Beech, both with a clean, close grain are still used for spoons, chopping boards and rolling pins. Clothes pegs are traditionally made from cleft Beech or split Willow. Sweeping besoms of Birch twigs wrapped round the end of a coppice pole were replaced with brushes – the bristles inserted into a Beech head.

Wood was with us from the cradle to the grave (Oak coffin for the rich, Elm for the poor); from clock cases to picture frames; from bedsteads to toilet seats; from matches (both the match and the box of Aspen until English manufacture succumbed to cheap lighters) to bellows backs (made of Elm); from Beechwood toys to Alder clog soles. Shoe lasts and saddle trees came from Beech, hat blocks from Lime. Even the word book may have come from the German for Beech (Buche), thin sheets of which supported the leather covers.

17th Century Elm water pipes were found intact, in London in 1930. Original village pumps (including the bucket) were also of Elm, long predating cast iron. Weapon use includes the longbow of Yew, dagger handles of Oak root and gunstocks of Walnut. Mats and rope came from the inner bark of Lime, shepherds' crooks from Hazel, walking sticks from Ash, Chestnut and Hazel.

Coopers made and repaired barrels in their millions. The best were made of Oak and Sweet Chestnut staves bound by hoops of Ash or Hazel (later iron). They were not only for liquids such as whisky, beer and cider (where they are still used) but also transported apples, cheese, crockery and cement! Basket makers depend on coppiced or pollarded Willow but new materials led to the plastic bag and are now widely used for objects such as lobster pots previously made of woven Willow.

Cricket bats are still made from Willow, billiard cues and hockey sticks from Ash but Hornbeam-headed golf clubs are becoming rare and most fishing rods are now of synthetic material. The quality of sound from woodwind or stringed Musical instruments depends on the wood – eg. the front of a violin from Spruce, the sides and back from patterned Sycamore. Pianos use many different species including Beech and Hornbeam.

The food value of trees is very important. In the past acorns and Beech nuts helped to fatten pigs and Hazel nuts were much sort for human consumption. Today the orchard fruits such as Apple, Pear, Plum and Cherry are the most significant. Wine is made from Elderberries and also Birch sap. Burning Birch twigs are still used to smoke hams or herrings and to add flavour to whisky. Medicinal products include Willow bark, from which Aspirin was developed, purgatives from Buckthorn, cold remedies from Limeflowers and artificial limbs from Willow.

With the rise of coniferous (especially Spruce) tree fellings the paper pulp industry is now an important user of trees. The food flavour vanilla is synthesised from a waste product of papermaking. Pulp is also used in the making of disposable nappies. Other modern products include hardboard (which contains some bark) and particle boards such as chipboard. Rayon is a fibre made from wood cellulose which also gives us cellophane, many adhesives and thickening agents and even an additive to washing powder which makes polyester fabric easier to wash!

Not all tree uses are obvious; Holly bark was valuable as a source of birdlime, used by fowlers to catch birds while the green shoots were fed to cattle and deer as winter feed. Watchmakers would be asked to 'pass the pith pot' – soft Elder pith was used to clean clock and watch mechanisms. Sadly even this use has been replaced by modern, mass-produced, multi-purpose products.

Introduced Tree Species

SPECIES WHICH ARRIVED VIA THE LAND BRIDGES (see p.13) are said to be native and on current evidence these are: Oaks (Sessile and English), Birches (both Silver and Hairy), Willows (Bay, Goat, Crack and White), Cherries (Bird and later, Wild), Limes (Small-leaved and later, Large-leaved), Wych Elm, Alder, Rowan, Aspen, Black Poplar, Ash, Hazel, Holly, Hawthorns (Common and Midland), Whitebeam, Crab Apple, Wild Service Tree, Field Maple, Beech, Hornbeam and Box plus the three Conifers: Scots Pine, Yew and Juniper. The Strawberry Tree is native to Ireland.

Some species may have arrived naturally, eg. as seed in bird droppings, after Britain became separated from mainland Europe c.5,500 B.C. Both Wild and Plymouth Pear are contenders. Other species such as Small- (or Smooth-) leaved Elm are possibly native as some pollen records pre-date Neolithic settlers.

Species brought to this country by man are known as **Introductions** and by the Iron Age may have included White Poplar and English Elm. Sweet Chestnut and Walnut were probably brought by the Romans along with Fig, which died out, and was reintroduced in the 16th Century. Seed or wooden objects found in dated archaeological sites do not prove that the tree was being grown in Britain at that time; imports of fruit and wood products further confuse the picture. The edible seeds of Stone Pine (*Pinus pinea*) found at Roman sites indicate it was the food that was imported, rather than the tree.

It is likely that monks introduced some European species during Anglo-Saxon times (410–1066) and that more arrived during the Middle Ages (1066–1536) but we have no written records until the mid-16th Century when books by William Turner give the names and localities for many plants (including trees) growing in Britain. Lyte's *Herball* of 1578 mentions Sycamore (as a garden tree) and Gerard published a list of the plants growing in his Holborn garden in 1596, a year before his famous *Herball*, which indicates the origin of some of the introductions.

From such records we conclude that the following were growing in this country by the end of the 16th Century:

Stone Pine (*Pinus pinea*)
Maritime Pine (*Pinus pinaster*)
Norway Spruce (*Picea abies*)
Italian Cypress (*Cupressus sempervirens*)
Holm Oak (*Quercus ilex*)
Sycamore (*Acer pseudoplatanus*)
Black Mulberry (*Morus nigra*)
Oriental Plane (*Platanus orientalis*)
Cherry Laurel (*Prunus laurocerasus*)
Cornelian Cherry (*Cornus mas*)
Lilac (*Syringa vulgaris*)
Laburnum (*Laburnum anagyroides*)

All these are native in mainland Europe, but the discovery and colonisation of Newfoundland and Virginia, set the scene for 17th Century introductions from the New World. This was the start of the age of plant hunters with the two John Tradescants leading the way. The elder John imported many fruit trees from Holland and France including Pomegranates and Peaches. He befriended Jean and Vespasien Robin, gardeners to the French King, and the two families swapped new plants. In 1621 *Robinia pseudoacacia* (False Acacia) came from America via the Robins to London.

Imports from the colonies, some brought back as seed by the younger Tradescant, included Black Walnut (*Juglans nigra*), American Plane (*Platanus occidentalis*), Swamp Cypress (*Taxodium distichum*), Red Maple (*Acer rubrum*) and Tulip Tree (*Liriodendron tulipifera*).

Trees continued to arrive from Europe and also the Middle East and included Horse Chestnut (*Aesculus hippocastanum*) about 1616,

European Larch (*Larix decidua*) about 1620, Norway Maple (*Acer platanoides*), Cedar of Lebanon (*Cedrus libani*) about 1640 and Manna Ash (*Fraxinus ornus*) near the end of the century.

The Tradescants grew many introduced trees in their garden at Lambeth and it is possible that it was here that hybridization between Oriental and American Plane gave rise to London Plane (*Platanus x hispanica*) – first described in the 1660s. In 1664 the book *Sylva* by John Evelyn was to influence the way landowners thought about trees as part of the landscape and encouraged the planting of trees.

18th Century newcomers included Turkey Oak (*Quercus cerris*) from S. Europe in 1735, and two early Chinese introductions – Tree of Heaven (*Ailanthus altissima*) in 1751 and Ginkgo (*Ginkgo biloba*). A seedling of the latter raised in 1754 was transferred to Kew in 1760. Lombardy Poplar (*Populus nigra* 'Italica') was introduced in 1758, five years before Rhododendron (*Rhododendron ponticum*) came in from S. Europe. In 1795 Archibald Menzies, a scientist working for the navy, introduced Monkey-Puzzle (*Araucaria araucana*) having some years earlier pocketed seeds served at a meal given by the Governor of Chile. It was to be 50 years before an adequate seed supply led to the Victorian craze for this tree.

Fig. 23: Monkey Puzzle tree

In the 18th and early 19th Century, Joseph Banks transformed scientific plant exploration with expeditions to Newfoundland, and, more famously with Captain Cook to Australia. On his return George III installed Banks as botanical adviser to Kew Gardens which he developed into a major scientific centre. He promoted plant hunting expeditions and seed swaps. Many exotic (non-native) British trees were first grown at Kew. In 1804 he was involved in the founding of the Horticultural Society (now Royal Horticultural Society) which later funded a number of plant hunters.

The opening up of the west coast of North America heralded a flood of new trees, many of them Conifers. In the 1820s and 1830s the Horticultural Society funded a number of expeditions to America by David Douglas who sent back the seed of many trees new to Britain (though some had been previously described by Archibald Menzies) including:

Douglas Fir (*Pseudotsuga menziesii*)
Noble Fir (*Abies procera*)
Grand Fir (*Abies grandis*)
Sitka Spruce (*Picea sitchensis*)

In a letter to William Hooker (later Director at Kew), Douglas wrote "You will begin to think that I manufacture pines at my pleasure" – among those he introduced were:

Monterey Pine (*Pinus radiata*)
Ponderosa Pine (*Pinus ponderosa*)
Sugar Pine (*Pinus lambertiana*)

To obtain seeds of Sugar Pine, Douglas shot the cones from high in the trees! He also collected seed of Coast Redwood (*Sequoia sempervirens*) but these were lost in a boat accident. The species had in fact already been introduced to Portugal from where seeds reached Britain in 1843.

Conifers from the American west coast grew well in the north of Scotland from where in 1849 local landowners funded a trip to Oregon by John Jeffrey. He sent seed of:

Western Hemlock (*Tsuga heterophylla*)
Western Red Cedar (*Thuja plicata*)
Nootka Cypress (*Chamaecyparis nootkatensis*)

Jeffrey disappeared but his search party found:

Lawson Cypress (*Chamaecyparis lawsoniana*) By this time nurseries such as Veitch's were also funding expeditions and their collector William Lobb sent back many of the same species as Jeffrey. Lobb collected seeds of Giant Redwood (*Sequoiadendron giganteum*) late in 1853 but another collector beat him to it by just four months.

The first half of the 19th Century saw the introduction of new trees from the North of the Indian subcontinent including Bhutan Pine (*Pinus wallichiana*) and Deodar or Indian Cedar (*Cedrus deodara*). In 1848 Joseph Hooker was funded by Kew (his father was Director!) to bring back plants from Nepal, Sikkhim and Bhutan. This he did, including a great many species of *Rhododendron.*

China was long inaccessible to Western botanists though from the 17th Century French Jesuit missionaries had sent back accounts and later herbarium specimens of the spectacular flora. In 1842 access was eased following the Treaty of Nanking and the Horticultural Society sent Robert Fortune to China. He took some Wardian cases – small enclosed greenhouses invented in 1829. Seedlings and small plants in these survived the long sea voyage from China. Previously only seeds had survived long sea journeys.

Fig. 24: Wardian case

Fortune introduced Golden Larch (*Pseudolarix amabilis*) and Japanese Red Cedar (*Cryptomeria japonica*). He put the Wardian cases to good use by importing Tea seedlings (which were exported to our colonies) and male plants of the Spotted Laurel (*Aucuba japonica*). He collected the latter in Japan enabling the female plants in Britain (originally introduced in 1783) to set red berries for the first time.

China was also a rich hunting ground for Ernest Wilson, funded by the Veitch nursery. In 1904 he successfully introduced *Davidia involucrata* – named after Armand David, the Jesuit priest who had first described it; it is commonly known as the Handkerchief Tree. He also introduced Paperbark Maple (*Acer griseum*) and various species of Rhododendron and Magnolia.

Fortune, Wilson and Veitch all visited Japan after it became more open to foreigners in 1854. Between them they brought back many cultivars of Japanese Maple (*Acer palmatum*) and Japanese Flowering Cherry (*Prunus serrulata*). In 1861 Veitch introduced Japanese Larch (*Larix kaempferi*) which crossed with European Larch to produce *Larix x eurolepis* in about 1904. This fast-growing, disease resistant hybrid is now our most widely planted Larch.

In 1888 on an estate near Welshpool a cross occurred between Nootka Cypress (*Chamaecyparis nootkatensis*) and Monterey Cypress (*Cupressus macrocarpa*); the resulting hybrid – Leyland Cypress (*x Cupressocyparis leylandii*) was named after the brother-in-law of the estate owner.

Among the more popular recent introductions none is more famous than Dawn Redwood (*Metasequoia glyptostroboides*) first described as fossil remains by a Japanese botanist in 1941. In the same year living specimens were reported from China but it was not until after the War that seeds were sent to the Arnold Arboretum in America from where they were sent to gardens round the world in 1948.

Most of the trees mentioned above are classed as exotics and do not spread outside gardens or plantations. Some introduced species have become naturalised – they spread without further help from man. These include: Rhododendron, Sweet Chestnut, Turkey Oak and Sycamore.

Trees in Legend, History and Folklore

THE STORY OF TWO TREES GIVING BIRTH TO MAN occurs in many parts of the world. In evolutionary theory related species are grouped on the same branch. The concept of a family tree may come from an earlier belief that a dead person's knowledge was retained by tree spirits and passed to future generations.

Mankind has long been dependent on trees for shelter, food, fuel and transport (see pp.19–21); spiritual links are equally deep-rooted. Sacred groves of trees used in ancient times for worship were mimicked by the trunk-like Doric columns of Greek temples. Pillars and fan vaulting of cathedrals are similarly tree-like. Legends depict trees with canopies in heaven, trunks on earth and roots in hell.

The Celtic calendar known as the Wheel of the Year relates to annual events with a different tree linked to each of 13 seasons. One was Duir from which the tribal philosophers and holymen took their name: Druids, or men of the Oak. Oak was sacred –not least when host to the mystic and healing Mistletoe. The Yule log burnt at the winter solstice was typically Oak. Sacred groves were often of Yew – its dark colour and poisonous foliage signified death; being evergreen and long-lived symbolized eternal life.

Adam and Eve ate from the Tree of Knowledge and Christ was crucified on a wooden cross. However many supposedly Christian customs have earlier antecedents. Druids brought evergreens into their homes in Winter for the wood spirits to rest out of the cold. In the midwinter Roman feast of Saturnalia people sent evergreen sprigs to their friends as tokens of good wishes. When St Augustine came to spread Christianity to Britain in 597 A.D. he sought integration with pagan sites and customs, thus churches were built near sacred Yews which continued to be venerated.

One tree legend is peculiar to an earlier Christian mission to Britain, led by Joseph of Arimathea who was said to have arrived in Glastonbury soon after Christ's death. When Joseph's staff took root, immediately producing leaves and flowers of Hawthorn, conversions followed. The Glastonbury Thorn (*Crataegus*

monogyna 'Biflora') whatever its true origin, is unique in its habit of flowering as usual in early summer and a second time at Christmas, hence its portrayal on a 1986 Christmas stamp. With the Gregorian calendar reform in 1752 the thorn was still in bud on Christmas day and many in the area continued to celebrate the old Julian date for Christmas by which time the blossoms were open.

In the 11th Century the Church tried to distance itself from what it saw as pagan rites and made it an offence to build a sanctuary round a tree. Trees however continued to be associated with preaching and in the 18th Century John Wesley drew large crowds to his 'pulpit' trees. The Rogation Week custom of 'beating the bounds', gospel readings under conspicuous trees marking a parish boundary, still echoed earlier pagan ceremonies.

Teutonic peoples had long worshipped trees prior to being encouraged by St Boniface to decorate a tree in praise of its maker. The Christmas link, associated with Martin Luther, was imported into Britain in 1841 by Prince Albert.

While Christmas subsumed Winter Solstice celebrations other seasonal festivals remained such as May Day; the tree symbolised by the decorated wooden May Pole, dancers representing the sylvan (wood) spirits. Lammas, on or near 1 August originated in Anglo-Saxon times as Loaf-Mass when the first loaf made from the new harvest was hung from an Oak. Lammas has now been merged with the more pagan Harvest Festival but Oak summer leaf burst is still known as lammas growth.

Woods were long feared as the hiding places of evil spirits and witches but certain trees gained a protective reputation. Farmers would drive livestock through a gate bedecked with Birch to prevent harm from witches (who 'flew' on Birch broomsticks). Rowan was highly regarded as a talisman against witches possibly due to the 5-pointed star mark on its berry, reminiscent of the magical pentagram symbol of protection.

Shakespeare's Macbeth is famous for the three witches (and Burnham Wood) but some scholars feel there is a more interesting, though muddled, reference from the sailor's wife who, on being asked by one of the witches to bring them some chestnuts, defiantly answers "Aroint thee witch" – the sense is much clearer as "A Rowan tree witch".

Trees associated with holy wells or places such as hermits' caves are often attributed with healing powers. One day near Oban I came across an ancient roadside Hawthorn with an odd trunk. Closer examination revealed hundreds of coins buried in the bark. The custom had started in the days of stage coach travel when passengers had alighted to add a coin to the lucky tree as a talisman against being robbed.

Some famous trees commemorate historical events. One such was the pollarded Oak near Boscobel House in Shropshire in which the then Pretender to the throne spent a day hiding from the Roundheads after the battle of Worcester in 1651. In 1660 on 29 May he become Charles 11 and this day became known as Oak Apple Day. Children arriving at school on that day without a sprig of Oak were made to pay a forfeit. The original tree has gone but a successor marks the spot.

It is fitting that the tree under which six agricultural labourers from Tolpuddle in Dorset met in 1834 to discuss action against their exploitation by the landed gentry was for once not Oak –so much the symbol of tradition, but Sycamore –a relative new comer. The oath procedure under which they set up the first agricultural trade union laid them open to a charge of mutiny and they were deported to Australia. The 'Martyr Tree', now adopted by the Trades Union Congress, still stands.

The story of Robin Hood and his supposed exploits in 13th Century Sherwood Forest hunting the King's deer, helping the poor and hiding from the Sheriff in Oak trees has lost little over the years even though academics argue over the details. Victorian day trippers arrived in their thousands to view some of the ancient oaks and today upwards of a million people come each year to see the Major Oak. Despite its name (from a local historian called Major Rooke) it is not the largest in the country and even at over 500 years old could hardly have sheltered an outlaw some 700 years ago.

Many place names reflect local woodlands or important trees hence Northern Ireland's (London)Derry from the Gaelic for Oak, and Sevenoaks in Kent –the latter having its number reduced by the Hurricane of October 1987. The frequency of Ash on the limestone in the Peak District is recorded in places such as Monyash and Ashbourne. Less obvious is Lindfield in Sussex; here the connection is with Lime, linden being an earlier name for the tree.

The original meaning of words and phrases associated with earlier tree customs is frequently forgotten. My department at Sheffield University was contacted by a local feminist demanding we rename the degree of Bachelor of Science. The word comes from the wreaths of berried Laurel awarded to good poets; the Latin for a Laurel berry being 'baccalaureus' (French 'bachelier'). That the term bachelor came from the same root is not denied but the Bachelor degree is apt for those of either gender as they are both, metaphorically at least, wreathed in glory.

Fig. 25: Laurel wreath

Woodlands in the last 900 years

THE NORMANS INTRODUCED MANY CHANGES IN LAND MANAGEMENT, not least the idea that it could be privately owned. By the 13th Century many English woods were private, and were fenced or ditched, to protect new coppice shoots from grazing animals.

The introduction of Fallow deer (possibly by Henry I) led to the setting up of deer parks. These were mostly woodland or a combination of grassland and scattered, pollarded trees, unlike the larger royal Forests and noblemen's Chases introduced initially by William the Conqueror.

Forests and Chases were not simply areas of dense woodland though they included such areas. They also encompassed wood pasture, grazing and arable land, and even towns and villages as exemplified by The New Forest. Forest areas had local laws. Those concerning the hunting of deer by the locals were draconian in nature and helped fuel legends such as that of Robin Hood. By the time of Magna Carta in 1216 (which prevented any more Royal Forests from being created) some 20% of England was covered by Forests and Chases. Though the deer belonged to royalty or their favourites, commoners had grazing rights.

From 1400–1750 woodland and wood pasture continued to be lost primarily to the needs of agriculture. From the 16th Century the enclosure of land, culminating in parliamentary acts of the 18th and early 19th Century, broke up wood pasture on commons and areas of old Forest. The planting of hedges as enclosures resulted in a huge increase in the frequency of Hawthorn, Blackthorn and some species of Elm, particularly in Southern England.

From woodland records it is evident that the time between coppice cuts lengthened, indicating a need for larger wood. By 1600 there were some 7 million people in Britain and the demand for wood and charcoal as fuel together with the need for timber to construct houses and naval vessels had increased dramatically.

In 1610 James I said "If woods are sufferd to be felled, as daily they are, there will be none left." The concern at the loss of trees and the value of those remaining had been growing over the 15th and 16th Centuries – a decline which various acts of parliament failed to prevent. John Evelyn's book 'Sylva' published in 1664 included a plea for the planting of trees and it is about this time that we get the first definite records of the planting of new woodland for economic gain.

Much of the planting was not of mixed woods but of single species; what we should call Plantations rather than woods or forests. Through the 17th Century such planting was not restricted to timber trees, there was also much planting of fruit trees in orchards. The 17th and 18th Centuries saw the beginning of the influx of exotic trees (see pp.22–24) and many of these were Conifers. Those from the west coast of America grew particularly well in parts of Scotland and here many of the landed gentry set up Conifer plantations (see fig.26). Between 1740 and 1830 the Dukes of Atholl in Perthshire planted 14,000,000 Larches. These plantations were the forerunners of our modern day 'forests' but had little effect on our existing woods, the acreage of which declined slowly.

Fig. 26: Conifer plantation

Plantations were not restricted to Conifers and included Beech, Oak, Ash and Sweet Chestnut. Shelter belts became popular and by the early 17th Century many country houses had planted avenues of trees on either side of their main access road.

Fig. 27: Avenue of Limes

Fig. 28: Orchard of Apple trees

Fashions were influenced by the arrival of new species such as Horse Chestnut. Later the 18th Century landscapers such as 'Capability' Brown instigated massive programmes of tree planting in clumps and belts around estates. In addition to native species, exotics such as Cedar of Lebanon were used.

From the 1840s with the coming of the Industrial Revolution the long-standing tradition of the coppice management of British woodlands began to decline. One reason for this was the expanding railway network making coal and coke more widely available – replacing firewood and charcoal. Another was the increased utilization of metal, where previously wood had been used, reducing the outlets for local wood craftsmen. Finally the lucrative use of Oak bark for tanning fell victim to chemical substitutes and cheap imports.

Throughout the 19th Century the importation of good quality, low-priced Coniferous timber from Scandinavia, Russia and even Canada, together with hardwood from parts of the Empire, reduced the incentive to grow timber trees. By 1914 woodland cover in Britain was down to only 5.7% of the land area (1.3 million hectares). The First World War and the German blockade on imports highlighted Britain's dependence on imported timber and resulted in the setting up of the Forestry Commission in 1919.

The main aim of the Forestry Commission was to produce a strategic timber reserve. The need was for timber (not wood) for new houses and factories, for railway sleepers, pit props and telegraph poles. The aim was to establish fast growing Coniferous plantations and encourage private landowners to do the same. Between the Wars some 25% of English land changed hands and new ownership and a shortage of labour accelerated the decline of coppice woods. The Second World War once again found the country very short of timber and after 1945 the Forestry Commission was given increased targets for buying land on which to establish Coniferous plantations.

For many years the maximum that could be paid for such land was £10 an acre and this resulted in the use of much marginal land, often upland moorland. Sadly with the introduction of planting incentives and tax avoidance schemes many Broadleaved woodlands were grubbed up and replaced by Coniferous plantations.

By 1990 the total area of woodland, including plantation, had risen to 2.1 million hectares (about 10% of the land area) but imports of timber still accounted for over 90% of our needs. 1.5 million hectares was under Conifers, much as monocultures of the following species:

Scots Pine (the only native species used)
Corsican Pine, Lodgepole Pine
Sitka Spruce, Norway Spruce
European Larch, Japanese Larch, Hybrid Larch
Douglas Fir.

Broad-leaved species have also been planted, often as closely-spaced monocultures. They include: Oak, Beech, Ash and Sycamore.

Whether Conifer or Broad-leaved, plantation woodland is very different from the permanent woodland it has, in many places, replaced. A plantation is not permanent and at harvest all or most of the trees are cut down at the same time and have to be replanted. There is no mosaic of woodland at different growth stages as in coppiced woodland and thus a much less diverse fauna and flora.

It has been calculated that between 1900 and 1970 the area of coppiced woodland decreased by more than 90%. Since 1945 over 50% of the remaining Ancient Woodland has disappeared, much of it to agriculture, and ironically, forestry. Ancient woodland is defined as woodland that has been in existence from 1600. As there was very little planting of new woods before this it can be surmised that an area of Ancient woodland is likely to have been wooded since the original Wildwood arrived.

The 20th Century has also seen problems for trees, whether in woodland or other habitats. Diseases have killed certain species, the most serious to date being Dutch Elm disease, which in 30 years from the mid-1960s has killed over 25 million Elms in Britain. Caterpillars have severely restricted the growth of certain Conifers, including non-native species. There is concern that Sweet Chestnut may succumb to a fungal disease while the Asian Gipsy Moth caterpillar could damage a wide range of species.

The effects of pollution including acid rain and the influence of summer drought (possibly resulting from climatic change) are further reducing the health of our tree stock. Recently urban trees have suffered from root damage caused by pavement trenches dug as part of the cable revolution.

More positive news for woodlands has been the work of various bodies (see list on p.183) including the National Trust, Countryside Commission, many local County Wildlife Trusts and, since 1972, the Woodland Trust, a charity devoted to buying and managing old woodland.

Twelve new Community Forests (using the term Forest in the old sense) have been launched since 1993, including the South Yorkshire Forest where Broad-leaved planting will be encouraged. The aim is also to provide recreation areas, wildlife havens and job opportunities. In addition a new National Forest, some 35 by 25km, midway between Derby, Leicester and Birmingham saw its first new plantings in 1990. The aim is for a third of the area to be under trees of which 60% will be Broad-leaved species.

Fig. 30: Pole lathe

The 1990s have also seen a revival in interest in some of the old woodland crafts as small areas of woodland return to coppice management. In addition to a return to producing charcoal there has been an increase in the use of pole lathes and the production of wattle hurdles. The Green Wood Trust organises practical courses for those with an interest in woodmanship.

Fig. 29: Elm dying of Dutch Elm disease

Woodland Wildlife

LONG-ESTABLISHED WOODLAND IS AN IMPORTANT WILDLIFE HABITAT. Many Ancient woods will have undergone hundreds (even thousands) of years of coppice management before a returning to high forest conditions in the last 100 years. Such woods typically contain a much richer ground flora (flowering plants, mosses, ferns etc.) than that found in more recently established woods.

It is thought that many Ancient woods stand on sites which have been wooded since the arrival of the Wildwood and will still contain remnants of the Wildwood flora. In contrast more recent woodland will only have acquired species which can readily colonize new areas, even when these are separated from established woods by open farmland or urban development.

Ecologists have studied the plants which grow beneath the tree and shrub layers and identified the strategies which make them suited to such sites.

Wood Anemone (*Anemone nemorosa*) grows rapidly in early spring (the shape of the emerging shoot enables it to push through dead leaves) and exploits the relatively high light conditions before the trees come into leaf. Anemone responds to coppicing by a marked increase in flowering but can survive for hundreds of years in deeper shade without flowering. Seed is regularly set but is not dispersed far from the plant. Vegetative reproduction (from the breaking up of the underground rhizome) is more common. As a result Anemone has a very low colonising ability and is typically associated with older woodland.

Many woodland plants are adapted to low light conditions (in summer the light intensity on a woodland floor can be less than 5% of that in open pasture land) and cannot compete with sun-loving plants in more open conditions. As the area of arable and grazing land expanded with the development of agriculture so such plants were restricted to woodland and other shady habitats.

Such plants often have poor seed dispersal, though some such as the hooked fruits of Wood Avens (*Geum urbanum*) are carried by animals. Very few have long distance wind-dispersed seed; there is very little wind on a woodland floor.

Certain plant species are either restricted to or rarely found outside Ancient woods. Their presence serves as a better indicator that a wood is indeed old than does the number of plant species which is influenced by soil type, proximity to a road etc. The pioneering work of George Peterken which was carried out in a number of woods in Lincolnshire listed species which were confined to Ancient woodland in that county including: Wood Sorrel, *Oxalis acetosella*; Common Cow Wheat, *Melampyrum pratense*; Herb Paris, *Paris quadrifolia*; Toothwort, *Lathraea squamaria*;Wood Millet, *Millium effusum*.

In addition two native trees were confined to Ancient woodland (and old hedges): Small-leaved Lime, *Tilia cordata*; Spindle, *Euonymus europaeus*.

Species almost confined to Ancient woodland included: Yellow Archangel, *Lamiastrum galeobdolon*; Sweet Woodruff, *Galium odoratum*; Wood Anemone, *Anemone nemorosa*; Wood Goldilocks, *Ranunculus auricomus*; Lily of the Valley, *Convalaria majalis*.

Peterken recorded the flora of woods of known age, making use of old maps and parish records. Many people have since used the presence of his indicator species to prove that a particular wood of unknown age is indeed an Ancient wood. Unfortunately an indicator species in Lincolnshire is not necessarily confined to Ancient woods in Somerset; the geographic range of a species and local climate being two variables. In some regions so-called Ancient woodland indicators occur in many Secondary woods, having apparently spread across fields via the hedge network.

Despite these limitations it is probable that a wood containing at least six of the above species is long established. The presence of curving or irregular boundaries and boundary banks, ditches or walls also indicates old woodlands; evidence that can be substantiated using local maps and records.

Many of the species mentioned on p.30 thrive under coppice management. After a cut, midsummer light levels at ground level increase by 20 times, and spring levels rise four-fold. In the second season after cutting there is a flush of flowering by Violets, Primroses, Wood Anemone and Yellow Archangel. The decline in coppicing has reduced the diversity of plants and the effect on the animal kingdom is equally dramatic.

Coppiced woodland contains a great diversity of habitat with a mosaic including some open areas, some older trees and access rides. Both the Nightingale and Garden Warbler require this diversity and the decline of the Nightingale population in Britain this century mirrors the decline of coppicing. Birds feeding in recently coppiced areas include White Throat and Tree Pipit while the more closed canopy (4–10 years after a cut) attracts Blackcap and the two species mentioned above.

Among small mammals, Woodmice inhabit recently cut areas but the populations of Shrews and Bank Vole is highest some 2–3 years after cutting. The Common Dormouse is not common in Britain; its main stronghold being coppiced woodland in south and west England. Apart from nuts from Hazel, which needs a long rotation to produce fruit, the Common Dormouse needs the diversity of other plants to obtain food and cover throughout the year.

Most butterfly species have larvae that feed on a restricted number of food plants. Many woodland species including Heath Fritillary, Silver Washed Fritillary and Chequered Skipper have become much rarer in the last 50 years. Many of the Fritillary species have larvae which feed on Violets; these flourish under coppicing but are shaded out in high forest conditions. The now very rare Heath Fritillary feeds on Common Cow Wheat, (see p.30) which grows in woodland that is open enough to encourage the herbs on which it is a semi-parasite. The Heath Fritillary is not a good flier and cannot easily cross open farmland in search of new habitats.

Other invertebrates including certain species of Hoverfly are also restricted to old woodlands and nests of the Wood Ant appear most frequently in coppiced woods, usually in areas cut some 2–5 years previously. Like the Nightingale and Silver Washed Fritillary, numbers of the Wood Ant have fallen this century.

Woodland is also an important habitat for the shade-loving mosses, liverworts and ferns. Many mosses and liverworts produce their spores in winter as this is the time of maximum light penetration. Older tree trunks and branches are colonized by some ferns, especially Common Polypody and by a large number of lichen species.

Fungi play an important role in woodland life and old mixed woodland contains many hundreds of species. Some are parasitic and kill trees, others have a mycorrhizal association with tree roots – ensuring a carbon food source for the fungus and adequate mineral uptake for the tree. Most parasitic and mycorrhizal species are very host-specific, so the greater the number of tree species the more potential for different fungi. Many fungi attack only older trees or dead wood. In a coppice wood this would be found in the standards, large boundary trees and in the old coppice stools.

Regardless of age or management of woodland there are other reasons why a wood tends to have a greater diversity of wildlife than a modern forestry plantation. A plantation usually consists of only one or a small number of species. This restricts the range of invertebrates, many of which feed on only one tree species, and also the number of bird species most of which are also specialised feeders. More importantly many plantations are of exotic species often introduced without all their associated species of insect and fungus. As a rough rule of thumb, the longer a tree species has been in the country the higher the number of associated invertebrate and fungal species. Finally the lack of permanence of a modern plantation restricts the diversity of its wildlife. Modern forests are not without their wildlife; some attract an interesting bird fauna but overall they are a second best to Ancient woodland.

Keys

THESE KEYS ARE INTENDED TO GUIDE YOU TO THE APPROPRIATE PAGES OF THE BOOK, where you can compare your specimen with the descriptions. Species described under the heading 'Cultivars, Related and Confusable Species' are not keyed out here nor are the many hundreds of other, less common, introduced trees.

At each number in the key you are offered two or more alternative descriptions: a), b), c) etc. Choose the description that fits your specimen. At the end of the line you will find either the name of the tree (and a page reference) or be told which number in the key to go to next. Refer to the Glossary (p.185) for an explanation of terms.

i. SUMMER FOLIAGE KEY TO CONIFERS AND THEIR RELATIVES

(Leaves with parallel veins, typically needle or awl-shaped or small, scale-like; often resinous).

1. a) leaves <4mm wide, all (or mostly) needle or awl-shaped: **2**
   b) leaves <4mm wide, all (most) scale-like: **11**
   c) leaves >4mm wide at base, triangular; leathery: **Monkey Puzzle** p.168
   d) leaves broad, soft; typically bilobed, veins like fan ribs: **Maidenhair Tree** p.36

2. a) needles arising singly: **3**
   b) needles in whorls or groups of 2 or more: **8**

3. a) needles on pegs: **Norway Spruce** p.154
   b) needles not on pegs: **4**

4. a) needles flattened, in 2-ranked sprays: **5**
   b) needles not or loosely 2-ranked: **7**

5. a) soft, oppositely-set needles on deciduous opposite branchlets which bear buds on outer side of stalk: **Dawn Redwood** p.144
   b) hard, spirally set needles arising alternately on shoot; buds in leaf axils: **6**

6. a) sharp-pointed needles longest at branchlet middle; scale leaves on leading and cone shoots. Waxy, grapefruit smell: **Coast Redwood** p.146
   b) blunt-tipped needles of various lengths, 2 blue-white bands below. Mouse-like smell (as Hemlock): **Western Hemlock** p.148

c) soft-pointed needles of various lengths, yellow-green below. 2nd year twig remains green. Smell not distinctive: **Yew** p.141

7. a) green needles, fruity aroma; oval, raised needle scars: **Douglas Fir** p.150
   b) grey-blue, stiff needles in upturned ranks; circular, raised needle scars: **Noble Fir** p.152

8. a) leaves awl-shaped, 90° to stem, most in whorls of three; apple-scented: **Juniper** p.166
   b) needles in whorls on short woody side shoots: **9**
   c) needles grouped in 2s, 3s or 5s: **10**

9. a) needles stiff, dark green (evergreen); in whorls of 10–20 (singly on leading shoots): **Cedar of Lebanon** p.156
   b) needles soft, pale green (deciduous); in whorls of 30–40 (singly on leading shoots): **Larch** p.158

10 a) needles in pairs: **Scots Pine** p.160
   b) needles in threes: **Monterey Pine** p.162
   c) needles in fives: **Weymouth Pine** p.164

11 a) pointed, spreading scales <8mm long, 3-ranked; aniseed smell: **Giant Redwood** p.170
   b) scales small (<3mm, longer on leading shoots), 4-ranked, in unequal-sized appressed pairs. Smell of pineapple when bruised: **Western Red Cedar** p.172
   c) scales tiny (<2mm), in 4-ranked unequal-sized pairs with white 'X' where leaves overlap below. Branchlets flattened, soft; smell of parsley: **Lawson Cypress** p.176
   d) scales tiny (<2mm), ridged and pointed; in 4 equal-sized ranks. Fern-like branchlets on orange twig. Smell not distinctive: **Leyland Cypress** p.174

ii. SUMMER FOLIAGE KEY TO BROAD-LEAVED TREES
(Trees with leaves having a blade at least 1cm wide; typically net-veined)

1. a) leaves in opposite pairs (or 3 together): **2**
   b) leaves alternate/clustered at apex: **11**

2. a) compound leaf: **3**
   b) simple leaf: **5**

3. a) leaflets palmate: **Horse Chestnut:** p.120
   b) leaflets pinnate: **4**

4. a) 3–7 toothed leaflets, upper pair sessile, smell unpleasant when crushed: **Elder** p.118
   b) 7–15 toothed leaflets all stalked, smell innocuous: **Ash** p.115

5. a) leaf palmately lobed: **6**
   b) leaf not lobed: **7**

6. a) leaf >8cm long; pointed, coarsely-toothed lobes; no latex in petiole: **Sycamore** p.125
   b) leaf <8cm long; round lobes, no/few blunt teeth; latex in petiole: **Field Maple** p.122

7. a) leaf <3cm long; margin entire: **Box** p.138
   b) leaf >3cm long: **8**

8. a) leaf with toothed margin: **9**
   b) leaf with entire margin: **10**

9. a) leaf glabrous, narrow ovate, small pointed teeth; side veins run to margin: **Spindle** p.136
   b) leaf glabrous, ovate, margin with fine round teeth, side veins curve to apex: **Buckthorn** p.134
   c) large (>6cm long) broadly ovate leaf, distinct veins, downy below: **Wayfaring Tree** p.130

10. a) leaf glabrous, sub-glossy: **Wild Privet** p.130
    b) leaf sparsely hairy on both sides; few prominent side veins all curve to apex: **Dogwood** p.132
    c) juvenile leaf matt, blue-green, aromatic (n.b. adult leaves are alternate): **Gum Tree** p.110

11. a) leaf compound: **12**
    b) leaf simple: **14**

12. a) leaf of 3 leaflets: **Laburnum** p.60
    b) leaf pinnate: **13**

13. a) 5–9 leaflets, margin entire: **Walnut** p.58
    b) 9–15 toothed leaflets: **Rowan** p.55

14. a) leaf lobed: **15**
    b) leaf not lobed: **21**

15. a) lobes lateral: **16**
    b) lobes palmate: **18**

16. a) leaf apex indented; one lobe each side, veins like fan ribs: **Maidenhair Tree** p.36
    b) leaf apex flat; two lobes each side: **Tulip Tree** p.68
    c) leaf apex lobed or pointed: **17**

17. a) leaf length <5cm; toothed, pointed lobes: **Hawthorn** p.64
    b) leaf length >5cm; entire, rounded lobes: **Oak** p.66

18. a) leaf thick, leathery: **Fig** p.62
    b) leaf not as above: **19**

19. a) hairs on leaf underside white, woolly: **White Poplar** p.72
    b) hairs on leaf underside sparse or only on veins: **20**

20. a) petiole >5cm, expanded base cups bud: **London Plane** p.70
    b) petiole <5cm; base not cupping bud: **Wild Service Tree** p.74

21. a) long leaves (>2 x breadth) **22**
    b) short leaves (<2 x breadth) **29**

22. a) leaf margin entire: **23**
    b) leaf margin toothed: **25**

23. a) length <7cm; matt above: **Gum Tree** p.110
    b) length >7cm; glossy above: **24**

33

24 a) underside pale green, glabrous; margin inrolled: **Rhododendron** p.104
b) as above; crushed leaf smells of bitter almonds (most leaves are toothed; see 28): **Cherry Laurel** p.102
c) underside and petiole with rust-coloured hairs: **Evergreen Magnolia** p.106

25 a) knobbly red glands near petiole base: **Wild Cherry** p.98
b) petiole without glands: **26**

26 a) leaf <1.5cm wide; small, regular marginal teeth, white hairs below: **White Willow** p.112
b) leaf >1.5cm wide; large or irregular marginal teeth, glabrous underside: **27**

27 a) leaf <10cm long; small marginal teeth, hairy petiole: **Strawberry Tree** p.108
b) leaf >10cm long: **28**

28 a) leaf rigid, glossy; teeth few, irregular; crushed leaf smells of bitter almonds: **Cherry Laurel** p.102
b) leaf pliable, glossy; prominent side veins (c.20 pairs) end in soft spines: **Sweet Chestnut** p.52

29 a) mature leaf hairy above: **30**
b) mature leaf glabrous above: **33**

30 a) rough textured leaf: **31**
b) smooth textured leaf: **32**

31 a) ovate leaf, unequal-sided blade base partially obscures short petiole: **Wych Elm** p.77
b) heart-shaped leaf with stout petiole: **Black Mulberry** p.42

32 a) margin with double, irregular teeth; white hairs on veins below: **Hazel:** p.82
b) margin fine-toothed, hairs in vein axils below: **Lime** p.44

33 a) leaf with at least some hairs below: **34**
b) leaf glabrous below: **37**

34 a) covering of hairs: **35**
b) hairy only on veins: **36**
c) hairy only in vein axils: **Alder** p.84

35 a) oblong-ovate, thick, glossy; entire or spine-edged leaves: **Holm Oak** p.50
b) broadly ovate leaf; toothed margin, white and felty below: **Whitebeam** p.80
c) broadly ovate; toothed margin, blue-green and downy below: **Goat Willow** p.90

36 a) margin double-toothed, c.15 pairs of parallel, impressed lateral veins: **Hornbeam** p.86
b) margin fine-toothed, lateral veins few, branching: **Crab Apple:** p.94

37 a) leaf rigid, thick, evergreen; margin often spiny: **Holly** p.47
b) not as above: **38**

38 a) margin entire (often wavy): **Beech** p.88
b) margin toothed: **39**

39 a) leaf outline lanceolate-ovate: **Bay Willow** p.92
b) leaf outline triangular/diamond-shaped: **40**

40 a) leaf margin with small, rounded teeth: **Black Poplar** p.40
b) leaf margin with double, pointed teeth: **Silver Birch** p.38

Broad-leaved Trees

Alternate – spiny or unusually shaped leaves (pp.36–53)

Maidenhair Tree
Ginkgo biloba

The sole survivor of a primitive group (it occurs as 200 million year-old fossils) which flourished before the advance of the Conifers to which, despite its leaf shape, it is related. Native to China it survived as a sacred tree in Buddhist temples. Deciduous; less distinctive in winter.

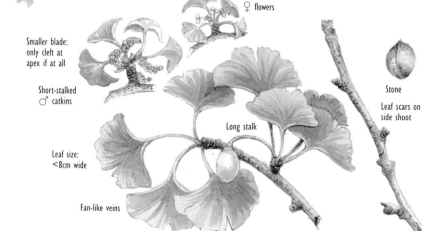

<30m

USES:
Edible kernel (eaten in Japan). Used herbally to improve circulation.

INTRODUCED via Japan in 1754. Frequently planted; less in the North. Either a slender, little-forked bole with short horizontal or ascending branches (pendulous tips) or much forked with a broader crown.

BARK: Deeply fissured, becomes fluted with age.

TIMBER: Pale yellow, light, not used commercially.

TWIG: New shoots green, brown by autumn; knobbly grey side shoots at right-angles.

BUDS: Small, conical, red-brown, glabrous.

LEAVES: Few, widely spaced. Blade cleft almost to the short petiole; most clustered on side shoots, on a long petiole. Thick but pliable. Matt green; gold in autumn.

FLOWERS: Most British trees are male. Female flowers like tiny acorns on a stalk which expands at its apex to form the fruit.

FRUIT: Pendulous, ripening yellow-brown. Flesh rots with a putrid smell to reveal plum-like stone with kernel.

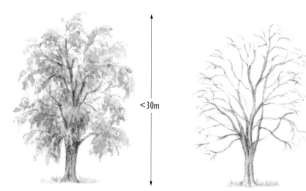

♀ flowers

Smaller blade:
only cleft at
apex if at all

Short-stalked
♂ catkins

Long stalk

Stone

Leaf scars on
side shoot

Leaf size:
<8cm wide

Fan-like veins

J
F
M
A
M
J
J
A
S
O
N
D

36

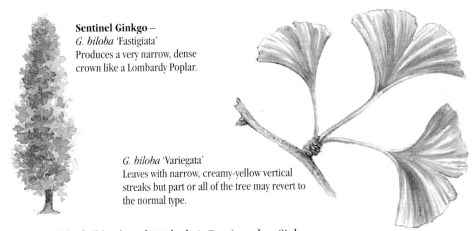

Sentinel Ginkgo –
G. biloba 'Fastigiata'
Produces a very narrow, dense crown like a Lombardy Poplar.

G. biloba 'Variegata'
Leaves with narrow, creamy-yellow vertical streaks but part or all of the tree may revert to the normal type.

The unusual leaf, (like that of Maidenhair Fern), makes Ginkgo instantly recognisable in summer. In winter the leafless, knobbly, short side shoots are similar to:

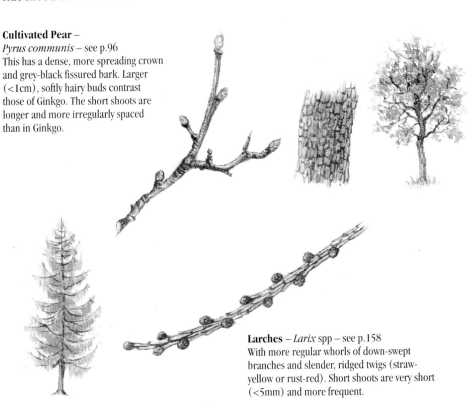

Cultivated Pear –
Pyrus communis – see p.96
This has a dense, more spreading crown and grey-black fissured bark. Larger (<1cm), softly hairy buds contrast those of Ginkgo. The short shoots are longer and more irregularly spaced than in Ginkgo.

Larches – *Larix* spp – see p.158
With more regular whorls of down-swept branches and slender, ridged twigs (straw-yellow or rust-red). Short shoots are very short (<5mm) and more frequent.

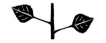

Silver Birch

Betula pendula (verrucosa)

DECIDUOUS
Betulaceae

A fast growing, pioneer tree; readily establishing in open habitats and able to grow at high altitudes. The small, widely-spaced leaves allow light to reach ground level resulting in a profuse ground flora. Short-lived, it often succumbs to Birch Bracket fungus. The similar Downy Birch is frequently mistaken for Silver Birch.

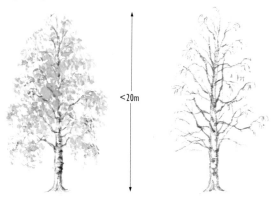

<20m

Horizontal lenticels

Diamond-shaped black patches

USES:
Twigs for besoms and horse jumps. Bark for roof shingles (wooden tiles). Sap for wine and shampoo. Wood for charcoal, bobbins, spools and reels.

NATIVE and common as open woodland on heaths and light soils. Also in mixed woods and gardens. Narrow oval, open crown, becoming more broadly domed. Pendulous tips.
BARK: Shiny red-brown when young, soon pinky-white. Later with deep black fissures.
TIMBER: Not durable. Pale. No obvious rings or grain.
TWIG: Thin, pliable and hairless. Purple bloom in early spring.
BUDS: Small, oval; angled from twig.
LEAVES: Spaced, small, variable but always taper-pointed. Outline triangular with a flat base or diamond-like with a wedge-shaped base. Thin, hairless. c.6 prs of side veins, each ends in a large tooth. 2 or 3 smaller teeth between each large tooth.
FLOWERS: Pendulous male catkins form late summer and elongate and open yellow in spring. Stalked green female catkins start erect.
FRUITS: Within the now pendulous, pale brown, female catkin. Hundreds of tiny seeds interspersed with scales.

J
F
M
A
M
J
J
A
S
O
N
D

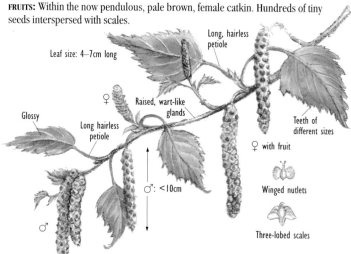

Leaf size: 4–7cm long

Long, hairless petiole

♀

Raised, wart-like glands

Glossy

Long hairless petiole

Teeth of different sizes

♀ with fruit

♂: <10cm

Winged nutlets

♂

Three-lobed scales

Downy Birch – *Betula pubescens*
Native on wet soil, especially peat. The commonest Birch in the Scottish Highlands. Rarely in gardens. A smaller tree. Erect branches lack pendulous tips. Twigs without glands but hairy when young. Bark brown or grey-white, peels in horizontal strips. Leaf more rounded at the corners, less taper-pointed with a regular, single-toothed margin and a downy petiole. Flowers and fruits similar.

Hybrids between *pubescens* and *pendula* are frequent and create problems for the beginner!

Downy young twig and petiole

Teeth all same size

Dwarf Birch – *Betula nana* (not illustrated)
Native on moors and bogs in Northumberland and Scotland. A shrub no more than a metre tall. Pubescent twigs; short-stalked leaves nearly circular in outline with deeply, blunt-toothed margins. Narrowly winged seed.

Introduced Birch species planted for their attractive bark include:

Szechuan Birch – *Betula platyphylla* var. *Szechvanica*
The chalky-white bark reaches well up the crown. Thick, glossy, blue-green leaves.

Autumn colours

Paper Birch – *Betula papyrifera*
White peeling bark reveals new orange-pink growth. Twig glabrous and warty. Larger, matt green leaf (<10cm), doubly-toothed margin and hairy petiole.

Another introduced tree has a Birch-like leaf:

Grey Alder – *Alnus incana* – see p.85
Grey bark, stalked buds and larger leaves with 9–12 prs of side veins which are pubescent on the undersurface. Cone-like fruits (old brown ones retained) prevent confusion with Birch.

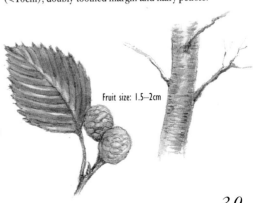

Fruit size: 1.5–2cm

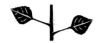

Black Poplar
Populus nigra ssp *betulifolia*

DECIDUOUS
Salicaceae

Uncommon in the wild, (it now rarely sets viable seed) but it was much planted in the industrial North due to its smoke tolerance. Often pollarded or damaged, giving an untidy look. Confused with introduced hybrid species (which grow faster). The 'Black' refers to its dark bark. White Poplar has lobed leaves, pale below – see p.72.

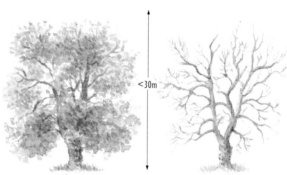

<30m

WILD south of a line from the Humber to the Mersey; also planted. Prefers damp soils. Short, swollen, burred bole. Broad, domed crown; branches ascend then curve down with almost vertical side shoots.

BARK: Deeply and coarsely-fissured, grey-brown to black.

TIMBER: Pale grey-white, light weight.

TWIG: Slender; initially hairy later smooth, grey-brown.

BUDS: Terminal large, scaled, sticky, brown; others appressed to stem, straw-coloured.

LEAVES: Shaped like an ace of spades, largest on burr shoots. Translucent toothed margin. Thick, glossy, paler below. Yellow-brown in autumn.

FLOWERS: Separate sex trees (see below).

USES:
Was used for cart bottoms, and brake blocks. Made into both matches and match-boxes.

FRUIT: Small green capsules; seeds with fluffy white down.

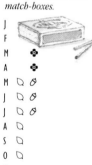

Bud: <1cm

J
F
M ❖
A ❖
M ◗ ⊘
J ◗ ⊘
J ◗ ⊘
A ◗
S ◗
O ◗
N
D

♀ catkins cream and green, loose-flowered

Petiole laterally flattened, no glands 3–6cm

♂ catkins short-stalked, soon fall

Green bracts and crimson stamens

Leaf size: 5–8cm x 5–8cm

Rounded, forward-pointing teeth

40

There are many introduced cultivars, hybrids and species of *Populus* including:

Lombardy Poplar – *Populus nigra* 'Italica'
Narrowly columnar, with a smoother bole and twigs; broader leaf. Male clone (cultivated from cuttings) thus no female catkins or fruit. The rarer female clone 'Gigantea' has a broader-topped crown and female catkins.

Black Italian Poplar – *P. x canadensis* 'Serotina'
Much planted male clone. Long unburred bole, more upswept lower branches, neater, rounded crown; smooth, angular twigs. Larger bud. Leaves emerge red-brown, very late then bright, glossy-green, matt below. Base flat. Longer smooth petiole. Purple-red male catkins. No females or fruit.

Glands at base of petiole

Grown for their attractive leaves and sweet smell from expanding buds and leaves are:

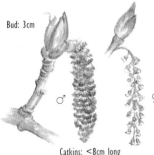

Bud: 3cm

Short petiole not laterally flattened

♂   ♀

Leaf size: <30cm

Catkins: <8cm long

Western Balsam Poplar – *P. trichocarpa*
Large tree with huge varnished, balsam-scented terminal buds; large flat-based, long-pointed oval leaves; margin finely toothed or entire. Underside pale, as if whitewashed; net-veined. Caterpillar-like male catkins. Slender, green female catkins. Woolly-seeded fruit.

Balm of Gilead – *P. candicans* (not illustrated)
As *trichocarpa* but suckering. Downy shoots and petioles, more heart-shaped leaves. Female only.

Lilac – *Syringa vulgaris*
Shrub with similar leaves borne in opposite pairs, no marginal teeth or laterally-flattened petiole. Showy fragrant pink/lilac/white flower-heads.

Lime – *Tilia x europaea* (not illustrated) – see p.44
Thinner leaf with heart-shaped base; paler, less shiny and more finely toothed. Hair tufts in vein axils below. Petiole round in cross section.

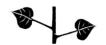

Common or Black Mulberry
Morus nigra

DECIDUOUS
Moraceae

Introduced from Asia before the 17th Century it was highly esteemed by the Victorians for its edible fruit. Old trees are still found in sheltered gardens and it is once again being more widely planted. When young it grows quickly but later appears very old, with a sinuous, often leaning bole. Sometimes confused with White Mulberry.

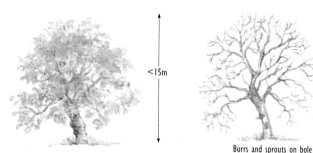

<15m

Burrs and sprouts on bole

USES:
Tarts, jam and wine. White Mulberry leaves are the preferred food plant of the 'silkworm' moth caterpillars.

INFREQUENT in parks and gardens; more in the South. As wide as it is tall. Short, often leaning bole. Branches twist giving an aged look; some reach the ground and take root.
BARK: Orange-brown, rough with peeling scales.
TWIG: Stout with scattered, large lenticels.
BUDS: Small (6mm), shiny red-brown.
LEAVES: Large ovate to heart-shaped; often curled, stiff, with a pointed tip. Margin irregularly, deeply double-toothed; larger teeth are rounded. Upper side deep-green, sub-shiny. Paler and softly downy below.
FLOWERS: On same or separate branches; short, pendulous, stalked male catkins; female catkins barely stalked, upright, bristly from the mass of stigmas.
FRUIT: Loganberry-like; a cluster of small fruits on a tiny stalk. Start hard and green, ripen orange to scarlet to deep purple-black and soft by late autumn.

A few leaves are 3-lobed

Flower size:
<1cm ♂

Leaf size: <18cm x 15cm

Hairy petiole

Upper surface of leaf roughly hairy

Broken twig exudes a milky juice

Pubescent twig

♀

J
F
M
A
M
J
J
A
S
O
N
D

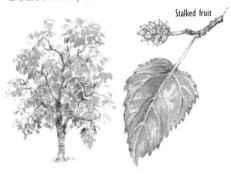

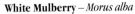

Stalked fruit

Very short petiole

White Mulberry – *Morus alba*
Less common Chinese introduction; a taller tree with smoother, finer shoots. Leaf not curling, glossy and hairless above and on a longer (3–4cm) petiole. Fruit start white, ripen yellowish pink or purple.

Red Mulberry – *Morus rubra* (not illustrated)
American species not well suited to our climate. Similar to *alba* but leaves more rounded, very downy below; fruit starts red before going purple.

Leaves of a similar shape and size are found on:

Wych Elm – *Ulmus glabra* – (right) see p.77
Very rough feel to the narrower hairy leaf which is widest above the middle, has more sharply toothed margins and a shouldered, often lop-sided base.

Red-tipped hairs

♂

Hazel – *Corylus avellana* – (left) see p.82
Young twig covered in long red-tipped hairs, leaf petiole with glandular hairs. Blade margin is sharply toothed and the upper surface is **softly** hairy.

Limes – *Tilia* spp – see p.44 (not illustrated)
Much taller trees; Common Lime has leaves with a glabrous upper surface, those of Large-leaved Lime bear long white hairs, neither are rough to the touch. Leaves have fine-toothed margins.

Handkerchief Tree – *Davidia involucrata* (above)
From China; instantly recognisable by its long white flower bracts but the leaf is Mulberry-like. Smooth, bright-green upperside; with dense white hairs below. Margin with pointed, triangular teeth.

Common Lime
Tilia x europaea (vulgaris)

DECIExcuous
Tiliaceae

A hybrid between Small-leaved and Large-leaved Lime. One of our tallest broad-leaved species, it is widely planted in parks, large gardens and streets where its basal sprouts and rain of sticky aphid honeydew cause problems to both pedestrians and car owners.

<45m

Burrs and sprouting shoots

USES:
Bark – rope and mats. Wood – piano keys, shoe lasts and carving. Flowers – honey and herbal cold remedies.

INTRODUCED and common; usually planted. Tall dome of ascending branches which arch down forming a dense canopy.

BARK: Smooth and grey, becoming finely fissured.

TIMBER: Pale yellow with little marking. Soft and light.

TWIG: Zig-zag growth form; smooth, glossy red-brown.

BUDS: Flattened, ovoid. One large and one small scale like a 'finger and thumb.'

LEAVES: 2-ranked. Broad. Heart-shaped or flat base – often lop-sided. 6–10cm x 6–10cm, those on sprout shoots <50% larger. Mid-green and smooth above, paler below. Patches of aphid honeydew may blacken with Sooty Mould.

FLOWERS: Clusters of 4–10 pendent flowers beneath a strap-like bract. 5 sepals, 5 petals, many orange anthers. Sweet smell.

FRUIT: Clustered, ovoid, pale green, pubescent, thick-shelled and faintly 5 ribbed. 8–10mm long.

J
F
M
A   ◌
M   ◌
J   ◌ ❖
J   ◌ ❖
A   ◌ ⌀
S   ◌ ⌀
O
N
D

Shiny red-brown bud

White hair tufts in underside vein axils

Smooth petiole 2–5cm

Side veins branch

Bract

Sharply fine-toothed

Red Nail Galls common

Flower size: 8–10mm

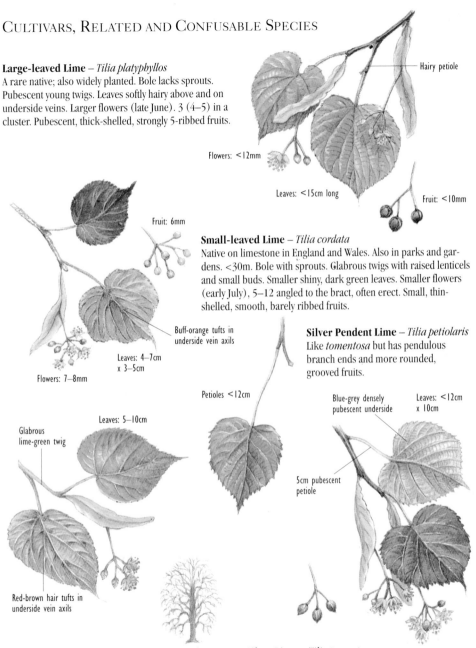

Large-leaved Lime – *Tilia platyphyllos*
A rare native; also widely planted. Bole lacks sprouts.
Pubescent young twigs. Leaves softly hairy above and on
underside veins. Larger flowers (late June). 3 (4–5) in a
cluster. Pubescent, thick-shelled, strongly 5-ribbed fruits.

Hairy petiole

Flowers: <12mm

Leaves: <15cm long

Fruit: <10mm

Fruit: 6mm

Small-leaved Lime – *Tilia cordata*
Native on limestone in England and Wales. Also in parks and gardens. <30m. Bole with sprouts. Glabrous twigs with raised lenticels
and small buds. Smaller shiny, dark green leaves. Smaller flowers
(early July), 5–12 angled to the bract, often erect. Small, thin-
shelled, smooth, barely ribbed fruits.

Buff-orange tufts in
underside vein axils

Silver Pendent Lime – *Tilia petiolaris*
Like *tomentosa* but has pendulous
branch ends and more rounded,
grooved fruits.

Leaves: 4–7cm
x 3–5cm

Flowers: 7–8mm

Petioles <12cm

Blue-grey densely
pubescent underside

Leaves: <12cm
x 10cm

Leaves: 5–10cm

Glabrous
lime-green twig

5cm pubescent
petiole

Red-brown hair tufts in
underside vein axils

Caucasian Lime – *Tilia x euchlora*
Infrequently planted. Densely twiggy with pendulous
lower branches. Glossy green, unequal-based leaves.
Yellow-white flowers in clusters of 3–7 (late July).
Pubescent, 5-ribbed, oval fruits.

Silver Lime – *Tilia tomentosa*
Much planted in parks. Grey young shoot. Crinkled,
dark green, hairless leaves. Margin sharply and unevenly
toothed. Clusters (7–10) of pale flowers (August).
Narcotic to bees. 5-angled, warty fruit.

Although much smaller in stature, the following trees have
similar shaped leaves:

Stout hairy petiole

Leaves: 12cm x 8cm

Black Mulberry – *Morus nigra* – see p.42
Distinguished by the larger leaves with double-toothed
margin; sub-shiny and deep green above, softly downy
below. Small green male and female catkins.
Loganberry-like fruit ripen purple-black and soft by
autumn.

Handkerchief Tree or Dove Tree –
Davidia involucrata
The large leaf has more pointed, triangular marginal
teeth. Bright green, smooth upperside and either dense
white hairs below or smooth and green (different
cultivars). Small head of purple flowers in May–June
is surrounded by two prominent yellow-white bracts.
Long-stalked green fruit like an unripe walnut, matures
dark purple. Introduced from China.

Leaves: <17cm x 15cm

Bract

Leaves: <25cm

Indian Bean Tree –
Catalpa bignoniodes
Has **opposite**, larger untoothed leaves which
emerge very late (June). Smooth above they
are hairy on the underside. Grown in large
gardens (mostly in the South) it has erect
showy Horse Chestnut-like flowerheads, each
frilly white flower having yellow or purple
markings. Fruit like very narrow brown bean
pods in hanging clusters; often overwinter.

Foxglove Tree – *Paulownia tomentosa* (not illustrated)
Also has **opposite**, untoothed leaves which can reach 35cm long. Pale green
above, densely pubescent below as is the long petiole. Flowers in May/June
(before the leaves emerge) as erect panicles of blue-purple, tubular, foxglove-
like flowers. A Chinese introduction mostly found in southern gardens.

Holly
Ilex aquifolium

A common evergreen tree or shrub in both town and countryside. A popular Christmas symbol. Problems with identification arise largely as a result of the many cultivars, confusion with Highclere Holly and in deciding on the sex of a plant – the well-known cultivar 'Golden Queen' is in fact male!

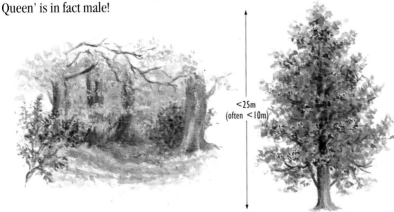

<25m
(often <10m)

NATIVE: Over most of Britain. Common as a shrub/small tree in woods, hedges and rocky ground. Also in gardens, parks and churchyards. Branches arch down (lowest ones to the ground), tips turn up. Untidy when old. Straight bole.
BARK: Silvery-grey, smooth; becoming bumpy with age.
TIMBER: Pure white and very close grained.
TWIG: Green and smooth, tinged purple in exposed plants.
BUD: Tiny, green, egg-shaped.
LEAVES: Glossy, thick and leathery with a pointed tip. Lower ones with undulating triangular marginal teeth each ending in a stiff spine. Upper ones flatter, less spiny or with entire margins. Short, green, grooved petiole.
FLOWERS: Separate sex trees. Fragrant clusters of small creamy-white, waxy flowers (pink tipped in bud). N.B. female flowers include stamens!
FRUIT: Clusters of small oval berries which ripen from green to orange-red by late autumn. Overwinter if not eaten by thrushes or fieldfares.

USES:
Foliage was fed to animals in winter. Bark produced sticky bird-lime (see p.21). Timber used in turnery, inlay and, when stained, as a substitute for ebony.

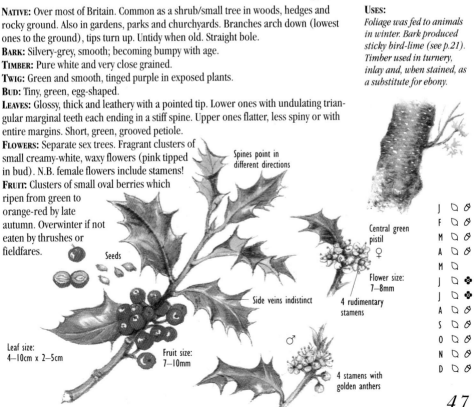

Spines point in different directions

Central green pistil ♀

Flower size: 7–8mm

4 rudimentary stamens

Side veins indistinct

Seeds

Leaf size: 4–10cm x 2–5cm

Fruit size: 7–10mm

♂

4 stamens with golden anthers

J	◗	♂
F	◗	♂
M	◗	♂
A	◗	♂
M	◗	
J	◗	❀
J	◗	❀
A	◗	♂
S	◗	♂
O	◗	♂
N	◗	♂
D	◗	♂

47

There are many cultivars of Holly and most are propagated vegetatively which results in a particular cultivar being either male or female. Examples include:

Most leaves spineless

Conical shape

'Pyramidalis'
A female cultivar bearing lots of fruit.

'Pendula'
Female with a
weeping form.
Branches reach
the ground.

Leaves with
more spines

'Bacciflava'
Female with many
bright-yellow berries.

'Golden Queen'
Male! (so no berries). Leaves with a yellow margin.

Small spines on
leaf blade

'Ferox' – **Hedgehog Holly**
Male with additional spines on the upper surface of
the leaf blade. Less common. Good for hedges.

Highclere Holly – *Ilex x altaclarensis*
There are many cultivars of this hybrid between Holly and Canary Holly; some occasionally naturalize in woodland near gardens. They have more vigorous growth, purple-grey bark, a purple tinge to the twig and petiole and flatter leaves (most also have larger leaves than *aquifolium*). The spines are smaller and all forward-pointing. The flowers are slightly larger. Examples include:

'Camellifolia'
Female with a pyramidal crown and large, mostly entire, Camellia-like leaves (purple when young).

'Hodginsii'
Most are male plants with large flat leaves; some with entire margins others with up to 9 spines each side. Both forms often on the same branch. Tolerant of salt and smoke so often planted in coastal and urban regions.

Purple twig

12cm x 6cm

Other trees or shrubs with holly-like **leaves:**

Oregan Grape – *Mahonia aquifolium*
Although rarely taller than 1.5m and bearing clusters of yellow flowers this garden and naturalised understorey shrub has glossy, prickly, evergreen leaves. Unlike Holly these are compound – there is no bud at the leaflet base.

Compound leaf

Desfontainia spinosa (not illustrated)
Garden shrub with opposite holly-like leaves and pendent, long, tubular, red-orange flowers.

No bud at leaflet base

Holm Oak – *Quercus ilex*
see p.50 (not illustrated here)
Easily distinguished when in fruit but has Holly-like evergreen, shiny, dark-green leaves and those on lower branches are broad and spiny toothed. They differ in being less stiff with 7–11 prs of prominent side veins and a felted white underside. Larger tree with dark grey, scaly bark.

Strawberry Tree – *Arbutus unedo*
see p.108 (not illustrated here)
Another shrub/small tree with dark green, oval, evergreen leaves but these have fine-toothed margins rather than spines and young twigs are hairy. Bell-like flowers and Strawberry-like fruits.

New Zealand Holly or **Daisy tree** – *Oleander macrodonta*
A garden shrub with a ribbed, angular, felty grey twig and a pale green-white underside to the Holly-like leaf which has an undulating margin bearing many (up to 20 per side) pointed lobes.
Fragrant Daisy-like flowers.

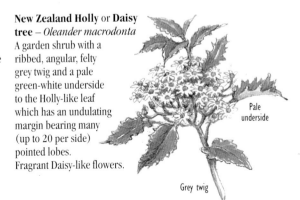
Pale underside

Grey twig

49

Holm Oak or Evergreen Oak
Quercus ilex

EVERGREEN
Fagaceae

I ntroduced some 400 years ago from the Mediterranean region, this sombre tree has very variable evergreen leaves, the more spiny ones being rather Holly-like. Grows best in coastal regions where it gets mild winters; heavy frosts damage the leaves which withstand salt-laden wind.

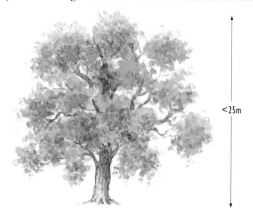

<25m

USES:
Used in its native region for furniture and tool making; the Romans are said to have used it for axles.

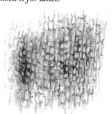

FREQUENT in southern parks and large gardens especially near the sea. Rarer in the North. Short, much-branched trunk gives a compact, broadly domed outline.

BARK: Thin, dark grey; flaking into rectangular scales.

TIMBER: Similar to but darker than Oak.

TWIG: Grey-brown, downy when young; densely leafy.

BUDS: Tiny; terminal, with whisker-like stipules.

LEAVES: Leathery but pliable; many shed early summer. Replacements pale and hairy, later shiny, dark-green. Young petiole downy. Blade on young/low branches broad, spiny-toothed; on old/upper branches narrower, with down-curled entire edges.

FLOWERS: With new leaves. ♀ tiny, grey-green, tipped pink on a stout woolly stalk.

FRUIT: Clusters of 1–3 pale-green, narrowly oval acorns.

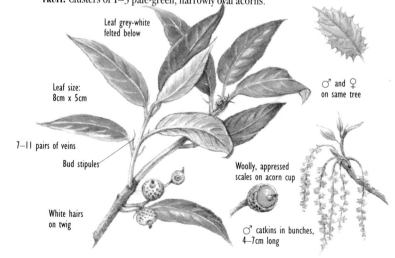

Leaf grey-white felted below

Leaf size: 8cm x 5cm

♂ and ♀ on same tree

7–11 pairs of veins

Bud stipules

Woolly, appressed scales on acorn cup

White hairs on twig

♂ catkins in bunches, 4–7cm long

J ▢
F ▢
M ▢
A ▢
M ▢ ✿
J ▢ ✿
J ▢ ✿
A ▢ ✿
S ▢ ✿
O ▢ ✿
N ▢
D ▢

Mossy cup

Leaf size: 4–6cm x 2cm

Lucombe Oak – *Quercus hispanica* 'Lucombeana'
Variable Turkey/Cork Oak hybrid. Leaves usually over winter especially when planted in the milder South West. Smaller leaves with c.5 prs of triangular, forward-pointing lobes each ending in a short spine. Acorns like Turkey Oak (see p.67) but the long cup scales are not parted.

Spreading cup scales

Cork Oak – *Quercus suber*
The thick corky bark is cut commercially in S. Europe but the untidy tree is rarely planted in Britain. Young shoots downy grey. Evergreen leaves shorter, more oval with 4–6 pointed teeth or entire margins.

Three small trees have similar evergreen leaves:

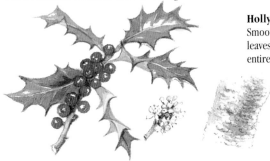

Holly – *Ilex aquifolium* – see p.47
Smooth bark, green twigs and glossy, very waxy, stiff leaves some with spreading spines others flat and with entire margins. Red berries only on female trees.

Prominent white midrib

Peeling bark

Phillyrea – *Phillyrea latifolia*
Outline similar to Holm Oak but the dark glossy leaves are **opposite**, matt-green below with obvious veins. Sweet-smelling flowers in the leaf axils and currant-sized, purple-black berries (see right).

Shallow-toothed margin

Strawberry Tree – *Arbutus unedo* – see p.108
Shrub-like. Leaf margins neatly saw-toothed. White, bell-shaped flowers opening in autumn as the previous year's globular fruits turn strawberry-coloured.

Spanish or *Sweet Chestnut*
Castanea sativa

DECIDUOUS
Fagaceae

A Roman introduction; its edible nuts seldom grow large enough to eat in northern Britain where self-sown seeds rarely germinate. Planted in parks, country estates and mixed woods. Some pure stands are found in S. England where it is still coppiced. Currently threatened by a fungus which has already killed many trees in France.

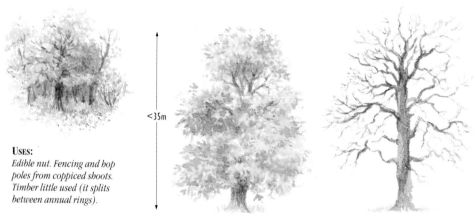

<35m

USES:
Edible nut. Fencing and hop poles from coppiced shoots. Timber little used (it splits between annual rings).

Deep spiralling fissures

INTRODUCED. Common; best on light, acidic soils. Tall, narrow-crowned. Straight, massive bole. Branches ascend and twist but spread when older.

BARK: Grey, smooth; later browner, fissured.

TIMBER: Like Oak but lacking a silver hue.

TWIG: Initially downy, grey-bloomed; later glabrous with longitudinal ridges.

BUDS: Small, few-scaled, shiny.

LEAVES: Two-ranked, leathery, very long and narrow. Dark-green, glossy. Lateral vein ends as soft, forward-pointing spine in the middle of a tooth. Yellow/brown autumn colours.

FLOWERS: Male catkin – cord-like, pale yellow, smells of semen; others with unopened male flowers at apex and clusters of green female flowers at the base.

FRUIT: Four spiny bracts open to reveal 2/3 flattened nuts.

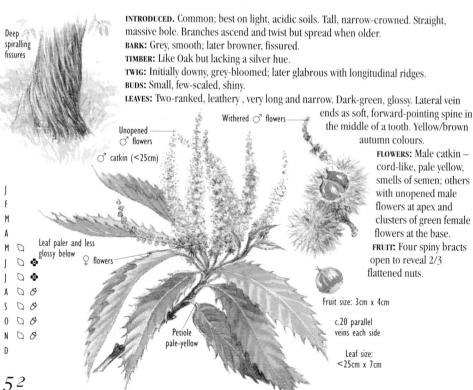

Withered ♂ flowers

Unopened ♂ flowers

♂ catkin (<25cm)

Leaf paler and less glossy below

♀ flowers

Petiole pale-yellow

Fruit size: 3cm x 4cm

c.20 parallel veins each side

Leaf size: <25cm x 7cm

J
F
M
A
M ▢
J ▢ ❀
J ▢ ❀
A ▢ ◈
S ▢ ◈
O ▢ ◈
N ▢ ◈
D

Unusual cultivars include: 'Laciniata'   'Albomarginata'

Whiskered
side bud

Some collections in S. England include a number
of Oak species with Chestnut-like leaves:

Chestnut-leaved Oak – *Quercus castaneifolia*
Leaves of a similar size and shape but only 10–12
prs of side veins. Veins downy on underside and
end in a spineless tooth. Smoother bark, large
brown terminal bud (part of a cluster). Single
acorn, half enclosed in a long-scaled cup.

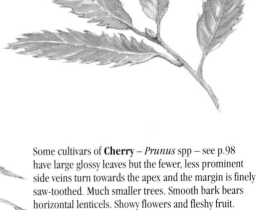

Japanese Chestnut Oak – *Quercus acutissima*
Leaves very like *Castanea* with 12–16 prs of side
veins and bristle-like teeth but with hair tufts in the
vein axils below. Also differs in its pale green
shoots and slender-pointed green buds. Acorns
not seen in Britain.

Some cultivars of **Cherry** – *Prunus* spp – see p.98
have large glossy leaves but the fewer, less prominent
side veins turn towards the apex and the margin is finely
saw-toothed. Much smaller trees. Smooth bark bears
horizontal lenticels. Showy flowers and fleshy fruit.

Broad-leaved Trees

Alternate – compound or lobed leaves (pp.55–75)

Mountain Ash or Rowan

Sorbus aucuparia

DECIDUOUS
Rosaceae

The name Rowan comes from rune – the Norse alphabet was carved on its wood. Being hardy it can grow high on mountains and does have an Ash-like compound leaf. Previously planted to ward off witch-craft, now grown for its showy flowers and colourful fruits. Easily confused with a number of introduced *Sorbus* species.

<20m

NATIVE: Commonest in the North and West. Wood edges, moors, cliffs and mountains especially on moist acid soil. Much planted by roadsides. Small, often multi-stemmed but sparsely branched. Ascending branches produce an open, irregular crown.

BARK: Smooth, shiny, silver-grey to purple-brown.

TIMBER: Grey-yellow, fine-grained, hard; takes polish.

TWIG: Initially downy then smooth, grey-purple.

BUDS: Large with an incurved pointed tip.

LEAVES: Pinnately compound. 6 or 7 (4–9) pairs of sessile, oblong, pointed leaflets and one stalked terminal leaflet. Red-green petiole rounded at its base but grooved among the leaflets. Orange/red autumn colours more frequent in the North.

FLOWERS: Large, flat-topped, erect or hanging clusters of small (<8mm) creamy-white, strong-scented flowers on woolly stems. 5 green sepals, (hairy outside) 5 petals, many stamens and a central stigma.

FRUIT: Dense hanging clusters of soft berries ripen from green through yellow and orange to bright scarlet by August. Retained into the winter.

USES:
Berries formerly used by fowlers as bait to trap birds and made into an ale and distilled to a spirit. Now made into jelly to serve with meat dishes. Wood is used by turners.

Flower head size: <15cm

Leaf size: <20cm x 12cm

Horizontal lenticels

Fruit size: <1cm

Bud size: 1.5cm

Evenly-toothed margin

Entire margin at base

Paler and lightly downy below

Leaf-scarred stalk

Purple, hairy-scaled bud

J
F
M
A
M
J
J
A
S
O
N
D

55

Many introduced *Sorbus* species are being planted (even in urban streets) for their compact shape, autumn leaf and winter berry colour. They differ in leaf size and in the colour of buds, leaves and berries.

1. Those with red winter buds:

Japanese Rowan – *S. commixta*
Pointed, shiny, red leaf bud. Large glossy leaves which turn purple and then red in autumn. Smaller, scarlet fruits.

Chinese Scarlet Rowan –
S. commixta 'Embley'
Pointed, shiny, deep-red buds hug the stem. Smaller, slenderer leaflets which turn red, then purple in autumn. Fruit as for *aucuparia*.

Sargent's Rowan – *S. sargentiana*
Ovoid, red, resinous buds; very large leaves, red in autumn. Hanging clusters of up to 200 smaller, bright-red fruit.

2. Those with different fruit colours:

S. aucuparia 'Fructo Luteo'
A cultivar with amber-yellow fruits.

Sorbus 'Joseph Rock'
Grafted on *aucuparia*.
Narrow outline. Bark with orange lenticels. Bright green leaf. Fruit yellow/pale orange.

Only toothed near tip

Hupeh Rowan – *S. hupehensis*
Distinguished by its open branching and blue-grey summer foliage. Broader leaflets are only toothed in the tip region. White or pale pink porcelain-like fruits.

3. Less commonly planted in parks and gardens:

<2cm

True Service Tree – *S. domestica*
With shredding, brown bark and green, rounded buds.
Drooping yellow-green leaves. Larger flowers and bigger
fruits, fewer in a cluster. Apple or pear-shaped.

Swedish Service Tree – *S. hybrida*
Mid-way between Swedish Whitebeam (see
p.80) and Rowan from which it is distinguished
by having usually only 2 (1–3) prs of
free leaflets at the leaf base, the
rest of the blade being a large
terminal lobe.

White underside

Two common native trees have leaves which can
be confused with Mountain Ash but they are
borne in **opposite pairs:**

Ash – *Fraxinus excelsior* – see p.115
A much taller tree. Bark lacks horizontal
lenticels. Broad, hairless, sooty-black
buds. Leaves with fewer, short-stalked
leaflets (3–7), the terminal pair usually the largest. Leaflets
shallowly and irregularly single-
toothed. Green petiole. The flowers and
fruits cannot be confused with Rowan.

Elder – *Sambucus nigra* – see p.118
Shrub-like. Green young twigs. Buds lack scales. 5 (or 7) toothed
leaflets are short-stalked and broader than *Sorbus*. Offensive
smell when crushed. Green, grooved petiole is keeled at its base.
Fragrant white flowers have 5 petals fused at the base (unlike
Sorbus). Smaller, rounder fruits turn black in late summer.

57

Common Walnut
Juglans regia

DECIDUOUS
Juglandaceae

The Romans planted Walnuts all over their empire and may have brought the tree to Britain though some authors consider it a 14th Century introduction. Unusual in woods, it is frequent in large gardens and parks but is less common in Northern England and Scotland.

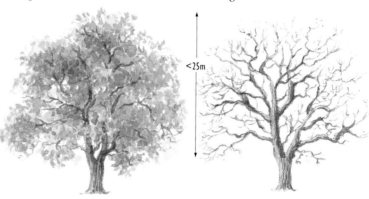

<25m

USES:
Edible fruits (nuts) and oil (also used in varnish). Timber (along with Black Walnut) is used in high class furniture, for veneers and gun stocks.

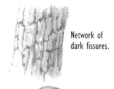

Network of dark fissures.

INTRODUCED: Frequent especially in the South. Ash-like bole. Open crown. Untidy, heavy ascending branches often twist.
BARK: Grey and smooth, later rougher.
TIMBER: Heavy, strong. Pale grey-brown with beautiful brown or grey veins.
TWIGS: Stout, smooth.
BUDS: Purple-brown, velvety, squat.
LEAVES: Pinnately compound with 7 (5–9) shiny, broad, untoothed leaflets; the apical one stalked and larger, the basal pr much smaller. Torn leaves release an acrid-smelling juice which stains skin brown. Dull brown in autumn. Leaflets fall separately.
FLOWERS: Separate sex flowers on the same tree. Pendulous male catkins on previous year's growth. Females in the new leaf axils. 2–5 small green, flask-shaped, short-stalked flowers.
FRUIT: 1 or 2 (3) plum-shaped drupes. Soft green husk covers the wrinkled, hard-shelled nut. Enclosed seed (kernal) is deeply fissured and in two parts, like a human brain.

J
F
M
A
M
J
J
A
S
O
N
D

Chambered pith

7–12 prs of curving side veins

♀ Forked, curving, yellow stigma

Small raised glands

5cm

V-shaped leaf scar with 'horse-shoe nail' markings

<10cm

♂

Green bracts and deep yellow stamens

Broad, grooved petiole base

Leaf size: <35cm

Kernal

58

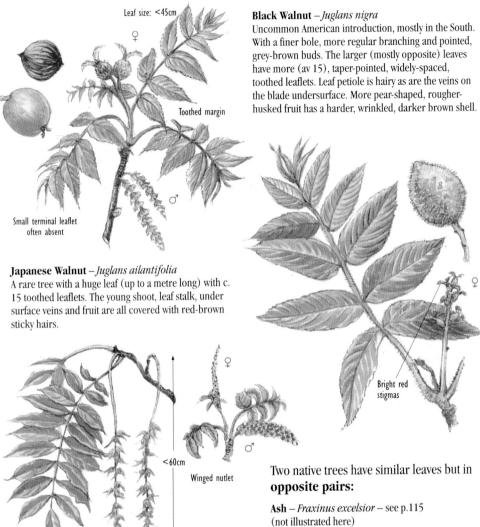

Leaf size: <45cm

♀

Toothed margin

♂

Small terminal leaflet
often absent

Black Walnut – *Juglans nigra*
Uncommon American introduction, mostly in the South.
With a finer bole, more regular branching and pointed,
grey-brown buds. The larger (mostly opposite) leaves
have more (av 15), taper-pointed, widely-spaced,
toothed leaflets. Leaf petiole is hairy as are the veins on
the blade undersurface. More pear-shaped, rougher-
husked fruit has a harder, wrinkled, darker brown shell.

♀

Bright red
stigmas

Japanese Walnut – *Juglans ailantifolia*
A rare tree with a huge leaf (up to a metre long) with c.
15 toothed leaflets. The young shoot, leaf stalk, under
surface veins and fruit are all covered with red-brown
sticky hairs.

♀

<60cm

♂

Winged nutlet

Caucasian Wingnut – *Pterocarya fraxinifolia*
Introduced. Suckers and branches low down. Pale grey bark
and buds lacking scales (the wrapped leaves are covered in
brown hairs). Long leaf with c. 21 (11–27) toothed, shiny,
bright green Ash-like leaflets. Petiole base <1cm wide. Thin
drooping female catkins; the scattered flowers with pink
stigmas. More compact male catkins. The tiny green nutlets,
surrounded by two paler circular wings, are bunched at the
lower end of the long hanging stalk.

Two native trees have similar leaves but in
opposite pairs:

Ash – *Fraxinus excelsior* – see p.115
(not illustrated here)
Also differs in the sooty-black buds, unscented
leaves with 3–7 coarsely-toothed leaflets and
clusters of flowers before the leaves emerge.

Elder – *Sambucus nigra* – see p.118
(not illustrated here)
Strongly-scented leaves with 5–7, ovate, toothed
leaflets, the largest at the end; borne from green
shoots. A shrub or small tree which bears masses of
5-petalled white flowers and bunches of black
berries in the autumn.

DECIDUOUS
Fabaceae

Common Laburnum or Golden Rain

Laburnum anagroides (L. vulgare)

Popular for its yellow pea flowers in early summer but all its parts (even roots) contain a dangerous alkaloid and its pea-like seeds have poisoned more children than any other plant in Britain. Voss's Laburnum is now more often planted, partly because being a hybrid, it sets fewer seeds and is thus less of a danger.

USES:
Turnery and musical instruments. Was used as an ebony substitute.

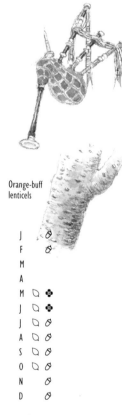

Orange-buff
lenticels

J
F
M
A
M
J
J
A
S
O
N
D

<8m

INTRODUCED (16th Century). Very common in gardens, parks and streets. Also bird-sown. A small tree more shrub-like when pruned. Slender, erect trunk; open crown of irregular, ascending, arched branches, thins with age.
BARK: Smooth, olive-green then brown; becoming lightly fissured.
TIMBER: Tan-yellow sapwood; hard, chocolate-brown, patterned heart wood.
TWIG: Grey-green, initially with long grey silky hairs.
BUDS: Tiny, egg-shaped, grey-brown with white silky hairs.
LEAVES: Bunched at shoot ends. Compound, oval-elliptical leaflets, often broadest above the middle. Smooth, matt grey-green above. Blue-green and initially with silky hairs below. Becoming smaller and sparser with age.
FLOWERS: c.30 golden-yellow, 'pea' flowers in hanging, downy-stalked racemes from leaf axils and shoot ends. Sweetly fragrant.
FRUIT: Clusters of pendant, 'jointed' (expanded over the seeds) hairy, green pods, later smooth, brown, twisted. 3–8 kidney-shaped black seeds inside.

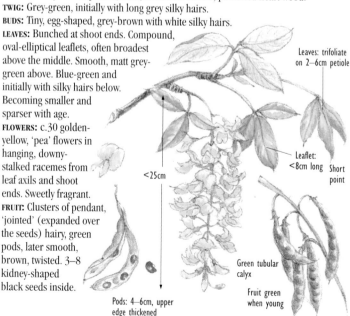

Leaves: trifoliate
on 2–6cm petiole

Leaflet:
<8cm long Short
point

<25cm

Green tubular
calyx

Fruit green
when young

Pods: 4–6cm, upper
edge thickened

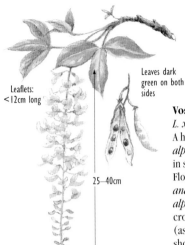

Leaflets: <12cm long

Leaves dark green on both sides

25–40cm

Scotch Laburnum – *L. alpinum*
Commoner in Scotland, often by roads. Taller (to 13m), with larger leaflets, sub-glossy above, less hairy below. Flowers 2–3 weeks later, longer slender racemes of well-spaced, smaller flowers. Pods with upper seam winged to a knife-like edge. Brown seeds.

Voss's Laburnum –
L. x watereri
A hybrid of *anagroides* and *alpinum*; leaves intermediate in size, glabrous below. Flowers as early as *anagroides* on long *alpinum*-type racemes, crowded with large flowers (as *anagroides*). Fruits few, shorter.

Curved fruits

Adam's or **Purple Laburnum** –
+ *Laburnocytisus adamii*
An odd graft of Laburnum and Purple Broom. Parts of the shrub have small purple fls and tiny leaflets (like the Broom); others have larger yellow fls and Laburnum leaves. Most are a mix of the two: pink/pale purple flowers and small, dark green Laburnum leaflets.

Blunt teeth

No other common trees have trifoliate leaves and yellow pea flowers but confusion is possible with:

Pair of spines

Paper-bark Maple – *Acer griseum*
Small tree, trifoliate leaves (middle leaflet stalked). Red-brown peeling bark. Small, open, pale green fls; in small erect clusters. Paired winged seeds, like Sycamore.

Downy

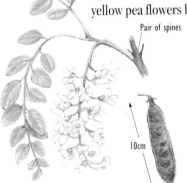

10cm

Veined wing around seed

False Acacia – *Robinia pseudoacacia*
Bark deeply fissured, twig ribbed, (spines absent in non-flowering cultivar 'Inermis'), leaf of 9–17 ovate, entire leaflets, white 'pea' fls (with yellow spots). Longer smooth, broader fruits – upper seam also winged.

Hop Tree – *Ptelea trifoliata*
Trifoliate leaves (middle leaflet stalked) smooth on both sides, dark green above and sometimes finely toothed. Unpleasant smell when crushed. Insignificant fls in erect clusters. Fruits like Elm.

Fig
Ficus carica

DECIDUOUS
Moraceae

A small tree, long grown in Mediterranean regions for its fruit. Well known for the shape of its leaves, depicted in works of art as cover for Adam's nakedness. Wild figs are pollinated by small egg-laying gall-wasps; domestic cultivars set fruit without the wasps. Fruit takes two summers to ripen and only well sheltered trees escape frost damage to maturing fruit.

<10m

INTRODUCED in gardens and parks, often on a south-facing wall. Self-sown e.g. by rivers where industrial outflows warm the water. Less frequent in the North. Small tree/ bush; open domed crown. Wide spreading, twisted branches from a very short bole.
BARK: Pale grey patterned with darker lines; like elephant hide.
TWIG: Stout, stubby, dark green with longitudinal ridges; large circular leaf scars.
BUDS: Terminal one large, pointed, green; others smaller, squat, red-brown.
LEAVES: Thick, leathery, variable in size and shape. Mostly large, with 3/5 palmate lobes; the middle one longest, the lower pair less deeply cut. Some leaves are oval or heart-shaped. Margin shallowly and irregularly blunt-toothed. Dark green and glossy (as if evergreen) but roughly hairy. Strong smell. Long, stout, yellow-green petiole.
FLOWER: Tiny male and female flowers hidden in the top of erect, fleshy, stalked pear-shaped structures.
FRUIT: Early ones are often frosted; later ones overwinter to swell and mature the following summer.

USES:
Valued for its fruit; fresh and dried. Syrup of figs is a mild laxative.

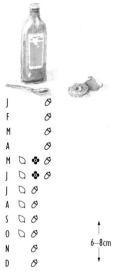

J	✿
F	✿
M	✿
A	✿
M	▢ ✾ ✿
J	▢ ✾ ✿
J	▢ ✿
A	▢ ✿
S	▢ ✿
O	▢ ✿
N	✿
D	✿

Petiole: 5–10cm

White hairs on main veins

'Seeds' among pink flesh

6–8cm

Leaf size: <25cm x 20cm

Indian Rubber Tree – *Ficus elastica*
A popular, mostly indoor, pot plant with evergreen, glossy, leathery, unlobed, entire leaves and stubby roots appearing from the aerial parts of the stem.

Leaf size: 30–40cm

Petiole: <50cm

Japanese Aralia – *Fatsia japonica*
A garden shrub. Stem Fig-like but covered with large v-shaped leaf scars. Very large palmate, evergreen leaves with 6–7 deep-cut, pointed lobes; dark green, leathery. Very long petiole droops in cold weather. Flowers in late autumn; terminal clusters of creamy-white, Ivy-like flower-heads. Small green pea-like fruits ripen black through the winter.

♀ flowers with pink stigmas

Castor-oil – *Ricinus communis*
Grown as a bedding plant or small shrub; occasionally naturalised. 5–7 pointed, palmately-lobed large leaves. Very long petiole attached to the middle of and at right angles to the blade. Erect clusters of green flowers (lower male flowers upper female flowers with pink stigmas) and spiny green fruits bearing brown and white mottled, poisonous, bean-like seeds.

Sharp-toothed margin

♂ flowers

Regular deeply-pointed, toothed margin

Mulberry – *Morus nigra* – see p.42
Large, roughly hairy leaves are occasionally 3 or 5 lobed but not leathery.

Paper Mulberry – *Broussonetia papyrifera*
Rare introduction with some lobed leaves (most ovate) but woolly underneath. Fissured brown bark, hairy young twigs. Male trees with stalked, curly cylindrical catkins, females setting fruits in globular clusters.

63

Common Hawthorn or May
Crataegus monogyna

DECIDUOUS
Rosaceae

The commonest hedgerow species (extensively planted 16–18th Century) where it rarely attains tree height. It also grows in scrub and open woodland. Over much of the country it now flowers about mid-May but under the old Julian calendar the flowers were open on May Day (1 May). Easily confused with Midland Hawthorn.

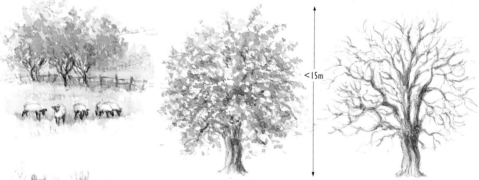

<15m

NATIVE and v. common. Often cut back to promote branching. Frequently multi-stemmed.
BARK: Grey-brown with orange-brown inner bark.
TIMBER: Very hard, pale with darker flecks.
TWIG: Purple-brown, later grey. Straight, similar-coloured, sharp spines from leaf axils.
BUDS: Tiny (2mm), dark brown, rounded.
LEAVES: 3–5 pointed lobes on each side, deeply cut (especially lower ones) $^1/_2$–$^2/_3$ to the midrib. Lobe edges at the leaf apex often coarsely toothed. Old leaves leathery, dark shiny green above; matt and paler below with hairs in the vein axils. Grooved pink petiole with tiny stipules at its base on young leaves.
FLOWERS: On erect stalks in flat-topped clusters of c.14. Each flower has 5 green sepals and 5 overlapping, white or pink-tinged, cupped petals. Strong, over-sweet fragrance.
FRUIT: Ovoid fleshy green haw ripens a deep maroon-red. Single seed.

USES:
Hedging. Young leaves eaten as 'bread and cheese'. Firewood for bread ovens. Walking sticks. Homoeopathic blood tonic.

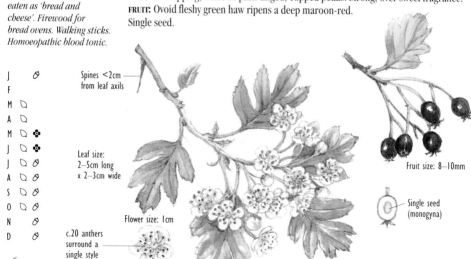

J	🌿
F	
M	🍃
A	🍃
M	🍃 ❀
J	🍃 ❀
J	🍃 🌿
A	🍃 🌿
S	🍃 🌿
O	🍃 🌿
N	🌿
D	🌿

Spines <2cm from leaf axils

Leaf size: 2–5cm long x 2–3cm wide

c.20 anthers surround a single style

Flower size: 1cm

Fruit size: 8–10mm

Single seed (monogyna)

64

Midland Hawthorn – *Crataegus laevigata (oxyacantha)*

Native in the Midlands and S.E. Britain, often on clay soils with Oak. More fluted, often twisted bole. Fewer thorns and larger, broader leaves. Lobes less deeply cut but with more extensive marginal teeth. Larger flowers fewer in a cluster, each with 2–3 styles. More rounded, crimson-coloured fruits bear 2/3 seeds. Hybridizes with *monogyna*.

Flower size: <2cm

Hawthorn cultivars include:

Glastonbury Thorn –

C. monogyna 'Biflora'
Thornless and flowering (but not fruiting) a second time close to Christmas. See p.25.

Paul's Scarlet –

C. laevigata 'Paul's Scarlet'
A double, red-flowered, infertile form often grown in parks and gardens.

Related and confusable species include:

Broad-leaved Cockspur Thorn –

Crataegus persimilis
Introduced and planted on road sides. A wide bush with broad ovate, unlobed, serrated, dark-green shiny leaves (pubescent on lower side veins). Brown shoot with many long thorns. Autumn colours orange-red-crimson. Dark red fruits (on pubescent stalks) fall in autumn.

Leaf size: 8cm x 6cm

Thorns: <4cm

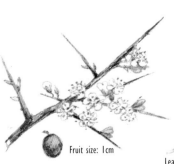

Fruit size: 1cm

Leaf size: 2cm long

Blackthorn – *Prunus spinosa*

A native hedgerow shrub with small **unlobed,** serrated leaves, dark brown-black twigs and spines. Hawthorn-like flowers appear in early spring, **before** the leaves. Fruits purple-black, bitter-tasting sloes, like small plums.

Firethorn – *Pyracantha coccinea*

A popular garden shrub often grown along a wall. Glossy unlobed, serrated **evergreen** leaves. Frequent spines which bear leaves. Dense heads of small white flowers in June. Masses of small red, orange or yellow berries.

65

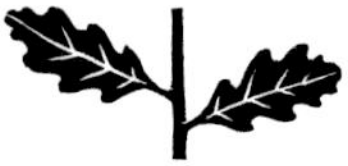

English Oak

Quercus robur

DECIDUOUS
Fagaceae

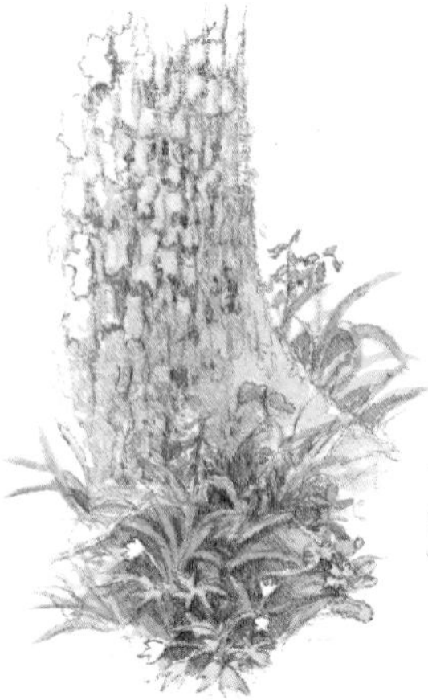

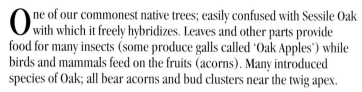

One of our commonest native trees; easily confused with Sessile Oak with which it freely hybridizes. Leaves and other parts provide food for many insects (some produce galls called 'Oak Apples') while birds and mammals feed on the fruits (acorns). Many introduced species of Oak; all bear acorns and bud clusters near the twig apex.

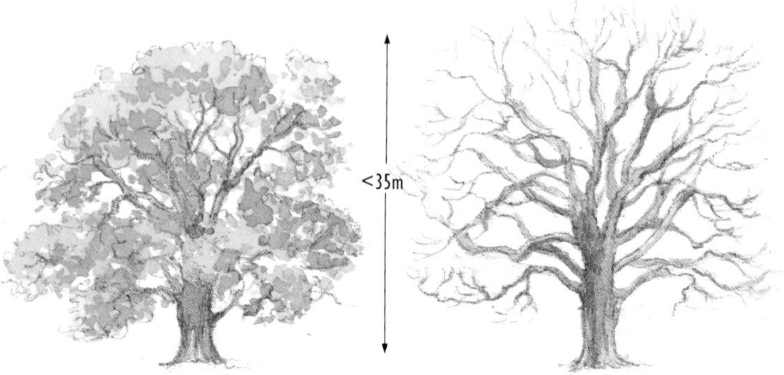
<35m

USES:
Buildings, ships, barrels, furniture, wheel spokes and for charcoal. Bark was used to tan leather.

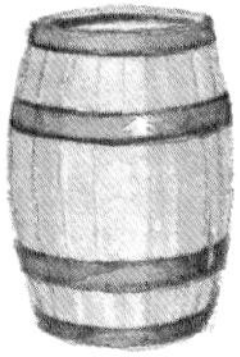

NATIVE on heavy, lowland soils. Planted in woods, parks and gardens throughout Britain. Broad bole bears massive, low branches at right angles. Wide crown when growing in open conditions

BARK: Grey; fissures delimit rectangular plates.

TIMBER: Yellow-brown; hard, very durable. Silver grain.

TWIG: Brown, then blue-grey, hairless.

BUDS: In leaf axils and clustered at twig apex. Oval, pale brown, hairless; many-scaled.

LEAVES: Bunched at twig ends, thick, curled, 4–6 prs of rounded, unequal lobes cut halfway to midrib. Short petiole hidden by auricles. 2nd flush of leaves (start pink-red) in August (Lammas Growth).

FLOWERS: Both sexes on same tree; male in bunches on the previous year's growth. Female, 1–5 tiny flowers on erect stalk from new shoot.

FRUIT: Acorn; often paired (1–4), stalked, green ripening to dark brown by autumn.

J
F
M
A
M
J
J
A
S
O
N
D

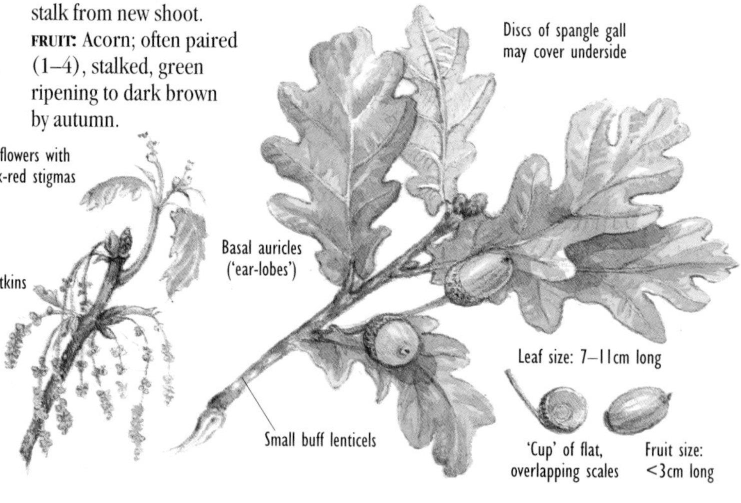
Discs of spangle gall may cover underside
♀ flowers with dark-red stigmas
♂ catkins
Basal auricles ('ear-lobes')
Small buff lenticels
Leaf size: 7–11cm long
'Cup' of flat, overlapping scales
Fruit size: <3cm long

CULTIVARS, RELATED AND CONFUSABLE SPECIES

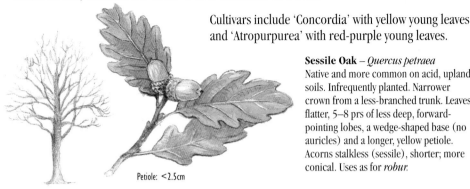

Cultivars include 'Concordia' with yellow young leaves and 'Atropurpurea' with red-purple young leaves.

Sessile Oak – *Quercus petraea*
Native and more common on acid, upland soils. Infrequently planted. Narrower crown from a less-branched trunk. Leaves flatter, 5–8 prs of less deep, forward-pointing lobes, a wedge-shaped base (no auricles) and a longer, yellow petiole. Acorns stalkless (sessile), shorter; more conical. Uses as for *robur.*

Petiole: <2.5cm

The most common introduced Oaks are:

Twisted stipules around bud and leaf bases

Leaf size: <12cm; deep triangular lobes

Turkey Oak – *Quercus cerris*
Hybridizes with native Oaks. Naturalised in the South. Taller, narrower crown; trunk often forks at about 6m; branches more erect. Bark grey with orange streaks, rougher. Rough twigs, few hairs. Longer, narrower leaves, dark green shiny, rough with 7–9 prs of lobes. Pubescent, short petiole. Acorn with 'mossy' cup ripens red-brown the following year.

Cup of green hair-like scales

Leaf size: <25cm x 15cm

Grey and downy beneath

Hungarian Oak – *Quercus frainetto*
Leaves larger with c.10 prs of deep lobes often with sub-lobes. Lobe size gradually decreases towards the short petiole. Acorns similar to *robur.*

A number of American species have been planted for their autumn colours, including:

Semi-circular indentations

Leaf size: 12–25cm

Red Oak – *Quercus rubra (borealis)*
Bark silver-grey, smoother. Leaves variable, large matt green on 2cm petioles; blade deeply cut into 7–11 prs of unequal lobes, with bristle-pointed ends. Tree turns uniformly red in autumn. Acorns ripen in 2nd year.

Saucer-like cup

Scarlet Oak – *Quercus coccinea*
Rarer with shorter, glossy green leaves, fewer, bristle-tipped lobes cut ¾ way to midrib. Long slender petiole. Leaves turn red sporadically; retained well into November. Squat acorns ripen in 2nd year.

Petiole: <4cm

For evergreen and other glossy-leaved Oaks see p.50

Tulip Tree
Liriodendron tulipifera

DECIDUOUS
Magnoliaceae

A timber tree in its native America but in Britain (introduced c.1650) it is grown for ornamental reasons, not so much for its tulip-like flowers (which can be overlooked) but for its unusually-shaped leaves which, like Aspen, tremble in the breeze. Readily identified by its leaves (but see the similar *L. chinense*) which lack a central pointed lobe, in contrast to Maples and Planes.

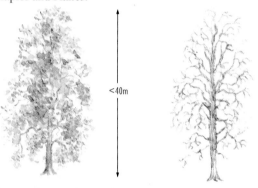

<40m

USES:
'Whitewood' used in North American house construction.

INTRODUCED in large gardens, less frequent from N. Midlands to Central Scotland. A narrow crown of regular branches, the lower pendant and upturned at the tips, the rest ascending. Bole massive, straight, often undivided.

BARK: Grey, smooth; later with shallow cracks; finally ridged, orange-brown.

TIMBER: Smooth-grained, pale creamy-yellow.

TWIG: Bloomed (lilac) then smooth, shiny red-brown with raised leaf scars.

BUDS: Large, long, often curved towards stem. 2 purple-red scales (stipules).

LEAVES: Large; long curved petiole. Blade variable; usually 4 (2–6) pointed lobes and a concave or flat, truncated apex. Outer edges of upper two lobes almost parallel. Glossy mid-green above, more blue-green below; hairless. Orange-yellow in autumn, fall late.

FLOWERS: High in crown at stem tips. Very fragrant. Initially cup-shaped, erect, short-stalked. 6 oval, waxy petals with a dark blue-green base, orange middle and pale-green/cream tip. Many long, fleshy creamy-yellow stamens surround the carpels which form a thin, green pointed 'spindle'.

FRUIT: Brown, flat; many in a Pine-cone like tuft. May break up after winter.

Leaf size: 10–15cm x 10cm

Flower size: 6–8cm

Midrib ends in whisker

Veins not palmate

Margins entire

3 spreading or reflexed sepals

J	�
F	�
M	☁
A	
M	☾
J	☾ ✿
J	☾ ✿
A	☾ ☁
S	☾ ☁
O	☾ ☁
N	☾ ☁
D	☁

Chinese Tulip Tree – *L. chinense*
Introduced 1901, much less common;
mostly in S. England. Has thinner leaves
which unfold a coppery-red and are
always 4-lobed; the apex is typically
flat. The smaller flowers (to 4cm)
have more uniformly-coloured petals,
usually pale orange.

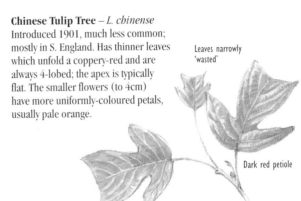

Leaves narrowly
'wasted'

Dark red petiole

L. tulipifera 'Aureomarginatum'
A rare, slow-growing cultivar. Young leaves
have a broad, yellow-orange border.

Other trees with similar-sized, lobed leaves include:

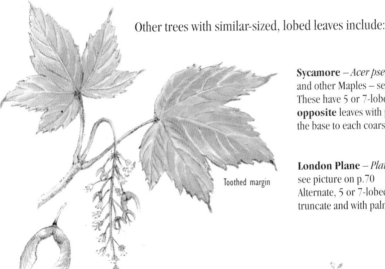

Toothed margin

Sycamore – *Acer pseudoplatanus*
and other Maples – see p.125
These have 5 or 7-lobed, not truncated,
opposite leaves with palmate veins, one from
the base to each coarsely-toothed lobe.

London Plane – *Platanus x hispanica* –
see picture on p.70
Alternate, 5 or 7-lobed leaves, toothed, not
truncate and with palmate venation.

Leaf size:
20cm x 20cm

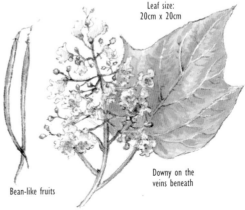

Yellow Catalpa – *Catalpa ovata*
Chinese tree with huge **opposite** broadly ovate leaves
with 3 (rarely 5) slender-pointed, entire lobes, a heart-
shaped base and a long red petiole. Pale yellow flowers
with red spots (petals bell-shaped at base, 5 spreading
frilled lobes at apex) in Horse Chestnut-like flowerheads.

Trees with similar flowers and fruits include
the related Magnolias, some of which have
greeny-orange flowers. Most of the cultivated
species have much larger, white or pink
flowers. The leaves are not lobed. See p.106

Bean-like fruits

Downy on the
veins beneath

London Plane

Platanus x hispanica (or *acerifolia*)

A hybrid (first record 1670) between two introduced Planes – American and Oriental. Widely planted, most notably in London. Regular bark replacement and shiny leaves help it tolerate dirty air; it also withstands heavy pruning and grows in compacted soil so is well suited to urban streets. The leaf can be confused with Sycamore and other *Acers* but these have opposite leaves.

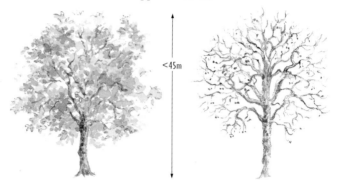

<45m

USES:
Turnery and tool handles. Cross-cut veneer gives a 'lacewood' pattern used in cabinet work.

GARDEN ORIGIN. More common in the South; slow growing in Scotland. Light loving, long-lived. Long bole bears large, often twisted, ascending branches which spread with age. Often pollarded.

BARK: Smooth, grey. Jigsaw-like pieces peel to reveal yellow/green underbark
TIMBER: Hard, fine-grained; pale brown with a pink hue.
TWIG: Slender, zig-zagging, initially downy, becoming glabrous, purple-brown.
BUDS: Red-brown, single-scaled with a curved, pointed tip.
LEAVES: Unfold browny-green, downy; later glabrous except on veins below. Large, leathery, shiny green; paler and matt below. Palmately lobed with 3, 5 or 7 pointed lobes cut <$^1/_2$ way to the base. Marginal teeth large, pointed and irregular. Pale brown in autumn. Petiole base encloses bud.
FLOWERS: As new leaves unfurl. Petalless; in separate sex clusters on same tree.
FRUIT: 1 or 2 burr-like brown bobbles on a long pendant stalk. Retained through winter, break up in spring.

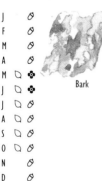

Bark

J	♂
F	♂
M	♂
A	♂
M	◻ ❖
J	◻ ❖
J	◻ ♂
A	◻ ♂
S	◻ ♂
O	◻ ♂
N	♂
D	♂

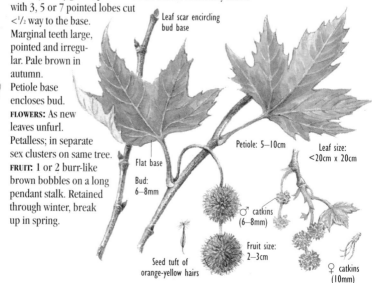

Leaf scar encircling bud base

Petiole: 5–10cm

Leaf size: <20cm x 20cm

Flat base

Bud: 6–8mm

♂ catkins (6–8mm)

Fruit size: 2–3cm

Seed tuft of orange-yellow hairs

♀ catkins (10mm)

The most common cultivar in London is 'Pyramidalis'. It has a conical shape, burred stem, slightly smaller, 3-lobed leaf and typically only one large fruit per stalk.

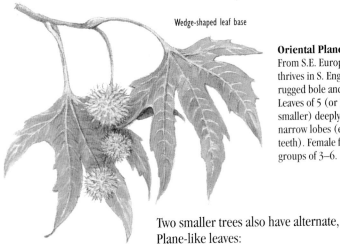

Wedge-shaped leaf base

Oriental Plane – *P. orientalis*
From S.E. Europe, much less common; only thrives in S. England. Smaller, with a short rugged bole and more spreading branches. Leaves of 5 (or 7 when the basal two are much smaller) deeply cut (to within 5cm of the base) narrow lobes (each with 1–3 large lobe-like teeth). Female flowers and fruits are borne in groups of 3–6.

Two smaller trees also have alternate, Plane-like leaves:

Sweet Gum – *Liquidambar styraciflua*
Gardens and parks southwards from the Midlands. Planted for its orange/red/purple autumn colours. Leaves shiny, deeply 5-lobed (3–7) with saw-toothed margins and a sweet, resinous fragrance on crushing. Heart-shaped base and a long slender petiole. A relative of Plane; its similar fruits are usually borne singly.

Leaf size:
15cm x 12cm

Wild Service Tree – *Sorbus torminalis* – see p.74
Uncommon native, occasionally planted. Leaves slightly smaller with spreading basal pair of lobes, those nearer the apex being only shallow. Unlike Plane the margins are **finely** toothed. Flowers and fruits not confusable.

Two trees have leaves of a similar shape and size to Plane but they are borne in **opposite pairs**:

Sycamore – *Acer pseudoplatanus* – see p.125
Norway Maple – *Acer platanoides* – see p.126

White Poplar
Populus alba

DECIDUOUS
Salicaceae

Probably an early introduction (pre-Iron Age) with further imports from Holland in the 16th Century where the alternative name 'Abele' comes from. This has also been used for the Grey Poplar; the two being frequently confused. In Britain sex helps – nearly all Grey Poplars are male.

Diamond-shaped lenticels

Dark, fissured base

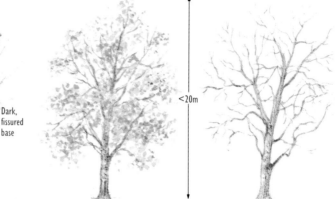

<20m

INTRODUCED and widely planted. Naturalised by the S. coast where it produces thickets. Suckering. Untidy crown often broadest near the top. Bole frequently leans.
BARK: Grey, smooth but for lenticels.
TIMBER: White. Little grain. Rough, porous, very light.
TWIG: Initially hairy then glossy brown with longitudinal ribs.
BUDS: Small, many-scaled. Hairy at base, glabrous at tip.
LEAVES: Vary in size and shape. Lead/sucker shoots bear palmately 5-lobed Maple-like leaves with irregular toothed margins. Upper surface thinly hairy – smooth and green by late summer, lower persistently felty-white. Side-shoot leaves more ovate with irregular, blunt, shallow teeth-like lobes, less white below. Red in autumn.
FLOWERS: Short-lived ♂ grey with red anthers, ♀ green.
FRUIT: Like a string of beads on a long hairy stalk. Small oval pods split in June to release fluffy seeds.

USES:
The best wood (as is Aspen) for making matches (and the box). 'Chip' punnets for soft fruit. Used in plywood.

J
F
M   ❖
A   ◗ ❖
M   ◗ ❖
J   ◗ ✎
J   ◗ ✎
A   ◗
S   ◗
O   ◗
N
D

Dense felty hairs on under-surface of leaf

♀ catkin:
3.5cm x 0.5cm

White woolly hairs on twig

Green stigmas

Petiole hairy below, rounded cross section

Leaf size: 3–9cm long

♂ and ♀ on separate trees

Cultivars include 'Richard II' with golden-yellow leaves and 'Pyramidalis' with a narrow, vase-shaped crown.

Leaves thinly grey-white, felty below

♂ catkin

Purple-red anthers

Leaf size: 6–8cm x 6–8cm

<40m

Prominent leaf scars

Long, laterally flattened petiole

Leaf size: 2–8cm x 2–8cm

♂

♀

Grey Poplar – *Populus x canescens*
Commonly planted (e.g. windbreak). Possibly a fertile hybrid – *Alba x tremula*. Rarely naturalised in damp woods. Taller, with few, heavy, ascending branches. Stouter twig. Older leaves on lead and sucker shoots dark-green, glossy above. Broadly ovate, margins coarsely toothed or shallowly 5-lobed. Petiole hairy, round in cross section. Side branch leaves rounder, smaller and smooth below. Large, irregular teeth, prominent venation. Petiole smooth, flexible and flattened laterally. Mostly only male catkins.

Aspen – *Populus tremula*
A small, native, suckering tree. Infrequent but commoner in the N. and in Scotland, on damp soil. Leaves mostly broad ovate to near circular. Vary in size, mostly smaller than the Poplars. Margin wavy, blunt toothed. Grey-green and not felty below. Long, slender, laterally flattened petiole on which blades tremble in the breeze. Sucker shoot leaves larger with shorter, round-sectioned petioles. Male and female catkins on separate trees.

Leaves of other Poplars differ in shape and lack a felty undersurface e.g.
Black Poplar – *P. nigra* – see p.40
The felty leaves and flexible petioles distinguish *alba* and *canescens* from species of *Acer* which have **opposite** leaves (e.g. **Sycamore** – see p.125)

Wild Service Tree – *Sorbus torminalis* – see p.74
A smaller tree than *alba*. Glossy alternate leaves with triangular lobes not felty below and on shorter, stouter petioles. Masses of white flowers and fleshy fruits.

73

Wild Service Tree
Sorbus torminalis

Service has nothing to do with churches, it is a corruption of the Latin, sometimes spelt sorvus. Also known as the Chequer Tree, with links to the pub name 'Chequers', which derives from Roman times when the chequer board was the symbol for a tavern. Often overlooked as its leaf shape is comparable with Sycamore.

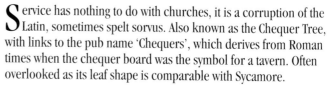

<12m

USES:
Fruits, rich in vitamin C, were eaten after being bletted (softened) by frost. Wood made cogs and stocks of crossbows. Still used for harpsichord jacks (string pluckers).

NATIVE in England and Wales but uncommon; rarely planted. On heavy marl or lime-stone. In hedges or Ancient Woods, survives from suckers; seedlings now rare. Small. Domed crown from ascending, spreading branches.

BARK: Grey-brown with shallow fissures and scaly plates.
TIMBER: Close-grained and tough.
TWIG: White-felted; later shiny red-brown, olive on underside.
BUD: Small (5mm), globular, shiny green. Broad-scaled.
LEAVES: Very variable, Maple-like. 3–5 prs of long-pointed lobes, large basal ones cut half way to the midrib and spreading; lobes smaller and less cut near the apex. Initially hairy below; later smooth, blue-green.
FLOWERS: In loose, downy-stalked clusters. White, rounded petals and yellow anthers.
FRUITS: Spherical or elongated, slightly angular. Green, slowly ripening to russet-brown, speckled with pale lenticels.

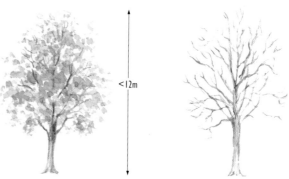

Finely double-toothed (except at base)

J
F
M
A
M ▢ ❖
J ▢ ❖
J ▢ ⌀
A ▢ ⌀
S ▢ ⌀
O ▢ ⌀
N ▢ ⌀
D ⌀

Leaf size: 10cm x 8cm

Petiole 2–5cm; felted when young

Fruit size: 1.5cm

Flower size: 1cm

Leaf shiny

74

No other **wild** *Sorbus* has a shiny, Maple-like leaf.
Planted species include:

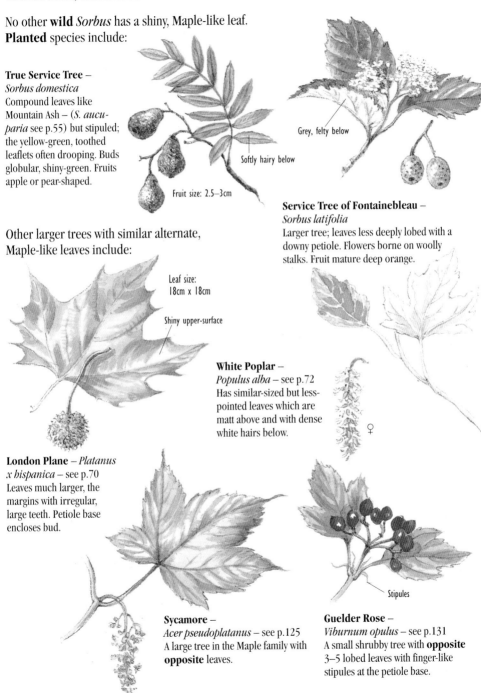

True Service Tree –
Sorbus domestica
Compound leaves like
Mountain Ash – (*S. aucu-
paria* see p.55) but stipuled;
the yellow-green, toothed
leaflets often drooping. Buds
globular, shiny-green. Fruits
apple or pear-shaped.

Fruit size: 2.5–3cm

Softly hairy below

Grey, felty below

Service Tree of Fontainebleau –
Sorbus latifolia
Larger tree; leaves less deeply lobed with a
downy petiole. Flowers borne on woolly
stalks. Fruit mature deep orange.

Other larger trees with similar alternate,
Maple-like leaves include:

Leaf size:
18cm x 18cm

Shiny upper-surface

White Poplar –
Populus alba – see p.72
Has similar-sized but less-
pointed leaves which are
matt above and with dense
white hairs below.

♀

London Plane – *Platanus
x hispanica* – see p.70
Leaves much larger, the
margins with irregular,
large teeth. Petiole base
encloses bud.

Stipules

Sycamore –
Acer pseudoplatanus – see p.125
A large tree in the Maple family with
opposite leaves.

Guelder Rose –
Viburnum opulus – see p.131
A small shrubby tree with **opposite**
3–5 lobed leaves with finger-like
stipules at the petiole base.

Broad-leaved Trees

Alternate – ovate, unlobed leaves (pp.77–96)

Wych Elm
Ulmus glabra

British Elms include native species, established introductions, hybrids and local varieties. Wych (meaning 'pliant') Elm is the most widely distributed but with other Elms, millions have died from Dutch Elm fungus since the mid-1960s. Elms have alternate, rounded winter buds and the leaf blade is frequently lop-sided at its base.

DECIDUOUS
Ulmaceae

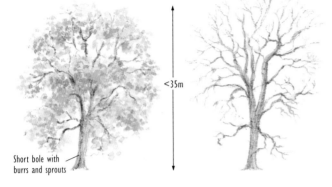

<35m

Short bole with burrs and sprouts

NATIVE and common (pre-1960s) in N. England and Scotland, often in river valleys; less frequent (though previously planted) in the South. Crown broad, irregular; initially bushy. Sinuous, heavy branches may reach the ground. No root suckers.

BARK: At first grey, smooth (glabrous); later brown with a network of deep fissures.

TIMBER: Warm-brown, feather-grained; difficult to split.

TWIG: Stout, red-brown, covered with short hairs.

BUDS: Stout, 6–7mm. 5–6 scales with rust-coloured hairs.

LEAVES: Variable. Most are on older shoots; ovate to almost rounded, broadest nearer the apex, short pointed; some have 2–3 tips from side shoulders. Those on young shoots may be much larger. Veins (12–18 prs) end in a large, pointed tooth. Upper surface with a beard-stubble texture from bristly hairs.

FLOWERS: Before leaves, high in crown. Sessile, purple-red clusters. Bisexual, petalless.

FRUITS: Clusters of 12–20 form before leaves mature. Seed central in a pale green (later brown), membrane-like oval wing, notched and downy at apex.

USES:
Chair seats, upmarket furniture, turnery and boat building. Formerly used for wheel hubs, water pipes and inexpensive coffins.

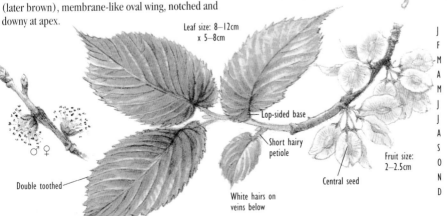

Leaf size: 8–12cm
x 5–8cm

Lop-sided base

Short hairy petiole

Double toothed

♂ ♀

White hairs on veins below

Central seed

Fruit size: 2–2.5cm

J
F
M
A
M
J
J
A
S
O
N
D

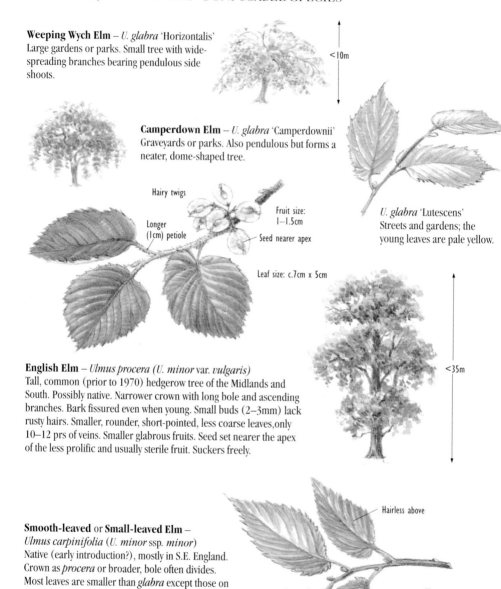

Weeping Wych Elm – *U. glabra* 'Horizontalis'
Large gardens or parks. Small tree with wide-spreading branches bearing pendulous side shoots.

<10m

Camperdown Elm – *U. glabra* 'Camperdownii'
Graveyards or parks. Also pendulous but forms a neater, dome-shaped tree.

Hairy twigs

Longer (1cm) petiole

Fruit size: 1–1.5cm

Seed nearer apex

Leaf size: c.7cm x 5cm

U. glabra 'Lutescens'
Streets and gardens; the young leaves are pale yellow.

English Elm – *Ulmus procera* (*U. minor* var. *vulgaris*)
Tall, common (prior to 1970) hedgerow tree of the Midlands and South. Possibly native. Narrower crown with long bole and ascending branches. Bark fissured even when young. Small buds (2–3mm) lack rusty hairs. Smaller, rounder, short-pointed, less coarse leaves, only 10–12 prs of veins. Smaller glabrous fruits. Seed set nearer the apex of the less prolific and usually sterile fruit. Suckers freely.

<35m

Smooth-leaved or **Small-leaved Elm** –
Ulmus carpinifolia (*U. minor* ssp. *minor*)
Native (early introduction?), mostly in S.E. England.
Crown as *procera* or broader, bole often divides.
Most leaves are smaller than *glabra* except those on young shoots. Bright green, shiny upper surface, white hairs in vein axils below. Often strongly asymmetric at base. Glabrous fruits with the seed close to the notched apex.

Hairless above

Fruit size: 8–15mm

Huntingdon Elm – *Ulmus x hollandica* 'Vegeta'
Formerly planted especially in E. Anglian hedges. Tall
(<35m), broad, rounded crown and strong, ascending
lower branches. Leaves nearly as long as *glabra* but narrower, more taper-pointed; 12–18 prs of veins. Smooth,
shiny upper surface; tufts of reddish hairs in vein axils
below. Longer (<2cm) petiole. Suckers freely.

Dutch Elm – *Ulmus x hollandica* 'Hollandica'
Widely planted before Dutch Elm disease. Branches
spreading, crooked and mostly high in crown. Twig
develops corky ridges. Leaves shorter, broader and less
taper-pointed than 'Vegeta'. Almost smooth above, hairy on
the 10–14 prs of veins (and in axils) below. Often buckled
with the marginal teeth raised. Suckers freely.

Other trees with similar-shaped leaves:

Glandular hairs

Black Mulberry –
Morus nigra – see p.42
A much smaller tree, the thinner
leaves are more rounded with a more
equal-sided, heart-shaped base and a
long hairy petiole. Marginal teeth are
less pointed. Upper surface is roughly
hairy but slightly shiny.

Hazel – *Corylus avellana* – see p.82
The leaf differs from *U. glabra* in being
paler green and soft to the touch (though
it is hairy above and on the veins below).
Basal lobes equal, only 6–8 prs of veins
and a longer petiole covered with
glandular hairs. A much smaller tree.

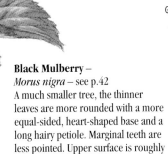

Lime – *Tilia* spp – see p.44
Tall crown and large leaves which
may be lop-sided at the base. They
differ in the flat or heart-shaped
base, much broader, thinner almost
hairless blade and being paler
green. Long petiole and 'finger and
thumb' shaped smooth buds.

Hop Tree – *Ptelea trifoliata*
(see picture on p.61)
Unusual, introduced small tree with trifoliate leaves more like Laburnum but with
Elm-like fruits. Those on *Ptelea* have
net-like veins on the membranous wing.

Whitebeam
Sorbus aria

DECIDUOUS
Rosaceae

Most beautiful in early summer when the emerging leaves look like Magnolia flower-buds. Mature leaves retain a white, felty undersurface resulting in less water loss; useful in dry urban streets where it is often planted. Variation in leaf shape and fruit colour encompasses some separate rare species but the Swedish and Orange-berried Whitebeam are the common lookalikes.

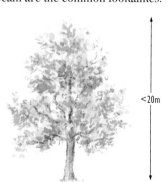

<20m

USES:
Fruits make a jelly served with meat dishes. Timber little used in Britain but on mainland Europe it was once used to make machinery cogs.

NATIVE south of Bedfordshire where it is frequent on basic soils (e.g. Downs) in scrub or woodland edges; naturalized and less common elsewhere. Planted by roads. Upswept branches form a dense oval crown. Shaded or crag trees often smaller, shrub-like.
BARK: Grey and smooth, becoming ridged and scaly.
TIMBER: Hard and heavy, similar to Hornbeam.
TWIG: Initially green, hairy, later smooth red-brown above and green below, with small, pale lenticels.
BUDS: Long (<2cm), pointed, green-brown, tipped with white hairs.
LEAVES: Broadly ovate with 10–14 prs of parallel side veins. Margins unevenly, singly or doubly, sharply toothed. Occasionally with shallow lobes. Yellow-brown in autumn.
FLOWERS: After the leaves unfurl. Terminal, branched flat-topped upright clusters. Flower stalk hairy. 5 hairy sepals, 5 white petals, lots of cream-coloured stamens and 2(3) styles. Heavy scent.
FRUIT: Spherical or elongated, bears 2 seeds. Green, ripening yellow to scarlet; warty from tiny corky lenticels. Soon eaten by birds.

J
F
M
A
M
J
J
A
S
O
N
D

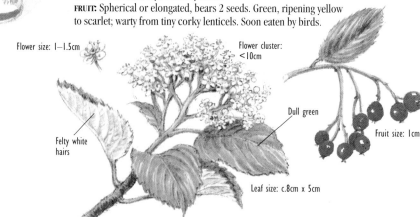

Flower size: 1–1.5cm

Flower cluster: <10cm

Dull green

Fruit size: 1cm

Felty white hairs

Leaf size: c.8cm x 5cm

Planted cultivars include 'Majestica' with larger,(<15cm) more elliptical leaves and bigger fruit. 'Lutescens' has a compact, egg-shaped crown and smaller leaves whose upper sides are covered in a creamy-white down in spring. Planted similar species found in parks and large gardens include *Sorbus thibetica* 'John Mitchell' with an almost round leaf (<18cm), entire for the basal third, the rest with blunt, uneven teeth. Russet-brown in autumn. Large round, yellow-brown fruits.

Leaf size: <20cm x 12cm

Felty, yellow-grey below

Swedish Whitebeam – *Sorbus intermedia*
Introduced and naturalised. Also some rare, native subspecies, chiefly in Scotland. Broader crown. Leaves dark, glossy green above. Basal 3–6 prs of lateral veins (total 6–9 prs) end in a rounded lobe cut ⅓ way to the midrib. Heavy flowering, the larger, orange-red fruits are more elongated and less speckled.

Orange-berried Whitebeam –
Sorbus croceocarpa
Frequently planted, grows to over 20m. It has *aria*-type leaves but yellow-orange fruits.

Grey felty under-surface

Service Tree of Fontainebleau – *Sorbus latifolia*
Occasionally planted. Bark shaggy, peeling. Leaf like a large, broad *intermedia* but with deeper, more triangular lobes. A number of rare, native subspecies with orange or brown fruits occur in the South-west.

Teeth restricted to apical region

White hairy under-surface

Wayfaring Tree –
Viburnum lantana – see p.130
This shrubby tree has leaves in **opposite** pairs each with a rounded base and with regular, fine-toothed margins. Green fruits in upright clusters ripen through red to glossy black.

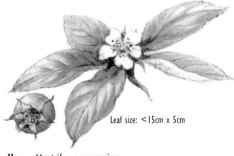

Leaf size: <15cm x 5cm

Medlar – *Mespilus germanica*
A shrub largely confined to old gardens. More elongated leaves with white woolly hairs below. **Solitary,** large (<6cm) white flowers. 5 green sepals are longer than petals. Large rose-hip like edible fruit bear dead sepals at apex.

Hazel
Corylus avellana

More often a multi-stemmed shrub than a tree. Much Hazel was formerly coppiced. The fruit are eaten by many species of animal and bird. Several cultivated varieties (e.g. Kentish Cob) and related species provide nuts for human consumption; most are now imported.

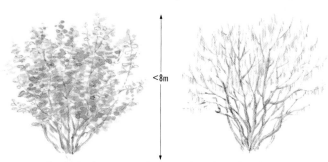

<8m

USES:
Nuts for food; coppiced rods for fences (hurdles), divining rods, walking sticks and firewood.

NATIVE except in the Shetlands. Common; forms wood scrub, prefers chalk or lime-stone. Woodland under-shrub, also in hedges and gardens. Typically many-stemmed.
BARK: Smooth with prominent lenticels. Peels in horizontal strips when old.
TIMBER: Bole rarely big enough to produce timber.
TWIG: Pale brown and sticky when young.
BUDS: Small (5mm), green, egg-shaped.
LEAVES: In two rows (all-round on young shoots). Variable, almost circular or broadly ovate, sometimes weakly lobed, rounded or heart-shaped base and a short-pointed tip. 6–8 prs of veins. Softly hairy above, paler with soft white hairs on yellow-green veins below. Yellow in autumn. Stout, short (1.5cm) green petiole covered in glandular hairs.
FLOWERS: Long before the leaves. Male catkins formed the previous autumn yellow as the flowers open. Female flowers look like the leaf buds until the bright red styles open.
FRUIT: Clusters of 2–4 pale-brown, woody-shelled, single-seeded nuts (cobs), in two deeply-toothed, sparsely hairy, green bracts.

J	✿
F	✿
M	✿
A	✿
M	◖ ✿
J	◖ ✿
J	◖ ✿
A	◖ ✿
S	◖ ✿
O	◖ ✿
N	◖
D	

♀ flower

Double, unequal triangular teeth

♂ catkins: 5cm

Red-tipped hairs

Leaf size: 10cm x 8cm

Fruit size: 1–1.5cm

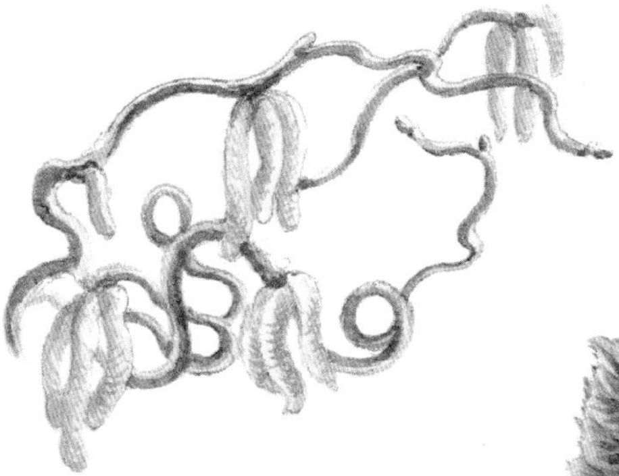

Garden cultivars include:
Weeping Hazel – *C. avellana* 'Pendula', infrequent.
Corkscrew Hazel – *C. avellana* 'Contorta' more common. Rarely above 3m. Twisted twigs and leaves.

Filbert – *Corylus maxima*
Grown in gardens and Kent orchards ('plats') for its larger, longer fruit which are totally encased in the tubular bract which extends beyond the nut, like a full beard (hence 'Filbert'). Leaves larger, more heart-shaped. Cultivar 'Purpurea' has purple leaves.

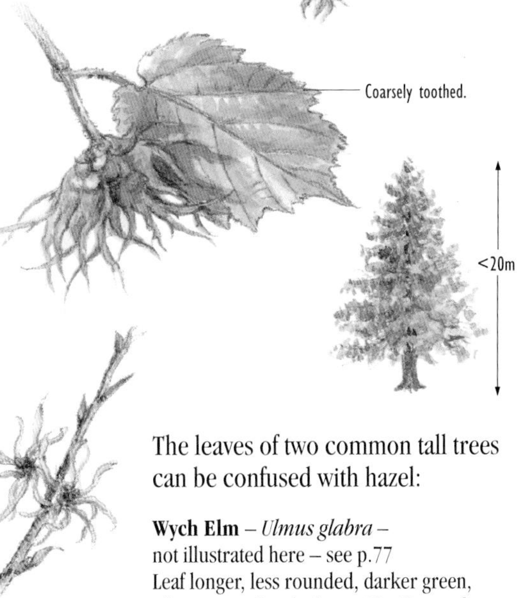

'Purpurea'

Turkish Hazel – *Corylus colurna*
An introduced tree with shaggy, brown fissured bark. Level, twisted branches bear larger, smoother, hanging leaves on long (2–6cm) reddish petioles. Broader fruits encased in raggedly-lobed bracts.

Coarsely toothed.

<20m

Witch Hazel – *Hamamelis mollis*
This garden shrub has a more pointed leaf with smaller teeth and a more downy undersurface. The yellow or red, spider-like, sweet-scented flowers open in winter on the bare twigs.

The leaves of two common tall trees can be confused with hazel:

Wych Elm – *Ulmus glabra* –
not illustrated here – see p.77
Leaf longer, less rounded, darker green, often unequal at the base. 12–18 prs of veins and a much rougher feel.

Lime – *Tilia* spp – not illustrated here – see p.44
Leaf more heart-shaped, paler green and softer. Long (5–6cm) slender, non-hairy petiole.

83

Alder

Alnus glutinosa

DECIDUOUS
Betulaceae

Alder thrives in nitrate-deficient, waterlogged soils with the help of large root nodules containing nitrogen-fixing bacteria. Its binding roots reduce the impact of river bank erosion and it grows with Willows in damp 'carr' woodland. Its timber is durable in water.

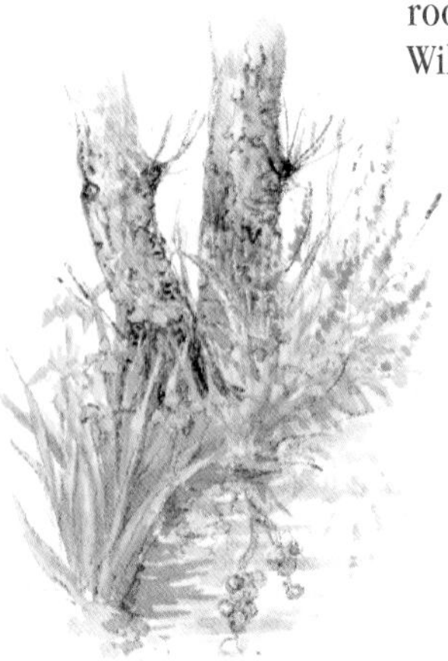

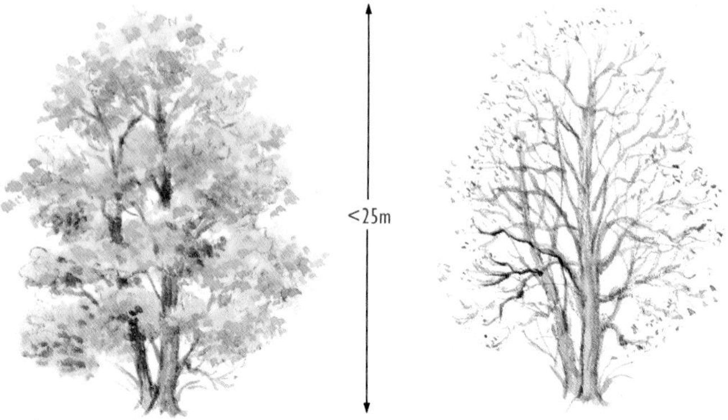
<25m

USES:
Clog soles, sluice gates, bridge piles. Best charcoal for gunpowder. Dyes from leaves, fruit and bark.

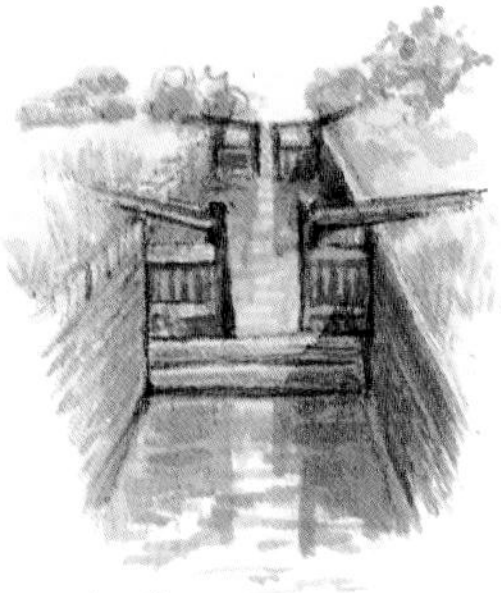

NATIVE and common by water. Crown open, straggly; little branched. Suckers to form a multi-stemmed shrub.
BARK: Grey, smooth, then brown-black, shallowly fissured into small squares. 'Bleeds' orange-red if damaged.
TIMBER: Pink when cut, ages yellow-brown; easily worked.
TWIG: Sticky (glutinous) green then purple-brown and glabrous.
BUDS: Stalked, erect, narrowed at the base, flattened, with 2–3 green/purple scales.
LEAVES: Initially sticky then glabrous except for the vein-axil creamy hair tufts below. Widest at or above the middle. Blunt end, midrib often ends in a notch. 6–7 paler veins each side. Wavy margin. Broad wedge-shaped base. Petiole with raised lenticels. Dark green/black in autumn.
FLOWERS: Before leaves. Catkins formed the previous autumn.
FRUIT: Cone-like, hard, green then brown. Persist long after winged seeds have been dispersed.

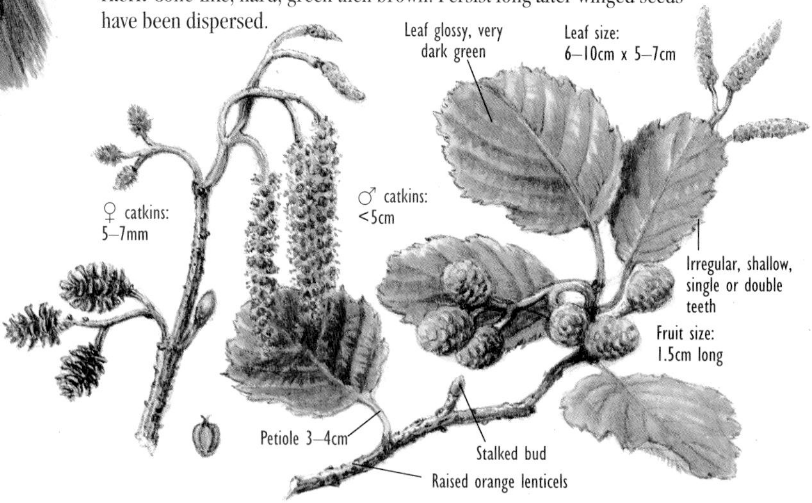
Leaf glossy, very dark green
Leaf size: 6–10cm x 5–7cm
♀ catkins: 5–7mm
♂ catkins: <5cm
Irregular, shallow, single or double teeth
Fruit size: 1.5cm long
Petiole 3–4cm
Stalked bud
Raised orange lenticels

J
F
M
A
M
J
J
A
S
O
N
D

CULTIVARS, RELATED AND CONFUSABLE SPECIES

Rare cut-leaved, cultivars include 'Laciniata' and 'Imperialis'. Three introduced Alders are being used for amenity planting:

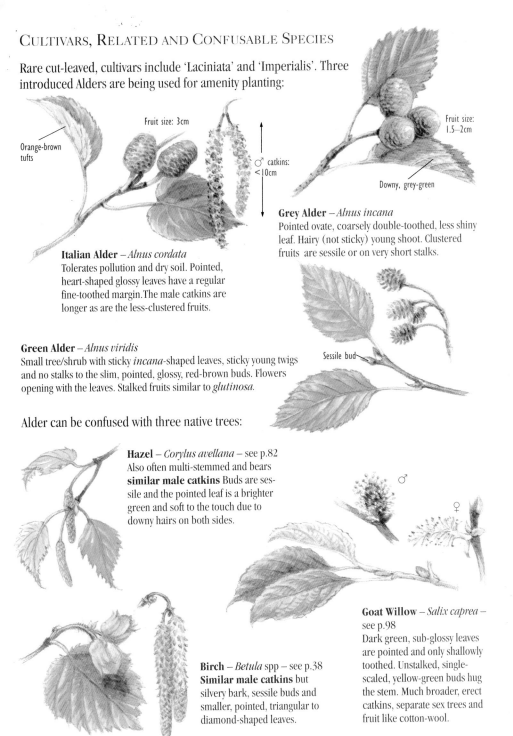

Fruit size: 3cm

Orange-brown tufts

♂ catkins: <10cm

Fruit size: 1.5–2cm

Downy, grey-green

Italian Alder – *Alnus cordata*
Tolerates pollution and dry soil. Pointed, heart-shaped glossy leaves have a regular fine-toothed margin.The male catkins are longer as are the less-clustered fruits.

Grey Alder – *Alnus incana*
Pointed ovate, coarsely double-toothed, less shiny leaf. Hairy (not sticky) young shoot. Clustered fruits are sessile or on very short stalks.

Green Alder – *Alnus viridis*
Small tree/shrub with sticky *incana*-shaped leaves, sticky young twigs and no stalks to the slim, pointed, glossy, red-brown buds. Flowers opening with the leaves. Stalked fruits similar to *glutinosa*.

Sessile bud

Alder can be confused with three native trees:

Hazel – *Corylus avellana* – see p.82
Also often multi-stemmed and bears **similar male catkins** Buds are sessile and the pointed leaf is a brighter green and soft to the touch due to downy hairs on both sides.

♂

♀

Birch – *Betula* spp – see p.38
Similar male catkins but silvery bark, sessile buds and smaller, pointed, triangular to diamond-shaped leaves.

Goat Willow – *Salix caprea* – see p.98
Dark green, sub-glossy leaves are pointed and only shallowly toothed. Unstalked, single-scaled, yellow-green buds hug the stem. Much broader, erect catkins, separate sex trees and fruit like cotton-wool.

85

Hornbeam
Carpinus betulus

A beautiful but frequently mis-identified tree which, especially when grown as a hedge, is often confused with Beech. Its male catkins are more like those of Birch, hence the Latin *betulus*. In the past it was often coppiced or pollarded. Produces our hardest native timber.

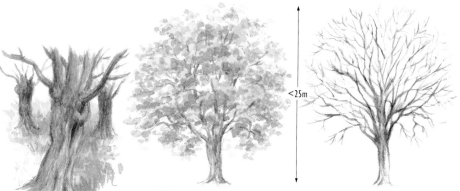

<25m

USES:
Butchers' chopping blocks, shoe lasts, skittles, wooden screws, industrial cogs and pulleys. Fuel for bakers' ovens.

NATIVE and frequent, often on clay, in the S. East, Somerset and Monmouth. Rarer and planted elsewhere; in woods, parks and streets and as garden hedging. Bole fluted, buttressed and oval in cross-section.

BARK: Grey. Initially smooth with metallic-blue and pale brown veins; later with vertical black fissures.

TIMBER: Hard, tough, heavy. Green-white, close-grained.

TWIG: Fine, slight zig-zag, brown with sparse hairs.

BUDS: Twig-hugging, slim; brown/green overlapping scales.

LEAVES: Not quite flat. c.15 prs of prominent, impressed side veins, initially downy below. Dark green above, paler below; slight gloss. Short red-brown petiole. Hedge plants and young trees retain russet-coloured leaves over winter.

FLOWERS: Drooping male catkins with yellow stamens and brown bracts. Short female catkins at apex. Crimson styles and leafy bracts.

FRUITS: Clusters of <16 small, oval ribbed nuts, each at the base of a large papery, three-lobed, green bract which turns yellow-brown by autumn.

J
F
M
A
M
J
J
A
S
O
N
D

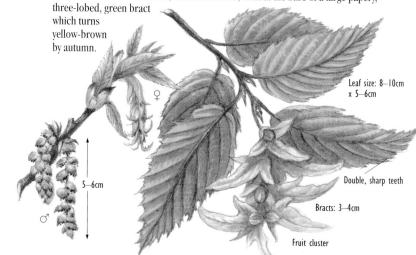

Leaf size: 8–10cm x 5–6cm

5–6cm

Double, sharp teeth

Bracts: 3–4cm

Fruit cluster

Cultivar 'Pyramidalis' or 'Fastigiata' (far right) is common as a street and park tree. Very dense branches from a 2m bole give a compact 'ace of spades' shape.

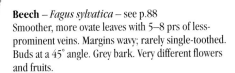

Hop Hornbeam – *Ostrya carpinifolia*
Increasingly planted. More fissured bark and green buds. Similar leaves, sparsely hairy above, have branching side veins. Clear yellow autumn colours. Hop-like fruits with simple, creamy, bladder-like bracts.

Beech – *Fagus sylvatica* – see p.88
Smoother, more ovate leaves with 5–8 prs of less-prominent veins. Margins wavy; rarely single-toothed. Buds at a 45° angle. Grey bark. Very different flowers and fruits.

Southern Beeches – *Nothofagus* spp
Large trees. Increasingly planted, some in plantations. Leaves and buds similar to Hornbeam. e.g:

Leaf size:
5–8cm x 3cm

♀

♂

Leaf size: <10cm

Finely-toothed margin

Roble Beech – *N. obliqua*
Leaves with 7–11 prs of paler side veins, margins irregularly and sharply single-toothed, base lop-sided; red in autumn. Bark cracking into small squares. Unstalked solitary male flowers. Fruits like small, unstalked Beech mast.

Raoul or **Rauli** – *N. procera*
Larger leaves with 15–22 prs of prominent veins. Bark with vertical grey-green fissures. Short-stalked fruit.

Hornbeam Maple – *Acer carpinifolium*
An uncommon shrub-like tree from Japan. Leaves are longer with >20 prs of side veins and are borne in **opposite** pairs. Smooth grey bark; flowers and fruits like maple.

Birches – *Betula* spp –
not illustrated here – see p.38
Similar-looking male catkins but very different bark, leaves and fruit.

Leaf: <18cm long

87

Beech
Fagus sylvatica

DECIDUOUS
Fagaceae

The dominant tree on the chalk of S. England. Dense shade restricts the ground flora but many fungi are associated with Beech. Makes a good hedge; was previously pollarded but is rarely coppiced. Confused with our native Hornbeam and several introduced species.

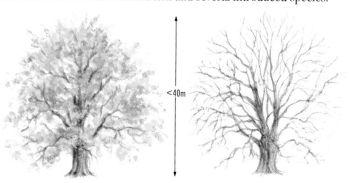

<40m

USES:
Furniture including legs and bentwood backs of chairs; toys, rolling pins, wooden spoons, parquet floors.

NATIVE only in the South and Midlands, planted elsewhere. Common on well drained soils. Trunk attains large girth. Bark: Unfissured, grey – rather like elephant hide. Often buttressed and stained with green algae.

TIMBER: Pink-brown, dark flecked; fine grained. Strong, hard. Not durable outside.

TWIG: Slender, purple-brown with lenticels, slightly hairy. Zig-zag growth form.

BUDS: Long, slender, pointed; all in one plane. Many overlapping scales.

LEAVES: Ovate, short-pointed. Emerge soft, pale green and hairy with a pair of brown stipules at the short petiole base. Later glossy above with 5–8 prs of parallel side veins ending in undulations or short teeth. Yellow to red-brown in autumn. Leaves retained on young trees and pruned hedges.

FLOWERS: As the leaves emerge. Short thick, hairy stalks bear 4 green, cup-like, bristly bracts with protruding crimson styles. Separate clusters of golden anthers on pendulous stalks.

FRUIT: Bracts turn brown and open to reveal 2 or 3 brown nuts, shaped like elongated pyramids.

J
F
M
A
M 🝙 ❁
J 🝙 ❁
J 🝙 ✿
A 🝙 ✿
S 🝙 ✿
O 🝙 ✿
N 🝙 ✿
D ✿

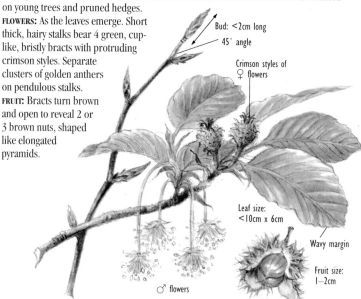

Bud: <2cm long

45° angle

Crimson styles of ♀ flowers

Leaf size: <10cm x 6cm

Wavy margin

Fruit size: 1—2cm

♂ flowers

'Mast'

Cultivars, Related and Confusable Species

The most commonly planted cultivars of *Fagus sylvatica* are:

Redder leaf of 'River's Purple'

Copper Beech – 'Purpurea'
Pink-red leaves mature purple-black.
Shaded leaves are often greener.

Fern-leaved Beech – 'Asplenifolia'
Leaves mostly elongated, deeply lobed or Willow-like. Some branches bear normal leaves.

Dawyck Beech – 'Dawyck'
<25m With a columnar shape, like
Lombardy Poplar but
maturing broader. Grafted.
Increasingly common.

Weeping Beech – 'Pendula'
Pendulous branches
produce either a low, very
wide crown or a tall, narrow
tree.

Species with Beech-like leaves include:

Toothed margins

Persian Ironwood – *Parrotia persica*
Parks and gardens; an introduced shrub/small tree.
Beech-like leaves have fewer side veins, which (unlike
Beech) branch. Grown for its crimson winter flowers,
orange-red autumn colours and flaking bark.

Hornbeam – *Carpinus betulus* – see p.86
Fluted trunk, smooth bark with grey and brown striations. Shorter buds hug the twig. Leaves more oblong, 10–15 prs of prominent side veins and double-toothed margins. Retains dead leaves when grown as a hedge. Native.

Oriental Beech – *Fagus orientalis* – not illustrated
A rare introduction with longer, less crowded leaves
with a wedge-shaped base and 8–12 prs of side veins.
Rich yellow in autumn.

Southern Beeches – *Nothofagus spp* – see p.87

Goat Willow

also known as *Palm*, *Great Sallow* or *Pussy Willow*

Salix caprea

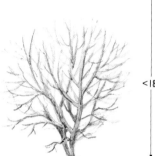

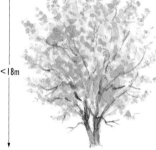

Most of the many Willow species are shrubs or have long, narrow leaves (see p.112). Goat Willow is a small broad-leaved tree bearing showy catkins ('like little cats' – hence 'Pussy' Willow) in spring. Flowers provide food for Honey Bees; cottony seeds a nest lining for Gold-finches. Readily hybridizes with others such as Grey Willow.

<18m

NATIVE and common; widespread. A pioneer species of cleared ground, scrub, hedges and water margins where it may be multi-stemmed. Tree-like in woodland edges.

BARK: Grey-brown, smooth or shallowly fissured.

TIMBER: Soft, pale-brown.

TWIG: Thick, short-jointed, brittle. Initially grey-haired, then smooth; green to red-brown.

BUDS: Single-scaled, glossy yellow, hug the twig. Large swollen catkin buds.

LEAVES: Ovate, short point twisted to one side (or under). Base rounded/wedge-shaped. Margin wavy with irregular, shallow, blunt-pointed teeth. Wrinkled above; dark green, hairless. Prominent net-veins below, blue-green and downy. Short hairy petiole.

FLOWERS: Short-stalked erect catkins, male and female on separate plants along young twigs. Initially silver-haired. ♂ catkin short, fat, golden-yellow. ♀ longer, greeny white.

FRUIT: Small, green capsules split to release tiny fluffy (snow-like) seeds.

USES:
Clothes pegs, rake teeth and axe handles. Willow bark was used to reduce fever prior to Asprin. Golden male catkins may adorn churches on Palm Sunday.

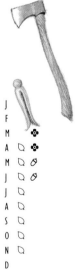

J
F
M ❖
A ☐ ❖
M ☐ ∂
J ☐ ∂
J ☐
A ☐
S ☐
O ☐
N ☐
D

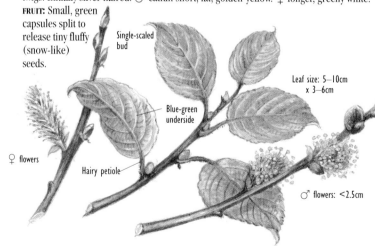

Single-scaled bud

Leaf size: 5–10cm x 3–6cm

Blue-green underside

♀ flowers

Hairy petiole

♂ flowers: <2.5cm

A popular small (<2m) weeping cultivar is 'Kilmarnock'. Stiffly pendulous branches bear showy male catkins (not illustrated).

Grey-felted below

Grey Willow or **Grey Sallow** – *Salix cinerea*
Favours damper ground; slightly smaller. More slender red-brown twigs remain hairy. Leaves smaller, long-pointed, more lanceolate. Toothed margins often rolled under. Lower surface grey-felted even when mature. Catkins smaller, narrower; open later.

Rusty Sallow – *Salix cinerea* ssp *oleifolia*
More common than Grey outside East Anglia and Lincolnshire. More tree-like and leaves with rusty-red hairs below; most obvious in late summer.

See p.112 for *Salix* species of tree stature with leaves much longer than broad.

Crab-apple – *Malus sylvestris,* **Cultivated apple** – *M. domestica* and **Pear** – *Pyrus communis* – see p.94
Leaves with a less-wrinkled, glossier upper surface, soon becoming smooth below. Margin of regular, fine-pointed, teeth. 5 free-petalled flowers, fleshy fruits.

Three native, small, bushy trees have leaves of a similar size and shape but smooth below. Buds many-scaled:

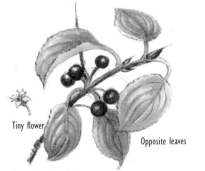

Tiny flower

Opposite leaves

Alder Buckthorn – *Frangula alnus*
Leaves not wrinkled, not wavy and with no marginal teeth. Smooth, black twigs. Insignificant flowers; fruit ripen from yellow to red-black.

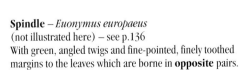

Purging Buckthorn – *Rhamnus cathartica* – see p.134
Leaves in **opposite** pairs. Regular fine-toothed margin and side veins curving towards the tip. Thorny twigs.

Spindle – *Euonymus europaeus*
(not illustrated here) – see p.136
With green, angled twigs and fine-pointed, finely toothed margins to the leaves which are borne in **opposite** pairs.

DECICUOUS
Salicaceae

Bay Willow or Laurel-leaved Willow

Salix pentandra

A beautiful willow, little known by botanists from S. England as its native distribution is from N. Wales and the N. Midlands northwards. Outside this range male trees are planted in gardens for their glossy leaves and fragrant showy catkins. The leaves resemble Bay Laurel (*Laurus nobilis*).

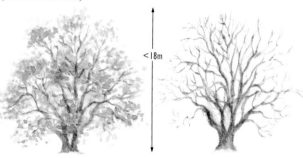

<18m

USES:
Brittle shoots are little used. Leaves have been used as a Bay substitute in Norway.

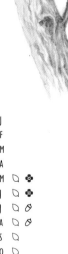

NATIVE but infrequent by northern streams and lakesides especially on peat soils. A broad, bushy shrub. Male trees throughout Britain in gardens.

BARK: Grey-brown with fine orange-brown cracks.

TWIG: Red-brown, glossy as if varnished.

TIMBER: Pale, brittle.

BUDS: Small, brown, glossy and sticky.

LEAVES: Bay-like, narrowly ovate, short-pointed, leathery. Finely and evenly saw-toothed margins, initially sticky. Deep glossy-green above, glossy, paler midrib. Matt, paler, blue-green below. Some much smaller leaves occur with the others. Aromatic (like Friars Balsam) when unfolding or crushed. Short, stout petiole with tiny warts (glands) at blade end.

FLOWERS: Late for a Willow; with the leaves. Fragrant, erect, short hairy-stalked catkins on separate sex trees. Male broad-based, hairy, dense-flowered, bright yellow; each flower with at least 5 stamens. Females thinner, shorter, hairless and green.

FRUIT: Green capsules releasing cotton-wool like seed.

J
F
M
A
M
J
J
A
S
O
N
D

♂

Catkin size: 2–6cm

Glossy midrib

Leaf size:
5–12cm x 2–5cm

Finely-toothed
margin

Glossy twig

♀

Two hybrid willows may occur naturally where *pentandra* is found but are also of garden origin and are introduced outside the natural range of *pentandra*:

Ehrhart's Willow – *Salix alba x pentandra*
(S. x erhartiana)
Male only; sometimes naturalised, especially in S.E. England. Less glossy twig and longer, narrower leaves which are initially thinly hairy on the upper surface. Male catkins longer and slenderer than in *pentandra*.

Shiny-leaved Willow – *Salix fragilis x pentandra*
(S. x meyeriana)
Male and female trees sporadically throughout England; probably introduced. More fissured bark but with glossy twigs and leaves; the latter slightly narrower than *pentandra*. Male flowers typically with 3–4 stamens.

The only other common tree-like Willows with an ovate leaf are **Goat Willow** – *Salix caprea* and **Grey Willow** – *Salix cinerea* (see p.90) These lack glossy stems and leaves and bear catkins earlier, before the leaves open.

Bay Laurel – *Laurus nobilis*
Introduced **evergreen**; grown in gardens as a pyramidal shrub for its scented leaves used in cooking. Will grow to a small tree if left unclipped. Leaves similar in size and shape to Bay Willow but thicker. Strong spicy scent when crushed and a wavy, non-toothed margin. Small yellow-green male and female flowers on separate plants in the leaf axils; female trees produce small oval berries which ripen from green to black.

Non-toothed margin

Crab Apple
Malus sylvestris

The ancestor of most cultivated apples and still used as graft stock for many cultivars. The hard fruits are too sour to eat raw. The 'skrab' (from the Norse for scrubby) apple is frequently confused with self-sown cultivated Apples (of which there are over a thousand different cultivars) and also with Pears *(Pyrus)*.

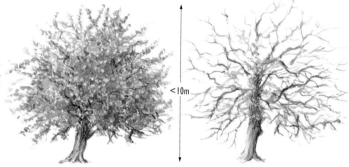

<10m

USES:
Jelly-jam and wine from the fruits. Wood for carving, inlay and turnery. Sweet-smelling firewood.

Probably **NATIVE** but infrequent. In hedges, woodland edges and mixed woods. Mostly on lime-rich soils. Small. Short bole with dense, twisted, spreading branches. Crown often one-sided.

BARK: Grey-brown. Fine fissures form rectangular plates.

TIMBER: Hard and very close-grained.

TWIG: Ribbed, red-brown. Short side shoots scarred from leaf and flower shoots, often bearing spines.

BUD: Pointed, red-purple with long grey hairs.

LEAVES: Variable in size and shape from oval to almost circular with a short-pointed apex. Initially hairy but soon glabrous above. Petiole c. half blade length, grooved, hairy; often dark-red at the base.

Leaf size: av. 6cm x 3cm

FLOWERS: Erect, stalked, sweet-smelling clusters of 3-7 flowers with 5 small green sepals (felted inner surface), 5 white (rarely pink tinged) petals, widest above the middle. Mass of yellow anthers, 3 stigmas.

Flower size: 2.5cm

Margin saw-toothed

FRUIT: Fleshy, firm, globular. Sepal remains at apex. Indented at junction with hanging stalk. Hard and sour. Dark brown seeds.

Hairy on the vein axils

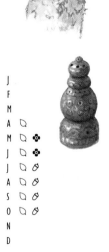

J
F
M
A
M
J
J
A
S
O
N
D

2–3cm spine

Fruit size: 2.5–3cm

Various non-native species and cultivars lacking spines are grown in gardens for their attractive flowers and fruits.

Malus 'John Downie' (not illustrated)
Popular in suburban gardens. White flowers and elongated, conical, orange-red fruits.

Purple Crab – *M. x purpurea*
A hybrid with a purple-green twig. The leaves emerge purple-green but age greener and more glossy. Crimson flowers, red-purple fruits. Oddly branched, untidy shape.

Siberian Crab – *Malus baccata*
Leaves more elongated. White fragrant flowers with narrow spaced petals and long-stalked, smaller, clear red or yellow, cherry-like fruits devoid of dead sepals.

Japanese Crab – *Malus floribunda*
With a twiggy, arching crown of downy shoots. Masses of early flowers. Deep pink bud, flowers emerge pink and fade to white. Red or yellow fruits.

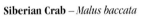

Fruit size: <1cm

Long hanging stalk

<15cm long

Cultivated Apple – *Malus domestica* (many cultivars)
Self-sown Cultivated Apples are frequent by roads and on waste ground. They often revert to bearing small, yellow, sour fruits more like Crab Apple but *domestica* has a downy, non-spiny shoot. Larger leaves are dark-green and smooth above; grey-green and hairy below. Relatively short petiole. Pinker flowers. Fruit colour, shape and size varies with the different cultivars; most ripen soft and sweet.

Fruit size: <12cm

Hairy flower stalks and sepals

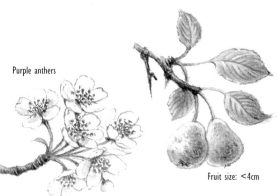

Purple anthers

Fruit size: <4cm

Wild Pear – *Pyrus pyraster*
Probably not native. Occasional in hedges and woodland edges in S. England. Often spiny, it differs from Crab Apple in being taller with almost black, more deeply fissured bark. Glossy leaves, more fine-toothed margin. Petiole as long as blade. Earlier (April) white flowers open before the leaves have unfurled. Inedible globular or elongated yellow/red-brown fruits lack a depression where the stalk attaches.

'Williams'

Cultivated Pear –
Pyrus communis (many cultivars)
Also grows from discarded seeds but is typically non-spiny and bears larger oval or rounded glossy leaves and larger pear-shaped, edible fruits.

Fruit size: <10cm

'Commice'

Margin entire

Fruit size: 3–12cm

Quince – *Cydonia oblonga*
A small, smooth-barked tree still grown in some Southern gardens. Leaves differ from Crab Apple in their entire margin and grey felty hairs below. Larger solitary, pink or white flowers. Downy green fruit ripens hard, yellow and very fragrant.

A small native tree with similar leaves is:

Goat Willow – *Salix caprea* – see p.90
The leaves are often wrinkled and the lower surface is covered with soft, downy hairs. Margins are irregularly, shallow-toothed. Single scaled, flattened yellow buds hug the stem. Flowers and fruits in catkins.

Male catkin

Broad-leaved Trees

Alternate – unlobed, long leaves (at least twice as long as broad; pp.98–113)

Wild Cherry
Prunus avium

Ohne of our most attractive native trees with distinctive bark, showy spring flowers and edible fruits. An ancestor of Cherry, cultivated for its fruit and related to many other *Prunus* species and cultivars, some of which are grown for their beautiful flowers.

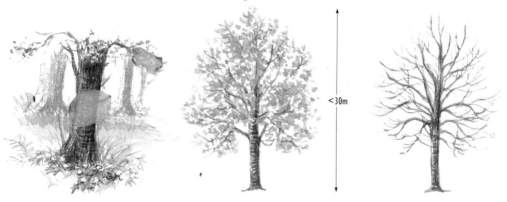

<30m

NATIVE: Most frequent in S. England in hedges and woodland edges; often on lime-rich soils. Planted in woods, parks, gardens and streets. Tall with a conical/rounded crown. Regular, whorled, near horizontal branches from a straight trunk; base often fluted.
BARK: Matures purple-brown, smooth and shiny. Peels in horizontal strips.
TIMBER: Brown with a green hue. Hard but light. Smells of Rose blossom when newly cut.
TWIG: Smooth, red-brown above, greyer below.
BUD: Large, many scaled, shiny red-brown.
LEAVES: Thin and limp. Base tapers to a long grooved petiole. Margin irregularly toothed. Emerge red-brown, mature smooth, dull matt green; paler and slightly hairy on veins below. Orange-red in autumn.
FLOWERS: Fragrant, with 5 white petals, c.20 yellow stamens and a single style.
FRUIT: Globular. Ripen from green to yellow to red to black. Glossy skin around sweet yellow flesh.

USES:
The wood is in demand for furniture, veneer and the manufacture of smoking pipes.

Horizontal lenticels

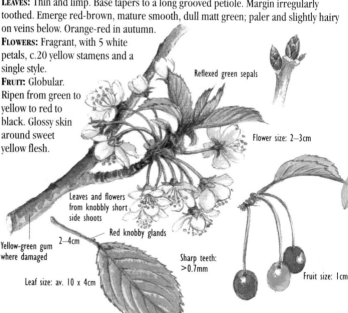

Reflexed green sepals

Flower size: 2–3cm

Leaves and flowers from knobbly short side shoots

Red knobby glands

Yellow-green gum where damaged

2–4cm

Sharp teeth: >0.7mm

Leaf size: av. 10 x 4cm

Fruit size: 1cm

J
F
M
A
M
J
J
A
S
O
N
D

More cherries are planted for their flowers and foliage than for their fruit. A range of species and cultivars vary in leaf colour (some are red-brown) and flowering times (autumn, winter and through spring to early summer). Some, like the native Bird Cherry (see p.103) produce flowers on a long spike. Flowers may be single or double and come in different sizes and colours. Some rarely or never set fruit, others produce red or black fruits, often small and sour.

Sargent's Cherry – *Prunus sargentii*
Frequent in streets, gardens and parks. Rounded crown. Graft union often swollen. Bark, bud and shoot dark red. Broader leaves more abruptly tapering to apical point emerge red-purple then yellow-green before orange/red in autumn. Early, (March–April) showy, pink flowers. Fruit as *avium*.

Japanese Cherries – Over 60 types formerly grouped as *P. serrulata* now classed as *Prunus* cultivars. Many are hybrids developed in Japan for their flowers – they rarely set seed and are propagated by grafting on *avium* stock. Examples include:

Notched tip to petal

Bristly margin

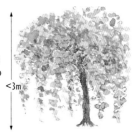

'Cheal's Weeping' – With deep pink very double flowers from late March. Branches arch to the ground.

<3m

'Kansan' – The commonest double pink-flowered form in streets and gardens. Profuse clusters of lilac pink flowers emerge mid–late April with the bronze-purple young leaves. Leaves larger than *avium* and the marginal teeth end in bristles – as do most Japanese Cherries.

Flower size: <6cm

Double white flowers

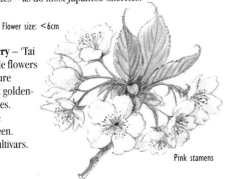

Great White Cherry – 'Tai Haku' – Large single flowers mid to late April. Pure white petals against golden-coppery young leaves. Mature leaves large (<20cm), dark green. Taller than other cultivars.

Pink stamens

Double Gean –
Prunus avium 'Plena'
A frequently planted large tree. Flowers later (early May), with long lasting, long stalked flowers. No fruit.

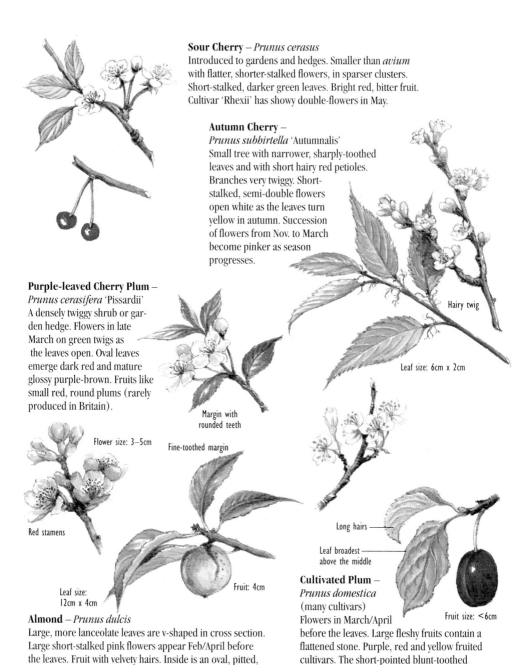

Sour Cherry – *Prunus cerasus*
Introduced to gardens and hedges. Smaller than *avium* with flatter, shorter-stalked flowers, in sparser clusters. Short-stalked, darker green leaves. Bright red, bitter fruit. Cultivar 'Rhexii' has showy double-flowers in May.

Autumn Cherry –
Prunus subhirtella 'Autumnalis'
Small tree with narrower, sharply-toothed leaves and with short hairy red petioles. Branches very twiggy. Short-stalked, semi-double flowers open white as the leaves turn yellow in autumn. Succession of flowers from Nov. to March become pinker as season progresses.

Hairy twig

Leaf size: 6cm x 2cm

Purple-leaved Cherry Plum –
Prunus cerasifera 'Pissardii'
A densely twiggy shrub or garden hedge. Flowers in late March on green twigs as the leaves open. Oval leaves emerge dark red and mature glossy purple-brown. Fruits like small red, round plums (rarely produced in Britain).

Margin with rounded teeth

Flower size: 3–5cm

Fine-toothed margin

Red stamens

Long hairs

Leaf broadest above the middle

Fruit: 4cm

Cultivated Plum –
Prunus domestica
(many cultivars)
Flowers in March/April before the leaves. Large fleshy fruits contain a flattened stone. Purple, red and yellow fruited cultivars. The short-pointed blunt-toothed leaves are subshiny. **Bullace** or **Damson** has pubescent, often spiny twigs, leaves hairy on both sides and small rounder purple fruits with a less flattened stone.

Fruit size: <6cm

Leaf size: 12cm x 4cm

Almond – *Prunus dulcis*
Large, more lanceolate leaves are v-shaped in cross section. Large short-stalked pink flowers appear Feb/April before the leaves. Fruit with velvety hairs. Inside is an oval, pitted, brown nut enclosing the kernal.

Some Cherries e.g. **Bird Cherry** produce their flowers and fruits on long spikes – see p.103.

The **leaf** of a number of trees can be confused with that of Wild Cherry:

Apple and **Pear** – see p.94
The leaves are broader with much less taper-pointed ends.

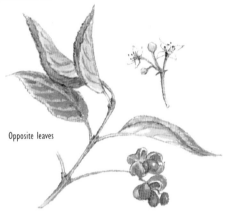

Opposite leaves

Spindle – *Euonymus europaeus* – see p.136
Rarely above 6m. The smaller, narrower leaves are **opposite** and with very finely toothed margins.

Smooth-leaved Elm – *Ulmus minor* – see p.77
The leaf is thicker and bears coarser, doubly serrate margins. It is unequal at the base and hairy on the undersurface veins.

The **fruit** of Wild Cherry can be confused with:

Cornelian Cherry – *Cornus mas*
Has opposite untoothed leaves with 3–5 prs of conspicuous side veins bending to the leaf tip. A small tree with spreading branches. Grown in gardens for the early flowers (Feb–March) in umbel-like masses surrounded by four, downy boat-shaped bracts. Fruit like a bright red oblong cherry.

I O I

Cherry Laurel
Prunus laurocerasus

EVERGREEN
Rosaceae

Laurel, as it is known, has an evergreen leaf similar to another introduction – Rhododendron. Both are shrubs or small trees that have become naturalised. The crushed leaves of Laurel smell of marzipan due to the presence of poisonous prussic acid. The flower and fruit spike is comparable with Portugal Laurel and some Cherries.

INTRODUCED in gardens and parks (e.g. as a hedge); also in woods for game-bird cover. Naturalised as an undershrub in woods on acid soil. Usually under 6m but over 10m if not pruned. Short bole; branches form a spreading bush.

BARK: Dark grey/black with small orange lenticels.

TIMBER: Not used. 'Laurel-wood' comes from an Indian tree.

TWIG: Smooth, pale green. Matures yellow-brown.

BUDS: Small, egg-shaped, bright green.

LEAVES: Large, evergreen, initially pale-green and soft, later stiff, leathery. Dark-green and glossy above, paler and less shiny below. Narrow ovate. Wedge-shaped base. Inrolled margin with a few irregular shallow teeth, most point towards the apex; rarely entire. Short, stout, green petiole. Strong smell of marzipan.

FLOWERS: c.30 fragrant flowers on an erect, short green-stalked spike. 5 dull-white petals fused at their bases.

FRUIT: Like small cherries. Purple-black, shiny when ripe. Flesh contains a single, poisonous stone.

USES:
Entomologists used the crushed leaves to kill captured insects.

J	◖	
F	◖	
M	◖	✿
A	◖	✿
M	◖	✿
J	◖	✽
J	◖	✽
A	◖	✽
S	◖	✽
O	◖	✽
N	◖	
D	◖	

Short point

Flower spike: <12cm long

Few irregular teeth

Leaf size: 20cm x 6cm

Style and stamens longer than petals

Flower size: 1cm

Fruit size: 1.5–2cm

CULTIVARS, RELATED AND CONFUSABLE SPECIES

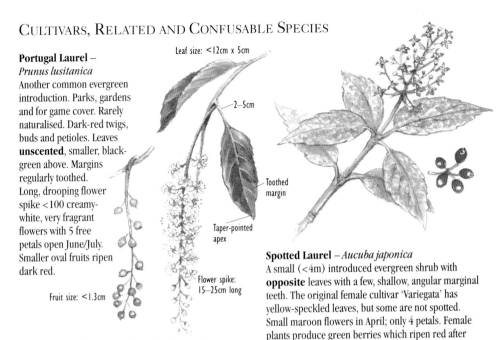

Portugal Laurel –
Prunus lusitanica
Another common evergreen
introduction. Parks, gardens
and for game cover. Rarely
naturalised. Dark-red twigs,
buds and petioles. Leaves
unscented, smaller, black-
green above. Margins
regularly toothed.
Long, drooping flower
spike <100 creamy-
white, very fragrant
flowers with 5 free
petals open June/July.
Smaller oval fruits ripen
dark red.

Leaf size: <12cm x 5cm

2–5cm

Toothed
margin

Taper-pointed
apex

Flower spike:
15–25cm long

Fruit size: <1.3cm

Spotted Laurel – *Aucuba japonica*
A small (<4m) introduced evergreen shrub with
opposite leaves with a few, shallow, angular marginal
teeth. The original female cultivar 'Variegata' has
yellow-speckled leaves, but some are not spotted.
Small maroon flowers in April; only 4 petals. Female
plants produce green berries which ripen red after
overwintering.

Two Cherries have smaller, deciduous leaves
but very similar flowers and fruits:

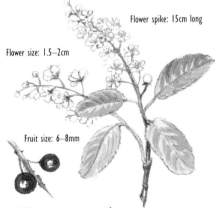

Flower spike: 15cm long

Flower size: 1.5–2cm

Fruit size: 6–8mm

Rum Cherry – *Prunus serotina*
Uncommon introduction. Similar to
padus but taller. More glossy leaves.
Shorter, upright, dense flower
spikes. Smaller flowers on shorter
stalks. Purple-black fruit retain
dead sepals at apex.

Orange/white hairs by
midrib

The large, glossy, evergreen leaves of Laurel
are confused with:

Bird Cherry – *Prunus padus*
Native in lime-rich woods in N. Britain. Also planted. A
small bushy tree with bitter-smelling bark, orange
lenticels and glossy brown shoots. Leaf with a rounded
base and fine-toothed margin. Green, smooth above;
paler and slightly hairy below. Almond-scented, small
white flowers in May, <40 on a spreading/drooping
spike. Small bitter-tasting fruits ripen glossy black.
Garden cultivar 'Watereri' has fewer, larger leaves and
longer, spreading flower spikes.

Rhododendron – *Rhododendron ponticum* –
see p.104 (not illustrated here)
Leaves always entire, with a tapered base. Large scaly
green buds. Showy flowers, dry fruits.

Evergreen Magnolia – *Magnolia grandiflora* –
see p.106 (not illustrated here)
Leaves are broader; paler below with rust-coloured hairs.
Large hairy, **single**-scaled buds. Spectacular flowers.

103

Rhododendron

Rhododendron ponticum

EVERGREEN
Ericaceae

There are some 800 species of Rhododendron. Plant hunters including Hooker, Forrest and Wilson collected many from China and the Himalayas to grace our gardens. Ranging from prostrate alpines to trees they include Azaleas. *Rhododendron ponticum* came from S. Europe in 1763. Naturalises (from seed and suckers) on peat, sandy and rocky soils. Regarded by some as a weed.

<8m

USES:
Cover for game birds.
Wood used in turnery.

INTRODUCED, locally abundant especially under Oak or Birch. A shrub, rarely to 8m. Short, sinuous, much-forked bole. Wide-spreading branches. Suckers freely.
BARK: Thin, grey-brown, shallowly fissured.
TIMBER: Brown with darker rings, hard.
TWIG: Smooth, green to orange-brown, finally grey-brown.
BUDS: Large (3–4cm) green, pointed, terminal buds with many overlapping scales.
LEAVES: Evergreen, glossy, grouped at twig ends. Widest nearer the shortly-pointed apex. Tapered wedge-shaped base. Margins often downturned. Prominent paler midrib. Stout, shallowly-grooved petiole, purple-red above, green below; often bent back so blade droops.
FLOWERS: In large clusters. Each with 5 small, fused sepals, 5 petals fused at base into a short tube, unequal spreading lobes.
FRUIT: Erect, narrow, dry capsule. Ripens from green to brown. Splits to release many tiny seeds.

J	◌
F	◌
M	◌
A	◌
M	◌ ❖
J	◌ ❖
J	◌ ◗
A	◌ ◗
S	◌ ◗
O	◌ ◗
N	◌
D	◌

10 stamens sweep upwards

Individual flowers: 5–6cm

Fruit

Brown spots

Yellow-green, sub-shiny below

Leaf size: 8–20cm x 4–6cm

Margins entire

R. ponticum is still the most common garden species of Rhododendron but there are now hundreds of introduced species and thousands of hybrids. Azaleas are species of Rhododendron – usually small shrubs; some are deciduous.

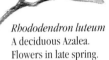

Rhododendron luteum
A deciduous Azalea.
Flowers in late spring.

Rhododendron 'Vanessa Pastel'
Evergreen, compact shrub with medium-sized leaves and loose, open trusses of pink flowers, flushed creamy-yellow and red in the throat. Flowers early summer.

Rhododendron arboreum
Evergreen tree <15m with red-brown, shredding bark. Large leaves (<20cm long) thinly hairy; silvery or rusty beneath. Tip abruptly pointed, midrib deeply impressed. Parallel, prominent side veins. Huge dense flower clusters on downy stalks from January to April. Deep bell-shaped white, pink or red flowers with darker spots inside.

Other introduced evergreens with similar leaves include:

Irregular shallow-toothed margin

Cherry Laurel –
Prunus laurocerasus –
see p.102
Glossy leaves of similar size, shape and colour. Smell of bitter almonds when crushed. Small (5–6mm) buds. Erect spikes of c.30 tiny white, fragrant flowers and red-black cherry-like fruit.

Evergreen Magnolia – *Magnolia grandiflora –*
see p.106
Leaf broader (<10cm) very thick and glossy; often with rust-coloured hairs below. Petiole with brown hairs. Large hairy buds with one scale. Young twig pubescent. Huge flowers borne singly. Fruit narrow, cone-like.

Evergreen Magnolia

Magnolia grandiflora

Magnolia species, hybrids and cultivars are grown for their showy flowers. Many are deciduous and do not reach tree size. From the Himalayas, Asia and N. and S. America, some like *grandiflora* are sensitive to frost and cold wind and do best grown against a south-facing wall.

<25m

USES:
Ornamental, grown mainly for its flowers.

INTRODUCED in parks and large gardens in England; mostly in the S. and W. To 25m but usually shorter. Trunk forks low down; branches spread widely.

BARK: Dark grey, smooth; later cracks into small scales.

TWIG: Stout, brown; with a rusty pubescence when young.

BUDS: Large (<1.5cm), pinched at the base; only one visible scale; green with brown hairs at the tip.

LEAVES: Large, broadest above middle; short-pointed apex. Evergreen, thick, leathery. Margin entire. Very glossy, dark green above, paler below. Prominent, pale midrib. Stout petiole with brown hairs.

FLOWERS: Sparsely, singly at shoot tip, erect; open cup-shaped, huge (<25cm). 3 petal-like sepals and 6–9 thick broad, bluntly pointed, creamy-white petals. Many golden stamens, central cone-like pistil. Sweetly fragrant.

FRUIT: Like a conical Globe Artichoke. Fleshy, felty scales on a stout, curved, orange-brown stalk. Scales open to reveal orange-red seeds dangling on fine stalks.

Rust-coloured hairs (absent in some cultivars)

Fruit: 5cm long

Petal and stamen scars

Leaf size: 10–25cm x 5–10cm

Circular leaf scar

J
F
M
A
M
J
J
A
S
O
N
D

Two commonly grown cultivars are:

M. grandiflora 'Exmouth'
Narrower leaf, less hairy
below. More hardy.

M. grandiflora 'Goliath'
Broader more twisted leaf;
larger flowers (<30cm).

Of the many more shrub-like species of
Magnolia the most commonly grown is:

Hybrid Magnolia – *M. x soulangiana*
To 6m. Leaf sub-shiny, deciduous; pale
green, finely hairy below. Flower buds with
grey silky hairs. Flowers before and as
leaves emerge; tulip-shaped when young.
Typically 6 petals and 3 shorter, spreading
petal-like sepals.

A related tree with a similar
flower and fruit is:

Swollen base to petiole

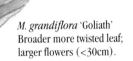

Two small introduced trees
with similar leaves to *M.
grandiflora* are:

Cherry Laurel –
Prunus laurocerasus – see p.102
The narrower leaves typically have a few
shallow marginal teeth, are not hairy
below and smell of bitter almonds when
crushed. Flowers and fruit in erect spikes.

Tulip Tree –
Liriodendron tulipifera –
see p.68
A tall tree with unusually shaped
leaves. The flowers look like a cross
between a Magnolia and a Tulip.

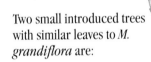

Sub-shiny below

Glabrous petiole

Rhododendron – *Rhododendron ponticum* –
see p.104
Leaves narrower, with a more tapered base. Hairless,
many-scaled flower buds. Showy clusters of purple
flowers in May/June.

Strawberry Tree

Arbutus unedo

An evergreen member of the Heath family. Native to the Mediterranean, parts of France and S.W. Ireland. This small tree or shrub is grown in gardens for its unusual autumn habit of bearing both flowers and fruits at the same time. Despite looking edible, the fruits taste unpleasant, hence *unedo* – 'I eat one (only)'.

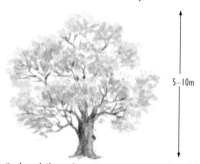

5–10m

NATIVE in Counties Kerry, Cork and Sligo where it grows as a spreading shrub. Planted, mostly in S. England and some sheltered coasts of Wales and Scotland in gardens, parks and churchyards. Dense, rounded, irregular crown. Many twisted, ascending branches; short, sinuous bole.

BARK: Rough, dull red-brown and grey. Ridged with age.

TIMBER: Dull brown with fine darker lines.

TWIG: Pink-red above, greener below.

BUDS: Tiny, but a conspicuous purple-red colour.

LEAVES: Oblong-ovate; wedge-shaped base and pointed apex. Leathery, glossy above; paler and subglossy below. Margins with small, unequal, forward-pointing teeth, those near the apex tinged red. Short hairy, pink-red petiole.

FLOWERS: Drooping clusters of c.15 flowers. Waxy urn-shaped flower with 10 stamens and 1 stigma. Fragrant.

FRUITS: 3–6 globular, white fleshy berries covered in soft pimples. Ripen (yellow to orange to red) over 12 months by which time more flowers are open.

USES:
The wood has been used for inlay and to make charcoal.

J
F
M
A
M
J
J
A
S
O
N
D

Red bract at stalk junction

Pale midrib

Glandular hairs

Leaf size:
4–10cm x 2–5cm

Flower size: 8mm

Fruit size:
1.5–2cm

5 joined petals

5 tiny green sepals

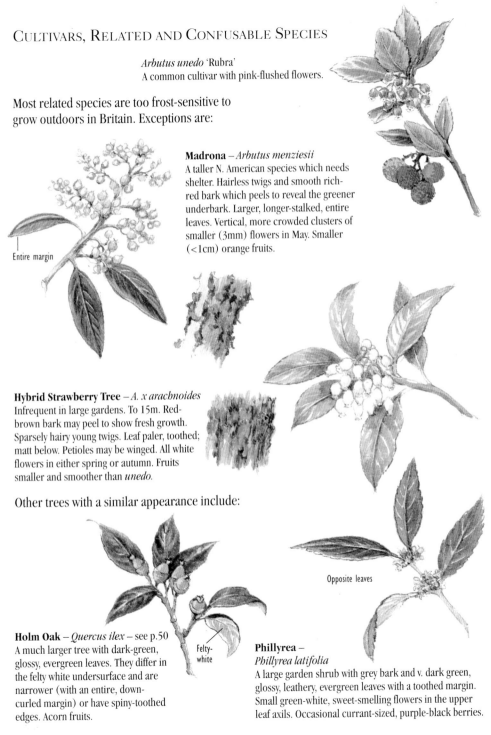

Arbutus unedo 'Rubra'
A common cultivar with pink-flushed flowers.

Most related species are too frost-sensitive to
grow outdoors in Britain. Exceptions are:

Madrona – *Arbutus menziesii*
A taller N. American species which needs
shelter. Hairless twigs and smooth rich-
red bark which peels to reveal the greener
underbark. Larger, longer-stalked, entire
leaves. Vertical, more crowded clusters of
smaller (3mm) flowers in May. Smaller
(<1cm) orange fruits.

Entire margin

Hybrid Strawberry Tree – *A. x arachnoides*
Infrequent in large gardens. To 15m. Red-
brown bark may peel to show fresh growth.
Sparsely hairy young twigs. Leaf paler, toothed;
matt below. Petioles may be winged. All white
flowers in either spring or autumn. Fruits
smaller and smoother than *unedo*.

Other trees with a similar appearance include:

Opposite leaves

Holm Oak – *Quercus ilex* – see p.50
A much larger tree with dark-green,
glossy, evergreen leaves. They differ in
the felty white undersurface and are
narrower (with an entire, down-
curled margin) or have spiny-toothed
edges. Acorn fruits.

Felty-white

Phillyrea –
Phillyrea latifolia
A large garden shrub with grey bark and v. dark green,
glossy, leathery, evergreen leaves with a toothed margin.
Small green-white, sweet-smelling flowers in the upper
leaf axils. Occasional currant-sized, purple-black berries.

Cider Gum
Eucalyptus gunnii

EVERGREEN
Myrtaceae

O f the many species and hybrid gum-trees from Australia some, like *gunnii* come from colder, highland areas and are better suited to the British climate. Most have peeling bark, no visible buds, aromatic leathery leaves and button-like flowers.

<30m

INTRODUCED in 1846 and the most commonly grown species. Not on chalk soils. Rapid growing. Single trunk and upswept branches.

BARK: Base rough, rest smooth pink/orange, peeling in long vertical strips. Exudes fragrant resin when damaged.

TIMBER: Little used in Britain.

TWIG: Yellow-white with a pink-grey bloom.

BUDS: Minute, no resting bud – expanding leaves stop growth in cold weather.

LEAVES: a) Juvenile (on young growth). Opposite, sessile, pale blue-grey, rounded; b) Adult. Alternate, pendant from a pale yellow petiole. Taper-pointed apex. Leathery with very little smell, dark blue-grey above, yellow-green below with prominent veins.

FLOWERS: Clusters of 3, small, short-stalked, button-like, blue-white flowerheads. Top-shaped in bud before the coned, green-red lid (fused petals) falls off to reveal masses of long stamens and central style.

FRUIT: Flat-topped, green then brown and woody. Top opens as 3/5 valves releasing tiny black seeds.

USES:
An ornamental tree in Britain. Grown in S. Europe for paper pulp. Eucalyptus oil is a decongestant and throat soother.

Grey
under-bark

Long white stamens

Leaf size: 8–10cm
x 3–4cm

Fruit size:
5mm

J	◌	⌀
F	◌	
M	◌	
A	◌	
M	◌	
J	◌	
J	◌	
A	◌	❖
S	◌	❖
O	◌	⌀
N	◌	⌀
D	◌	⌀

3–6cm long

Juvenile   Adult

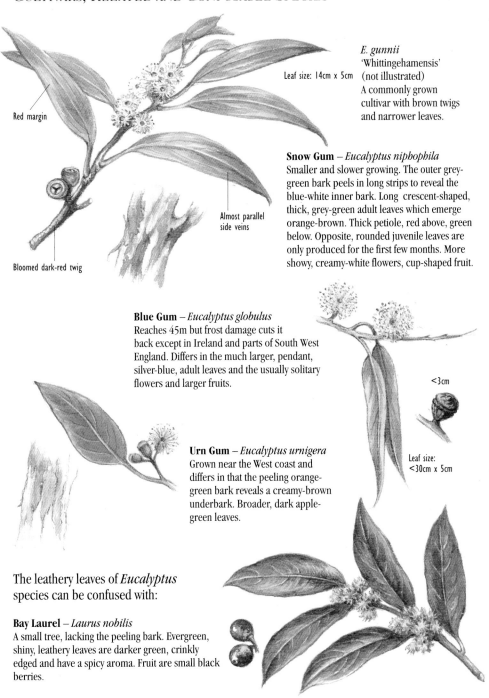

Red margin

Leaf size: 14cm x 5cm

E. gunnii
'Whittingehamensis'
(not illustrated)
A commonly grown
cultivar with brown twigs
and narrower leaves.

Almost parallel
side veins

Bloomed dark-red twig

Snow Gum – *Eucalyptus niphophila*
Smaller and slower growing. The outer grey-green bark peels in long strips to reveal the blue-white inner bark. Long crescent-shaped, thick, grey-green adult leaves which emerge orange-brown. Thick petiole, red above, green below. Opposite, rounded juvenile leaves are only produced for the first few months. More showy, creamy-white flowers, cup-shaped fruit.

Blue Gum – *Eucalyptus globulus*
Reaches 45m but frost damage cuts it back except in Ireland and parts of South West England. Differs in the much larger, pendant, silver-blue, adult leaves and the usually solitary flowers and larger fruits.

<3cm

Urn Gum – *Eucalyptus urnigera*
Grown near the West coast and differs in that the peeling orange-green bark reveals a creamy-brown underbark. Broader, dark apple-green leaves.

Leaf size:
<30cm x 5cm

The leathery leaves of *Eucalyptus* species can be confused with:

Bay Laurel – *Laurus nobilis*
A small tree, lacking the peeling bark. Evergreen, shiny, leathery leaves are darker green, crinkly edged and have a spicy aroma. Fruit are small black berries.

White Willow
Salix alba

DECIDUOUS
Salicaceae

USES:
Baskets, fencing and firewood. Cricket bats and artificial limbs (from S. alba 'Coerulea').

O ne of the commonest larger Willows. (See those with broader leaves on pp.90–93.) Willows have simple, unlobed leaves and single-scaled appressed buds. Many grow in wet ground and are often coppiced or pollarded. White Willow is frequently confused with Crack Willow with which it hybridizes.

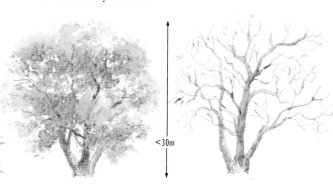

<30m

NATIVE and widely planted though less in the West. Rarer than *fragilis* in the South. Best on deep, riverside soils. Broad, dense crown with ascendant branches from a stout bole. Often pollarded.

BARK: Grey-brown with a diamond network of ridged fissures.
TIMBER: Pale greyish-yellow, light; does not split.
TWIG: Slender, pliant, initially hairy then smooth; olive-brown.
BUDS: Small, hairy, pointed (often off-centre), flat to the stem.
LEAVES: Narrow with a pointed, tapered apex and tapered base. Initially covered in silvery-white hairs on both sides, underside retaining these, upper side becoming smooth and dull green.
FLOWERS: Spreading, short-stalked, narrow, yellow male catkins. Shorter green female catkins on separate trees.
FRUIT: Catkins of small green capsules containing cotton-tufted seeds.

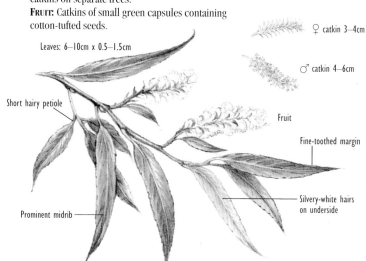

♀ catkin 3–4cm

♂ catkin 4–6cm

Leaves: 6–10cm x 0.5–1.5cm

Short hairy petiole

Fruit

Fine-toothed margin

Prominent midrib

Silvery-white hairs on underside

J
F
M
A
M
J
J
A
S
O
N
D

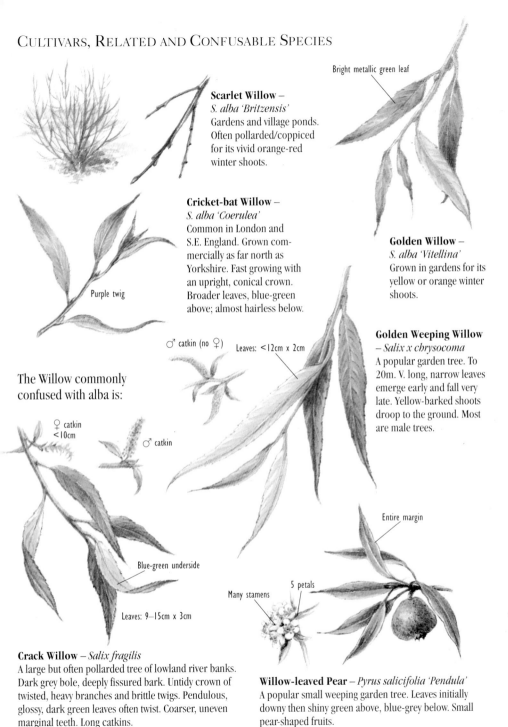

Bright metallic green leaf

Scarlet Willow –
S. alba 'Britzensis'
Gardens and village ponds.
Often pollarded/coppiced
for its vivid orange-red
winter shoots.

Cricket-bat Willow –
S. alba 'Coerulea'
Common in London and
S.E. England. Grown com-
mercially as far north as
Yorkshire. Fast growing with
an upright, conical crown.
Broader leaves, blue-green
above; almost hairless below.

Golden Willow –
S. alba 'Vitellina'
Grown in gardens for its
yellow or orange winter
shoots.

Purple twig

♂ catkin (no ♀)   Leaves: <12cm x 2cm

The Willow commonly
confused with alba is:

Golden Weeping Willow
– *Salix x chrysocoma*
A popular garden tree. To
20m. V. long, narrow leaves
emerge early and fall very
late. Yellow-barked shoots
droop to the ground. Most
are male trees.

♀ catkin
<10cm

♂ catkin

Entire margin

Blue-green underside

5 petals

Many stamens

Leaves: 9–15cm x 3cm

Crack Willow – *Salix fragilis*
A large but often pollarded tree of lowland river banks.
Dark grey bole, deeply fissured bark. Untidy crown of
twisted, heavy branches and brittle twigs. Pendulous,
glossy, dark green leaves often twist. Coarser, uneven
marginal teeth. Long catkins.

Willow-leaved Pear – *Pyrus salicifolia 'Pendula'*
A popular small weeping garden tree. Leaves initially
downy then shiny green above, blue-grey below. Small
pear-shaped fruits.

Broad-leaved Trees

Opposite leaves (pp.115–139)

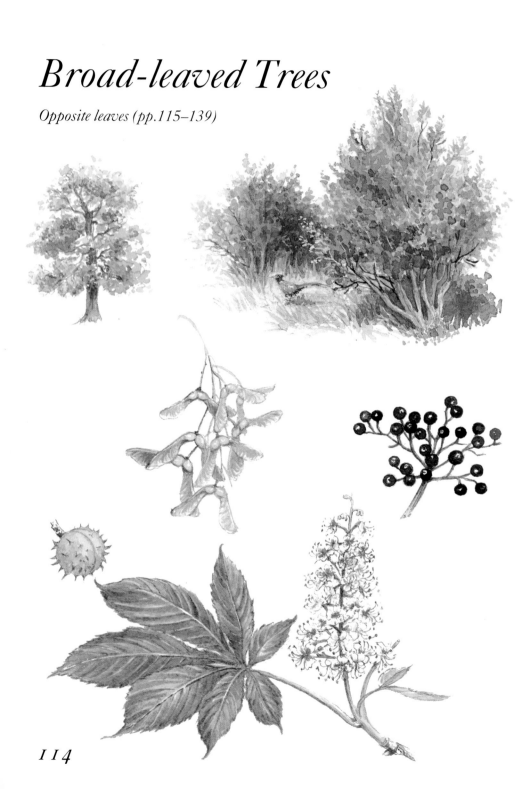

Ash

Fraxinus excelsior

ommonest on base-rich soil. On the limestone of the Peak District it is found in place names such as Monyash. Its leaves emerge late and fall early; one result of this is a rich ground flora in Ash woods. Its compound, pinnate leaves are often confused with other trees with the same leaf form but its black opposite buds are diagnostic.

DECIDUOUS
Oleaceae

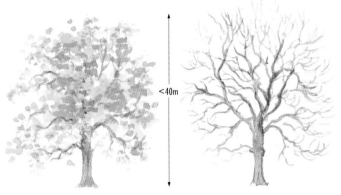

<40m

NATIVE and common. Prefers damp, calcareous soil. Tall; domed crown, trunk often forks. Lower branches sweep up but twigs bend down.

BARK: Smooth and grey; later vertically fissured.

TIMBER: Coarse-grained, white. Absorbs shock.

TWIG: Grey-green with paler lenticels.

BUDS: Matt-black, paired on flattened twig. Larger terminal bud.

LEAF: Pinnate with one terminal and 3–7 opposite prs of pointed, ovate leaflets, terminal pr the largest. Margins with irregular, forward-pointing teeth. 6–8 prs of side veins curve to apex. Glabrous above – woolly hairs either side of the paler midrib below. Green even in autumn. Green, lightly grooved petiole.

FLOWERS: Before the leaves. No petals. All male (each with two stamens) or all female (with longer stalks bearing flask-shaped pistils), or mixed. Many trees bear both sexes but on separate twigs.

FRUIT: Bunches of 'keys'. Seed at stalk end of twisted, notched wing. Brown by autumn, often persist.

USES:
Wheel rims, ladder rungs, tool handles, oars, hockey sticks, tennis rackets and billiard cues.

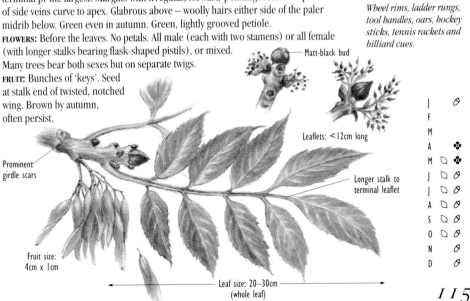

Matt-black bud

Leaflets: <12cm long

Prominent girdle scars

Longer stalk to terminal leaflet

Fruit size: 4cm x 1cm

Leaf size: 20–30cm (whole leaf)

J	✿
F	
M	
A	❀
M	▱ ❀
J	▱ ✿
J	▱ ✿
A	▱ ✿
S	▱ ✿
O	▱ ✿
N	✿
D	✿

Weeping Ash – *F. excelsior* 'Pendula'
A popular cultivar, grafted on Common
Ash and producing twisted branches with
terminal sections hanging vertically. In
large gardens, parks and churchyards.

Narrow-leaved Ash – *Fraxinus angustifolia*
Has brown buds and leaves bunched at twig ends.
Lanceolate leaflets, glabrous beneath. Thinner,
yellow petiole. Most frequent in city parks. Not
native.

Brown bud

Manna or Flowering Ash – *Fraxinus ornus*
Introduced. Fewer (5–9) leaflets, all obviously
stalked and only toothed near the apex. Hairy
brown buds. Fragrant, dense heads of creamy-
white flowers (with petals) not opening until
May or June. Narrower 'keys'. 'Knuckles' on
trunk. Frequent in parks and gardens.

Lobed leaflet base

Leaf length:
<60cm

Tree of Heaven – *Ailanthus altissima*
Of similar size and shape to Ash but the longer alternate leaves have more (c.20), narrow leaflets on
1cm reddish stalks, the pairs not quite opposite and
the leaflet base irregularly heart-shaped. Shiny
green above and with a rank smell when crushed.
Separate sex trees. Winged fruits with central seed.
Mostly in Southern streets and gardens. Introduced.

Three trees have **alternate** compound leaves:

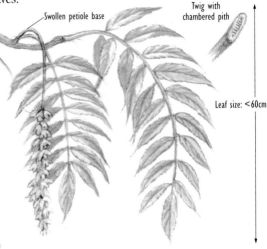

Swollen petiole base

Twig with chambered pith

Leaf size: <60cm

Caucasian Wing-nut – *Pterocarya fraxinifolia*
Much longer leaves with typically 21 bright green, stalkless, narrow-pointed, leaflets. Middle leaflets largest, all have margins with forward pointing teeth. Brown long bud has no scales – only two compressed leaves. Spaced, winged, circular green fruit on very long hanging stalk. Frequently suckering. Introduced. Often planted by water.

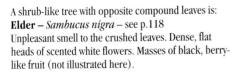

Leaflet size: 6cm x 2cm

Mountain Ash or **Rowan** –
Sorbus aucuparia – see p.55
A small native tree, the leaves typically have 7 (up to 9) pairs of evenly toothed, smaller unstalked leaflets and a stalked terminal one. Purple, downy buds. Clusters of 5-petalled flowers and orange-red berries.

Black Walnut – *Juglans nigra* – see p.58
Large leaf with more widely-spaced, bright green, drooping, finely serrated, lanceolate leaflets (av. 14). These are not quite opposite; the longest pair is in the middle and the terminal one is absent or small. Hairy on veins below, on the petiole and the buds. Hanging male catkins. Hairy, green globular fruit contains wrinkled nut. Large gardens and parks. Introduced.

Leaf size: <45cm

A shrub-like tree with opposite compound leaves is:
Elder – *Sambucus nigra* – see p.118
Unpleasant smell to the crushed leaves. Dense, flat heads of scented white flowers. Masses of black, berry-like fruit (not illustrated here).

Elder

Sambucus nigra

This small tree grows like a weed on rich, disturbed soil especially near rabbit warrens and badger setts. It carries its poisonous, unpleasant-smelling leaves for all but the most severe winter months. Various cultivars and related, introduced species share the smell of Elder – formerly used to deter flies annoying domestic animals.

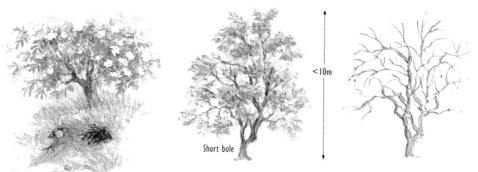

<10m

Short bole

USES:
Dyestuffs and medicines from bark, leaf, flower and fruit. Drinks from flowers and fruit. Hollowed twigs made musical pipes, the removed pith being used to clean watch mechanisms.

NATIVE: Common (rarer in Scotland) in hedges, woodland clearings and near houses. Typically an untidy bush.

BARK: Grey-brown, deeply furrowed and becoming corky.

TIMBER: Hard and pale yellow.

TWIG: Green and smooth when young, easily snapped.

BUDS: Lack protective scales, open early.

LEAVES: Compound with 5 (3–7) ovate, toothed leaflets. 'Cat urine' smell when bruised. Retained, with little colour change, until early winter.

FLOWERS: In erect flat clusters. Individual flowers tiny. Sickly sweet smell.

FRUIT: Berries ripening from green to shiny black (rarely yellow or white). Each contains 3 leathery seeds – distributed by birds.

Long stalk of terminal leaflet

Yellow stamens

5 petals fused at base

Naked bud

Flower head: 10–20cm (across)

Fruit size: 6–8mm

No stalk (upper leaflets)

Warty lenticels

White pith

Grooved petiole keeled at the base

Short stalk (lower leaflets)

J
F
M
A
M
J
J
A
S
O
N
D

CULTIVARS, RELATED AND CONFUSABLE SPECIES

Red-berried Elder – *Sambucus racemosa*
Introduced. Naturalised from Derbyshire northwards, commoner in Scotland. Smaller shrub. Much smaller flowerheads and red berries.

Narrower leaflets

Stalked glands

Pale brown pith

Cut-leaved Elder – *S. nigra* 'Laciniata' (not illustrated)
With finely divided fern-like leaves. Also sold in a variegated form.

American Elder –
Sambucus canadensis
Introduced. A suckering shrub with fewer lenticels on the twigs, more convex flowerheads opening later (July) and purple-black berries.

Golden Elder – *S. nigra* 'Aurea'
A cultivar with yellow leaves.

Dwarf Elder – *Sambucus ebulus*
(also known as Dane's Elder)
Possibly native, an unusual perennial **herb** (<2m). More (9–13), narrower leaflets per leaf.; smaller flowerhead, petals pink-tinged in bud. Black, poisonous berries.

Purple stamens

Stipules

Two trees have similar opposite, compound leaves but lack the offensive Elder smell:

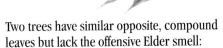

♂

♀

Box-Elder *or* **Ash-leaved Maple** –
Acer negundo (left)
Introduced. Leaflets more irregularly-toothed or even shallowly-lobed. Petiole yellow or pale pink. Male and female flowers on different trees in early March (before the leaves), Maple-like fruit.

Manna Ash – *Fraxinus ornus* – see picture on p.116
Introduced. Tall, smooth-barked tree. Leaves with 5–9 stalked leaflets, on a slender grooved petiole which is hairy at the joints. Fragrant flower heads of creamy-white flowers with very narrow petals. Fruits like slender Ash keys.

Horse Chestnut

Aesculus hippocastanum

Native to N. Greece. Arrived in Britain in the 17th Century from Turkey where its fruits were used to treat sick horses. The sticky winter buds, unusual leaf, spectacular flower heads and pretty autumn colours all ensured its popularity. Seed called 'conkers' (from 'conqueror' or 'conche' – an older game played with snails).

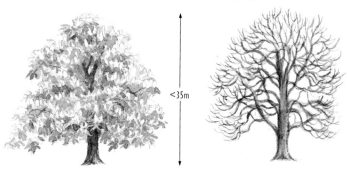

<35m

USES:
Chemicals from the seeds treat varicose veins and piles. A component of a well-known make of foam bath.

INTRODUCED. Common; less so in Scotland. Densely branched, domed crown; sturdy bole. Old trees with side branches which sweep down before turning up at the ends.
BARK: Grey-brown, smooth; later darker and cracked into elongated rectangles.
TIMBER: Soft and lacking strength.
TWIG: Stout, light brown with paler lenticels.
BUDS: Paired plus large terminal one, oval, sticky, red-brown. Vein scars like nail holes.
LEAVES: Compound; (3), 5 or 7 sessile, oblong, prominently veined, pointed palmate leaflets on a long, grooved petiole. Irregularly double-toothed, dark green, paler below, glabrous when mature. Middle leaflet largest. Yellow/gold/scarlet in autumn.
FLOWERS: Long, erect branched clusters of <100 showy flowers (5 fls per branch, only 1 or 2 open together). 5 small green sepals. 4 or 5 unequal-sized (largest at the top) overlapping, crinkly-edged petals each with coloured blotch. Usually 7 curved stamens (just longer than petals) with white filaments and orange anthers.
FRUIT: Green, spiny outer husk splits into 2 or 3 segments to reveal one globular or 2–3 flattened, shiny red-brown 'conkers'.

Fruit size: <5cm; matt area known as 'buck's eye'

Leaflets broadest above the middle

Coloured blotch: starts yellow, reddens with age

Middle leaflet size: <25cm x 8cm

<30cm

Horseshoe-shaped leaf scars

Brown down on new leaves

J
F
M
A
M
J
J
A
S
O
N
D

Fruit size 3–4cm

A. hippocastanum – 'Baumannii' (not illustrated) Double, longer-lasting flowers and no fruit thus not damaged by conker hunters! Usually grafted.

Red Horse Chestnut – *Aesculus x carnea* Commonly planted; a fertile hybrid (so rarely grafted). Smaller tree, matt grey-green buds (some shoots lack a terminal bud); 5/7 smaller, short-stalked leaflets broadest at the centre. Darker green, often crinkled, with a more sharply-toothed edge. Smaller flower clusters. Flowers with 4 equal, plain pink/dull-red petals. Stamens just longer than petals. Smaller russet-husked fruit with no or few spines. Cultivar 'Briotii' has shiny leaves and bright red flowers.

Indian Horse Chestnut – *Aesculus indica* Smaller sticky buds; 5 or 7 narrower (not touching), slightly glossy, dark-green, finely-toothed, pendant, stalked leaflets (middle one much larger) and pink-red petiole. 4-petalled flowers (June/July) – only blotched on the 2 upper, longer petals. Pear-shaped fruits with a thinner, rough but not spiny, russet-coloured husk. Wrinkled, black-brown seeds.

Up-turned stamens protrude <2cm

Leaflet 6–12cm long

Yellow or Sweet Buckeye – *Aesculus flava* American, infrequently planted. Slightly smaller tree. Non-resinous buds and stalked glossy, dark green leaflets; red-brown downy beneath. Open tubular flowers of 4 yellow petals in short erect heads. Stamens shorter than petals. Fruit often irregular, smooth.

Red Buckeye – *Aesculus pavia* From American, rarely >4m. Non-resinous buds. 5 smaller, double-toothed leaflets. Thin tubular flowers with 4 red, non-spreading petals. Smooth fruit.

Field Maple

Acer campestre

DECIDUOUS
Aceraceae

Native to England and Wales; introduced to Scotland and Ireland. An inconspicuous small tree most frequent in hedgerows and woodland edges, occasionally in gardens. Sometimes taken for a small Sycamore and confused with other trees with lobed leaves. The Bird's-eye Maple used in veneers is cut from the Sugar Maple (see p.126).

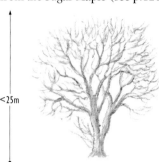

<25m

Small square platelets

USES:
Before the spread of Sycamore it was used for bowls and platters and for the backs and sides of violins.

J
F
M
A
M ◻ ❖
J ◻ ❖
J ◻ ∅
A ◻ ∅
S ◻ ∅
O ◻ ∅
N ◻
D

NATIVE and common on lime-rich soils in S. and E. England, infrequent in Wales and the North. A small bushy tree. Branches low down to give a round-headed outline from a short sinuous bole. Upturned branch ends.

BARK: Rough, grey-brown with shallow fissures.

TIMBER: Creamy or yellow-white, fine-grained.

TWIG: Straight, slender. Paler with corky wings when old.

BUDS: Minute, pointed; red-brown with a grey, hairy tip.

LEAVES: Small, usually wider than long, thick, deeply 3 or 5 round-lobed. Upper lobes sublobed or with a few large blunt teeth; heart-shaped base. Emerge pink-red then mid-green to dull grey-green. Yellow or purple in autumn. Glabrous above, downy below.

FLOWERS: Clusters of widely-spaced small yellow-green flowers at the twig apex. 5 sepals, 5 small petals. Some male – 8 stamens, others female – 2 curled styles.

FRUIT: Stalked bunches; pairs of winged seeds; almost smooth wing often bright red, maturing brown. 2 seeds at 180° (unlike Sycamore).

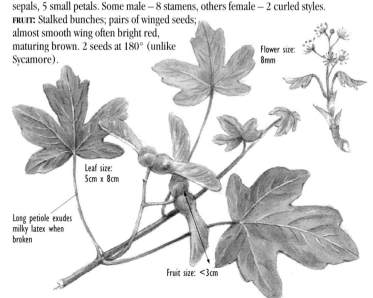

Flower size: 8mm

Leaf size: 5cm x 8cm

Long petiole exudes milky latex when broken

Fruit size: <3cm

Cultivars, Related and Confusable Species:

Introduced small-leaved Maples include:

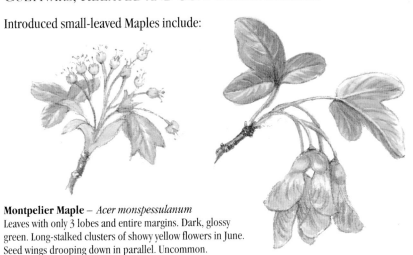

Montpelier Maple – *Acer monspessulanum*
Leaves with only 3 lobes and entire margins. Dark, glossy
green. Long-stalked clusters of showy yellow flowers in June.
Seed wings drooping down in parallel. Uncommon.

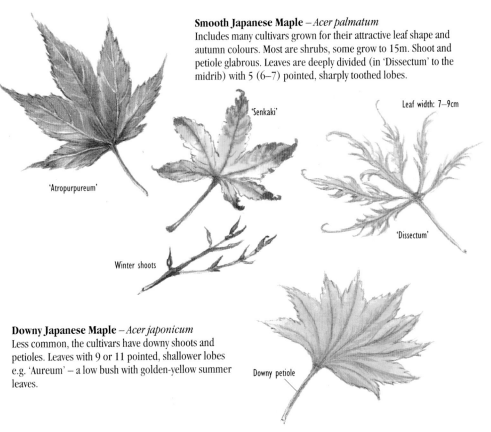

Smooth Japanese Maple – *Acer palmatum*
Includes many cultivars grown for their attractive leaf shape and
autumn colours. Most are shrubs, some grow to 15m. Shoot and
petiole glabrous. Leaves are deeply divided (in 'Dissectum' to the
midrib) with 5 (6–7) pointed, sharply toothed lobes.

'Senkaki'

Leaf width: 7–9cm

'Atropurpureum'

'Dissectum'

Winter shoots

Downy Japanese Maple – *Acer japonicum*
Less common, the cultivars have downy shoots and
petioles. Leaves with 9 or 11 pointed, shallower lobes
e.g. 'Aureum' – a low bush with golden-yellow summer
leaves.

Downy petiole

Paper-bark Maple – *Acer griseum*
Increasingly common in parks and gardens. Red-brown bark flakes off both the bole and larger branches. Leaves emerge pink then yellow to green and finally orange-red in autumn. The unusual leaves are compound (trifoliate), but each roundly-lobed leaflet can be confused with a *campestre* leaf, though this is much broader. Paired fruits hang down like a coat hanger.

Leaflet size:
4cm x 2cm

Other trees with Maple-like but **alternate** leaves:

Thick white hairs on underside

White Poplar – *Populus alba* – see p.72
Leaf underside and latex-free petiole covered in thick white hairs. Leaves vary in size, often larger than Maple. Slender catkins and fluffy seeds.

Wild Service Tree –
Sorbus torminalis – see p.74
A rare native with toothed, triangularly-lobed leaves. Clusters of 5-petalled white flowers and brown-speckled, berry-like fruit.

Hawthorn – *Crataegus monogyna* – see p.64
Shiny green leaf usually longer than wide on a short, grooved petiole with stipules at the base. Lobes with a pointed tip and coarsely toothed at the apex. 5-petalled white flowers and red, berry-like fruits.

Sycamore
Acer pseudoplatanus

DECIDUOUS
Aceraceae

I ntroduced from mainland Europe in the Middle Ages. Widely
planted in woods, parks and gardens. Naturalised; growing quickly
from seed. Some regard it as a weed. It was confused with the biblical
Ficus sycomorus and is also mistaken for other members of the Maple
family. The Planes have alternate leaves.

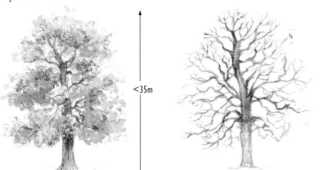

<35m

USES:
*Kitchen utensils, draining
boards, rollers and
furniture. Wood with
attractive grain is used for
violin backs and sides.*

ABUNDANT; tolerates salt spray and city pollution. Big, domed crown may be wider than
tall, with many large, densely-foliated branches. Bole becomes stout with age.
BARK: Smooth, grey; later whorled and cracked. Peeling to reveal pink under-bark.
TIMBER: Creamy-white, close-grained.
TWIG: Y-forked, stout and smooth. Longitudinal lenticels.
TERMINAL BUDS: Large, plump, with green scales edged pink.
LEAVES: Large, broader than long. 5 (3–7) pointed lobes cut $^1/_3$–$^2/_3$ to the midrib.
Margins unevenly, coarsely blunt-toothed. Emerge orange-red, pubescent; mature nearly
glabrous. Pale blue-green underside, upper side very dark green. May be covered with
aphid honeydew, black blotches of tar-spot fungus (*Rhytisma acerinum*) and red finger
galls (*Phytoptus*). Long petiole, often tinged red, base
encircles a bud. No latex.
FLOWERS: In hanging clusters, <100 small,
flowers. 5 sepals and 5 tiny petals. First open
mostly female, middle ones mostly male with
8 pale stamens. Those at the apex
often sterile. Copious nectar.
FRUIT: Short-stalked
bunches, paired like coat-
hangers. Oval seed has a
smooth, papery
wing, broadest at
the apex. Green
(tinged red) later
pale brown.

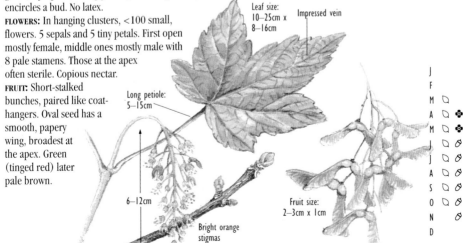

Leaf size:
10–25cm x
8–16cm

Impressed vein

Long petiole:
5–15cm

6–12cm

Bright orange
stigmas

Fruit size:
2–3cm x 1cm

J		
F		
M	▢	
A	▢	✤
M	▢	✤
J	▢	∂
J	▢	∂
A	▢	∂
S	▢	∂
O	▢	∂
N		∂
D		

125

A. pseudoplatanus
'Brilliantissimum'
A slow-growing, bushy-
headed graft planted for
its leaf colour – pink then
yellow and finally green
and white.

A. pseudoplatanus 'Atropurpureum'
Leaf underside dark purple. Widely planted.

Several introduced Maples also have opposite, large,
palmately lobed leaves, the most common being:

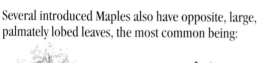

Prominent,
whiskered points

Fruit size: 4–5cm

150°

Norway Maple – *Acer platanoides*
Planted and naturalised. Less domed. 5 shallow-lobed, angular
toothed, similar-sized leaves. Thin; bright green above – rich yellow-
brown in autumn. Slender grooved petiole exudes milky latex when
cut. Showy (larger petals) erect inflorescences before the leaves.
Fruits yellow. Cultivars grown for leaf colour and shape.

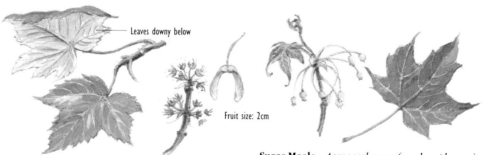

Leaves downy below

Fruit size: 2cm

Red Maple – *Acer rubrum*
With red-brown shoots, buds and petioles. Slightly
smaller green leaves with reddish veins. Red in autumn.
Small, red-petalled flowers (before the leaves) and
smaller fruits on slender drooping stalks.

Sugar Maple – *Acer saccharum (saccharophorum)*
Rarer but confused with above. Darker green leaf has
more rounded unwhiskered teeth. No milky latex when
cut. Smaller, non-petalled flowers in drooping clusters
with the young leaves. Fruit rarely ripens in Britain,
wings (3–4cm) almost parallel. Source of maple syrup.

Milky latex

Caucasian Maple – *Acer cappadocicum*
Short bole and more rounded crown. Produces root
suckers. Glossy leaves emerge pink then green and
yellow by autumn. Leaves with 5 deep, long-pointed
lobes but smooth margins. Flowers and fruits similar
to *platanoides* but later.

Silver Maple – *Acer saccharinum*
Large gardens and urban plantings. Deeply 5-lobed leaf, the
pointed lobes set with irregular large teeth. Emerge orange-
pink then light green above but silver-white with hairs below
on a thin pink petiole. Greenish-red petalless flowers in
separate sex clusters open in March (before leaves). Fruits
at 180° angle but often only one develops.

The following have similar-shaped leaves borne **alternately**:

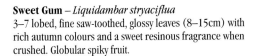

London Plane – *Platanus x hispanica* –
(or *acerifolia*) see p.70
Leaf large (to 20cm x 20cm) with triangular-shaped
lobes bearing scattered, large, pointed teeth. Glossy
above, downy on the veins below. Flaking bark and
globular flowers and fruit.

Sweet Gum – *Liquidambar stryaciflua*
3–7 lobed, fine saw-toothed, glossy leaves (8–15cm) with
rich autumn colours and a sweet resinous fragrance when
crushed. Globular spiky fruit.

Tulip Tree – *Liriodendron tulipifera* – see picture on p.68
With 4-lobed, flat-ended, non-palmately veined, untoothed
leaves and tulip-like, green and orange flowers.

127

Wild Privet
Ligustrum vulgare

A semi-evergreen small shrub (most leaves fall in winter). The related evergreen Garden Privet makes a better hedge and Glossy Privet does reach tree size. Both *vulgare* and *ovalifolium* take readily from cuttings but are susceptible to Honey Fungus (*Armillaria mellea*), especially on very acid soils.

<1–3m

USES:
The berries were formerly used to produce a dye.

NATIVE: Locally common on lime-rich soils and near the coast, especially in the South. In open woods, scrub, hedges and by walls. Shade tolerant. A straggly, branched, thicket-forming shrub.

BARK: Smooth, grey-brown.

TIMBER: Stem size too small for timber production.

TWIG: Slender, grey-brown, initially densely pubescent. Often arches and roots at the tip.

BUDS: Oval, brown.

LEAVES: Opposite or in whorls of three. Lanceolate, pointed with a wedge-shaped base. Entire margin. Dark green and 'polished' above; paler green and with a prominent midrib below. Shades of purple/brown in autumn/winter.

FLOWERS: Erect, branched terminal clusters (panicles), of sickly-sweet scented, tiny dull-white flowers. 4 petals, the lower halves fused as a basal tube, the upper half as free spreading lobes.

FRUIT: Stalked, egg-shaped, poisonous berries ripen from green to a glossy, purple-black by November. Persist over winter.

Petals fade red-brown

3–7cm

Hairy flower stalk

Leaf size:
3–7cm long

Fruit size:
6–8mm

J (◖)♂
F (◖)♂
M ◖
A ◖
M ◖
J ◖ ✤
J ◖ ✤
A ◖ ♂
S ◖ ♂
O ◖ ♂
N ◖ ♂
D (◖)♂

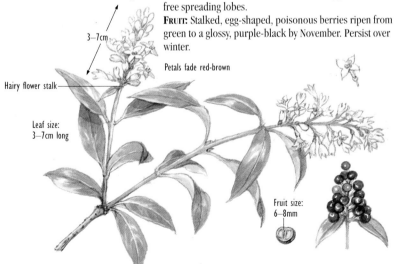

Golden Privet – 'Areum' is a popular cultivar with a green leaf centre and a margin of golden-yellow.

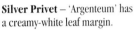

Silver Privet – 'Argenteum' has a creamy-white leaf margin.

L. vulgare 'Aureum'
A cultivar with dull, yellow leaves now less-often planted.

Garden or **Oval-leaved Privet** – *Ligustrum ovalifolium*
Introduced from Japan. A popular hedge plant also used for game cover as it only sheds its leaves in very cold weather or in badly polluted air. Denser growth of twigs and leaves. Young shoots and flower stalks not hairy. Stiffer, more erect, broader ovate leaves with more rounded ends. Larger flowerheads in July. Flower tube 2–3 times as long as the spreading lobes. Fruits similar to *vulgare*.

12–20cm

Glossy or **Chinese Privet** –
Ligustrum lucidum
Introduced to streets and parks in the South. A densely-foliated, round-domed tree to 15m with a short, sinuous, fluted bole with grey-brown bark and smooth, grey twigs. Large leathery glossy leaves. Pale green flower buds in spring, open as fragrant, lilac-white panicles from late summer to December. Small blue-black, bloomed berries.

Leaf size:
8–12cm x 4cm

Privet is not readily confused with any other shrub or tree except:

Box – *Buxus sempervirens* –
see p.138
Grows wild especially on lime-rich soil. Much used for hedging. Differs in the smaller round-ended, thick, shiny, opposite leaves (smelling sweet when wet) borne in flat ranks. Small, yellow, petalless flowers and brown, horned fruit.

3cm x 1cm

Most garden plants used as hedging such as Escallonia and Firethorn have alternate, toothed leaves. An exception is:

Leaf size:
1cm long

Shining Honeysuckle – *Lonicera nitida*
A densely leafy shrub with small, dark green (greyish below), opposite, closely set, blunt-tipped, sessile leaves with a rounded base. Stem purple-tinged, hairy. Pairs of small, fragrant, creamy-yellow flowers in April in leaf axils. Small, purple, semi-transparent berries.

Wayfaring Tree
Viburnum lantana

I n the 16th Century John Gerard wrote of the delight to the wayfarer on seeing this small tree. An earlier name, 'Hoary Withy', referred to the leaf underside (as if covered in hoar frost) and the pliant twigs. The leaf hairs cut water loss enabling the tree to grow on dry soil. The related *opulus* has a more maple-like leaf.

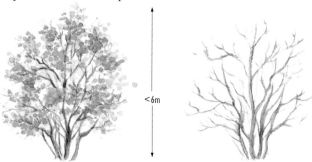

<6m

USES:
Young shoots made baskets, older shoots pipe stems and the berries ink.

NATIVE and locally frequent in S. and S.E. England, introduced and rare further north. Hedges and woodland edges, usually on chalk or limestone. Also in gardens. A small spreading tree with a slender, much forked stem.

BARK: Pale brown, becoming deeply fissured.

TIMBER: Insubstantial.

TWIG: Pliable. Green then red-brown but covered in grey down (star-shaped hairs under a lens).

BUDS: Naked (no scales), small, green with brown tips, hoary.

LEAVES: Ovate, rough to the touch, decussate. Regular, finely sharp-toothed margin. Sparsely hairy above, paler below with prominent veins. Red-purple in autumn. Short, grooved downy petiole.

FLOWERS: Erect, terminal, slightly domed umbels of small fragrant flowers.

FRUIT: Erect head of oval, laterally-flattened berries. Ripen from green to red to shiny black by September. Very sour smell and taste – poisonous to humans.

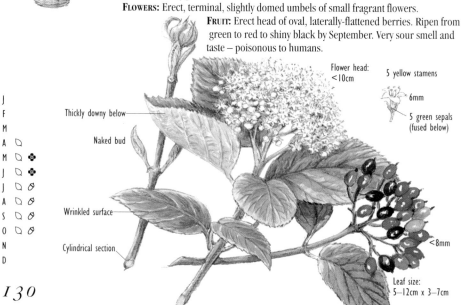

J
F
M
A
M
J
J
A
S
O
N
D

Thickly downy below

Naked bud

Wrinkled surface

Cylindrical section

Flower head: <10cm

5 yellow stamens

6mm

5 green sepals (fused below)

<8mm

Leaf size: 5–12cm x 3–7cm

Evergreen leaves

Laurustinus – *Viburnum tinus*
A popular garden shrub with smaller, narrower, more pointed, entire, glossy, **evergreen** leaves. Heads of pink-budded white flowers from late autumn to early spring. Blue-black berries.

Central, small (6mm) fertile flowers

Outer circle of large (20mm) flat, sterile flowers

Leaf size: 10cm x 12cm

Guelder Rose – *Viburnum opulus*
Native. Frequent in most areas in hedges and as a woodland undershrub on moist soils. A small (<4m) Y-branched shrub. Smooth, angular twigs with scaly buds. Leaves with 3–5 pointed lobes, deeply and irregularly toothed. Flat-topped flower head. Globular, translucent, scarlet berries.

Sparsely hairy below

Finger-like stipules

Snowball Tree – *V. opulus 'Roseum'*
Common garden cultivar originating in Guelderland (Netherlands). Differs in the more showy, globular, Hydrangea-like heads of all sterile flowers. No fruits; propagated by layering.

Globular fruit

Unevenly, singly or doubly toothed

Whitebeam – *Sorbus aria* – see p.80
Differs in the leaves being **alternate**, with a wedge-shaped base. Long, scaly buds. Similar flower clusters but with larger flowers (<1.5cm) with many stamens. Larger (1cm) hanging fruit ripen scarlet.

Silver Lime – *Tilia tomentosa* – see p.44
The toothed leaves are white and woolly below but are heart-shaped and **alternate**. A much taller tree with very different flowers and fruit.

Dogwood
Cornus sanguinea

A much-branched shrub often confused with Buckthorn. The genus contains several popular garden species. Its bitter fruits were said to be fit only for dogs and it was known as Dagwood – its branches made animal prods or dags. The 5,000 year old 'man in the ice' found on the Austrian-Italian border in 1991 carried arrows made of *Cornus*.

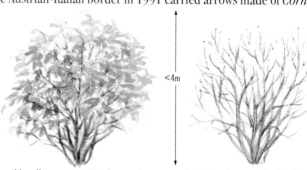

<4m

Wrinkled bark

USES:
Dogs (wooden meat skewers) were made from the wood. Bitter-tasting berries supplied lamp oil.

NATIVE and locally common. Mostly on calcareous soils in S. and Central lowland Britain. In hedges, and woodland edges. A suckering, erect, much-branched, round-headed shrub, occasionally a small tree.

BARK: Grey-green. Foetid smell when damaged.

TIMBER: Tough and hard.

TWIG: Smooth; dark-red above, green below.

BUDS: Opposite, red-brown, appressed to stem.

LEAVES: Ovate. Long pointed tip, rounded base. Margin entire but wavy. Close-pressed hairs on both sides. Dark green with red-purple tinge. Deep-red in autumn. 3–4 prs of prominent, inset, side veins. Grooved petiole, dark-red above.

FLOWERS: Erect, branched, flat-topped cluster of small fragrant flowers. 4 tiny green sepals, 4 slim, pointed, creamy-white petals, 4 stamens.

FRUIT: Upright cluster of glossy berries. Green ripening purple-black by September.

J
F
M ◗
A ◗
M ◗
J ◗ ✤
J ◗ ✤
A ◗ ⊘
S ◗ ⊘
O ◗ ⊘
N
D

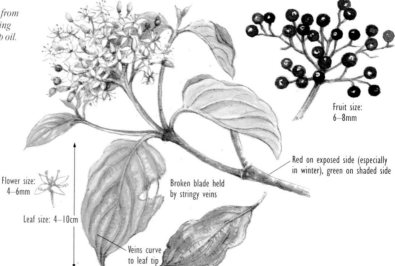

Fruit size:
6–8mm

Red on exposed side (especially in winter), green on shaded side

Flower size:
4–6mm

Broken blade held by stringy veins

Leaf size: 4–10cm

Veins curve to leaf tip

Introduced species, coppiced to produce more shoots
are grown for their coloured winter bark. The larger
leaves have 6–7 prs of curving side veins. Fruits white.

Red-barked Dogwood –
Cornus alba
First year shoots bright red
in winter; not suckering.

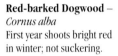

Red Osier Dogwood – *Cornus stolonifera*
As *alba* but suckering. Cultivar 'Flaviramea'
has yellow-green shoots.

Fruit

Showy bracts

Brown hair tufts

Japanese Dogwood – *Cornus kousa*
Tall shrub with larger glossy leaves. Pronounced wavy
margins. Tiny green flowers in a globular cluster
surrounded by 4 large, spreading, pointed, creamy-white,
petal-like bracts. Long-stalked raspberry-like fruits.

Flower size: 4mm

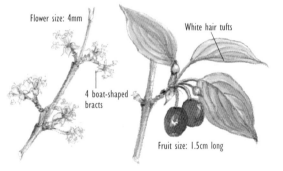

White hair tufts

4 boat-shaped
bracts

Fruit size: 1.5cm long

Cornelian Cherry – *Cornus mas*
Garden shrub with level or downswept branches; young
twigs green. Short-stalked leaves. 3–5 prs of arching side
veins. Flowers before the leaves. Yellow clusters of tiny, 4-
petalled flowers. Cherry-like fruits ripen in good summers.

Alder Buckthorn – *Frangula alnus* – see p.135
(not illustrated here)
Leaves similar in shape to *Cornus* but **alternate** and with
6–10 prs of side veins which do not curve to the apex.
Flowers and fruits in small groups of 1–3. Native.

Buckthorn – *Rhamnus catharticus* – see p.134
Leaf has toothed margin. Long and short shoots,
some ending in thorns. Untidy clusters of fewer
flowers and flatter, black berries. Native.

Buckthorn or *Purging Buckthorn*

Rhamnus cathartica

DECIDUOUS
Rhamnaceae

The twigs of this shrubby tree have short, opposite, often thorny branches, in the form of a cross (hence its reputation as a protection against witchcraft), and were thought to resemble the horns of a Roe Deer buck – 'Buck thorn'. It is confused with other shrubby trees such as Alder Buckthorn; all can be separated on leaf characters.

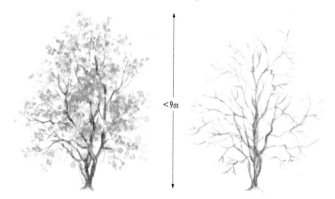

<9m

NATIVE and locally frequent in scrubby woodland on chalk and limestone in central and S.E. England, also in Fens. Rarer in the West, not in Scotland. A small untidy tree. Short narrow bole; regular 90° branches, with foliage near to the ground.

BARK: Brown/black with areas of orange underbark. Scaly.

TIMBER: Red-brown, flame-like grain; creamy sapwood.

TWIGS: a. Long (growth) shoots with opposite buds in leaf axils. May end in a short thorn. b. Short, knobbly prs of opposite shoots at 90° to long shoots. Bear leaf, flower and fruit clusters. Some end in a short thorn.

LEAVES: Ovate, glabrous; widest at middle, short-pointed tip and broad wedge-shaped base. 2–4 prs of prominent side veins curve to apex. Pale brown in autumn. Long (<2cm) grooved petiole.

USES:
Purgative from bark and fruit. Sap green pigment from the berries.

FLOWERS: Dioecious. Small, fragrant. 4 (5) narrow, pointed, yellow-green petals. Males: 4 stamens. Females: 4-lobed green stigma and rudimentary stamens.

FRUIT: Clustered fleshy, berry-like fruits; apex slightly flattened. Sharp taste. Contain 3–4 seeds.

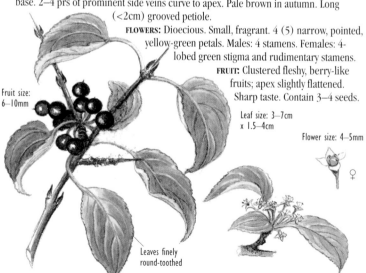

Fruit size:
6–10mm

Leaf size: 3–7cm
x 1.5–4cm

Flower size: 4–5mm

♀

Leaves finely
round-toothed

J
F
M
A
M
J
J
A
S
O
N
D

Mediterranean Buckthorn – *Rhamnus alaternus* (right)
Garden shrub (<5m) lacking spines. Smaller evergreen, alternate, leathery, glossy, leaves. Honey-scented flowers lack petals. Smaller, pear-shaped, black fruit. Cultivar 'Argenteo-variegata' with grey marbling and creamy-white leaf margins is commonest.

Teeth at apex

Entire wavy margin

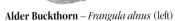

Alder Buckthorn – *Frangula alnus* (left)
Native. Commoner than *Rhamnus* in the west; on damp, acid soils. No thorns or short shoots. Yellow underbark. Leaves **alternate** widest nearer apex, shiny above. 6–10 prs of side veins run to margin. Yellow to orange-red in autumn. Dioecious. Flowers with 5 green sepals, 5 white-green petals, 5 stamens. Sparser green fruit ripen black via yellow and red. 2-seeded.

Other shrubs similar in **some** characters are:

Sea Buckthorn –
Hippophae rhamnoides
Densely branched. Silvery-grey twigs, long, sharp thorns and narrow, entire, **alternate,** willow-like silvery-green leaves. Tiny, stalkless, petalless, green flowers. Sessile orange berry-like fruit. Native. Planted on sand-dunes and in urban parks.

Blackthorn – *Prunus spinosa* – see p.65
Thorny but with much smaller **alternate** leaves and showy 5-petalled white flowers before the leaves emerge. Fruit like a small purple-black plum.

Leaves opposite

Spindle – *Euonymus europea* –
see p.136
No thorns. Similar opposite, toothed, ovate leaves are much narrower with a taper-pointed apex and 8–10 prs of parallel side veins. Similar small flowers. Ribbed pink fruits and orange seeds.

Dogwood – *Cornus sanguineus* – see p.132
Leaves with 4–5 upcurved side veins as *Rhamnus* but entire as *Frangula;* red in autumn. No thorns but red bark on first-year twigs. Small 4-petalled white flowers in flat-topped head. Erect clusters of purple-black fruit.

Spindle
Euonymus europaeus

DECIDUOUS
Celastraceae

A small tree, easily overlooked until autumn when its leaves turn purple-red and its pink, angled fruits split to reveal orange-coated seeds. These are attractive to children but like the rest of the tree (and related species) are poisonous, being violent purgatives. The only common tree species with narrowly ovate, finely-toothed, opposite leaves.

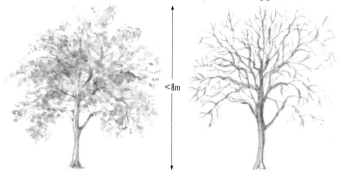

<8m

USES:
Skewers, knitting needles and shoemakers' pegs. Spindles (superseded by the spinning wheel).

NATIVE in hedges, scrub and woodland edges. Most frequent in S. England on chalk and limestone. Planted in parks and gardens. Bushy, with multiple slender stems. Upward arching, twiggy branches.

BARK: Grey and smooth then brown with pink fissures.

TIMBER: Hard and white.

TWIG: Smooth and rounded; later 4 longitudinal ridges create a squarer cross-section. Finally browner with corky outgrowths.

BUDS: Small, slightly flattened.

LEAVES: Opposite, long, thin, hairless. Apex taper-pointed, base wedge-shaped. 8–10 prs of veins run to margins. Crushed leaf smells unpleasant.

FLOWERS: Erect clusters of 3–8 flowers. 4 tiny green sepals, 4 narrow, green-white petals. Occasional male only (infertile pistils) or female only (rudimentary anthers) plants.

FRUIT: Spreading, initially matt green but pink by late September, splitting to reveal 4 fleshy, orange-coated white seeds.

J
F
M
A
M
J
J
A
S
O
N
D

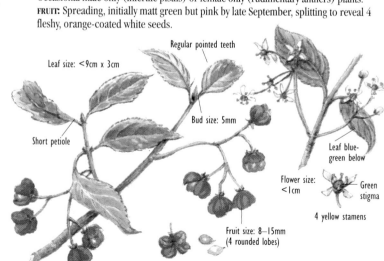

Regular pointed teeth

Leaf size: <9cm x 3cm

Bud size: 5mm

Short petiole

Leaf blue-green below

Flower size: <1cm

Green stigma

4 yellow stamens

Fruit size: 8–15mm
(4 rounded lobes)

CULTIVARS, RELATED AND CONFUSABLE SPECIES

Cultivars of *europaeus* include 'Atropurpureus' with leaves which turn deep purple by early summer and a vivid red by autumn.

The most frequently planted Spindle is:

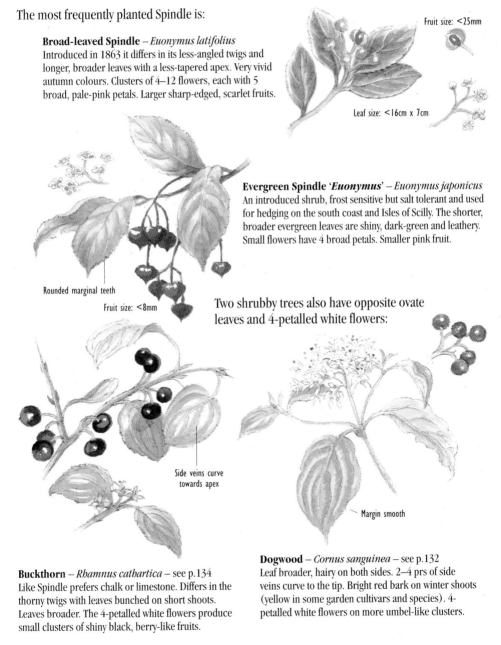

Broad-leaved Spindle – *Euonymus latifolius*
Introduced in 1863 it differs in its less-angled twigs and longer, broader leaves with a less-tapered apex. Very vivid autumn colours. Clusters of 4–12 flowers, each with 5 broad, pale-pink petals. Larger sharp-edged, scarlet fruits.

Fruit size: <25mm

Leaf size: <16cm x 7cm

Evergreen Spindle 'Euonymus' – *Euonymus japonicus*
An introduced shrub, frost sensitive but salt tolerant and used for hedging on the south coast and Isles of Scilly. The shorter, broader evergreen leaves are shiny, dark-green and leathery. Small flowers have 4 broad petals. Smaller pink fruit.

Rounded marginal teeth

Fruit size: <8mm

Two shrubby trees also have opposite ovate leaves and 4-petalled white flowers:

Side veins curve towards apex

Margin smooth

Buckthorn – *Rhamnus cathartica* – see p.134
Like Spindle prefers chalk or limestone. Differs in the thorny twigs with leaves bunched on short shoots. Leaves broader. The 4-petalled white flowers produce small clusters of shiny black, berry-like fruits.

Dogwood – *Cornus sanguinea* – see p.132
Leaf broader, hairy on both sides. 2–4 prs of side veins curve to the tip. Bright red bark on winter shoots (yellow in some garden cultivars and species). 4-petalled white flowers on more umbel-like clusters.

137

Box

Buxus sempervirens

EVERGREEN
Buxaceae

W̲ell known as a garden hedge and shrub, Box is native on lime-rich soils in southern England where it grows as a small tree. Long-lived with overlapping, small, evergreen leaves it is easily shaped and has been much used in topiary. The many cultivars include dwarf ones used as edging to flower-beds. The hard, heavy wood sinks in water.

USES:
Rulers, chessmen and illustrators' wood blocks.

<10m

NATIVE: Shade tolerant; often under Beech. Dense crown and a leaning, twisted, often multi-stemmed bole. Rarely above 5m in gardens.
BARK: Smooth, pale brown then cracking into small, grey corky squares.
TIMBER: Even-grained, pale yellow.
TWIG: 4-angled, green with dense white woolly hairs.
BUDS: Lost in leaves, green, pubescent. Tiny.
LEAVES: In one plane, thick, leathery, small, broadest around middle, base wedge-shaped, apex shallowly-notched or rounded, margin entire, down-rolled. Dark green, glossy above; yellow-green, less shiny below. Sweet-smelling when warm and wet.
FLOWERS: Small pale yellow clusters in leaf axils, no petals; 5–6 stalkless male flowers surround one, short-stalked female.
FRUIT: Green, urn-shaped, with 3 split horns, then (in good summers) brown and papery. Top splits into 3, releasing glossy black seeds.

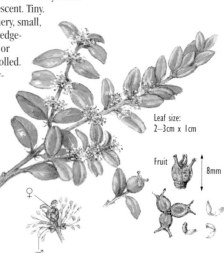

Leaf size:
2–3cm x 1cm

Fruit

8mm

J	◗	
F	◗	
M	◗	❁
A	◗	❁
M	◗	⊘
J	◗	⊘
J	◗	⊘
A	◗	⊘
S	◗	⊘
O	◗	⊘
N	◗	
D	◗	

Edging Box – *B. sempervirens* 'Suffruticosa'
A dwarf cultivar used as a hedge around flower-beds and graves.

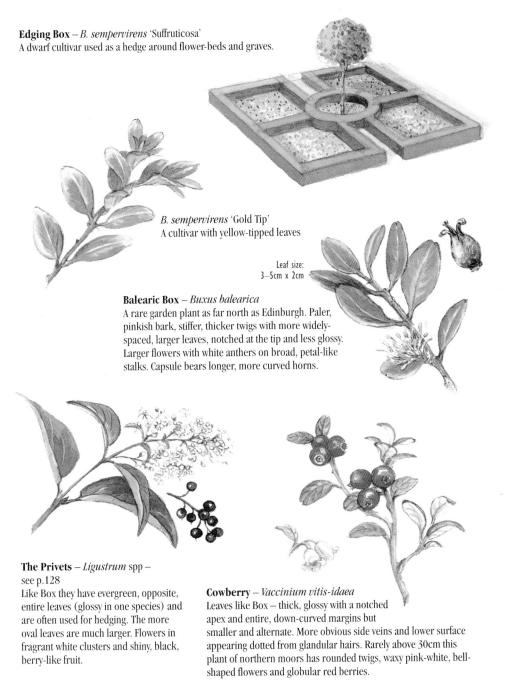

B. sempervirens 'Gold Tip'
A cultivar with yellow-tipped leaves

Leaf size:
3–5cm x 2cm

Balearic Box – *Buxus balearica*
A rare garden plant as far north as Edinburgh. Paler, pinkish bark, stiffer, thicker twigs with more widely-spaced, larger leaves, notched at the tip and less glossy. Larger flowers with white anthers on broad, petal-like stalks. Capsule bears longer, more curved horns.

The Privets – *Ligustrum* spp –
see p.128
Like Box they have evergreen, opposite, entire leaves (glossy in one species) and are often used for hedging. The more oval leaves are much larger. Flowers in fragrant white clusters and shiny, black, berry-like fruit.

Cowberry – *Vaccinium vitis-idaea*
Leaves like Box – thick, glossy with a notched apex and entire, down-curved margins but smaller and alternate. More obvious side veins and lower surface appearing dotted from glandular hairs. Rarely above 30cm this plant of northern moors has rounded twigs, waxy pink-white, bell-shaped flowers and globular red berries.

139

Coniferous Trees

(pp.141–178)

English Yew
Taxus baccata

EVERGREEN
Taxaceae

Very slow growing and long-lived, some are considered to be over 2,000 years old. Many early Christian churches were built on the sites of pagan meeting places – often among Yews. Lacks resin but the foliage and seeds (but not the fleshy 'berries') contain a poisonous alkaloid. Some cultivars are more well-known than the native type.

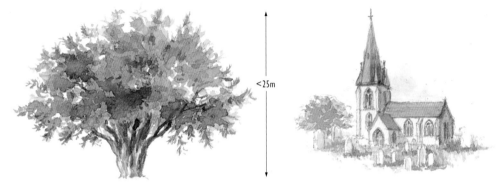

<25m

NATIVE but local (rare in Scotland), mostly on lime-rich soil. Shade tolerant. Planted in churchyards and gardens for hedging and topiary. Often multi-stemmed, with shoots coalescing to give a fluted trunk which hollows with age.

BARK: Smooth, red-brown. Jigsaw-like flakes reveal purple-red underbark.

TIMBER: Strong, pliable and durable. Dark brown with pronounced annual rings.

TWIG: Green at first but orange-brown by the 3rd year.

BUDS: Egg-shaped, green and tiny (2–3mm).

LEAVES: Spirally arranged on upright shoots but 2-ranked on the horizontal shoots (petioles twist). Flattened, of mixed lengths. Short soft-pointed apex. Base narrows to green stalk arising from stem ridge.

FLOWERS: Usually on separate sex trees. Clusters of pale yellow globular male catkins on under surface of previous year's growth. Bud-like females near shoot ends.

FRUITS: Like a small green acorn before the cup-shaped, fleshy aril develops, almost engulfing the single dark green (ripening brown) seed. Aril turns a bright pink-red by September.

USES:
The best wood for long bows. Used for veneers and turnery. Foliage contains a precursor for a cancer drug.

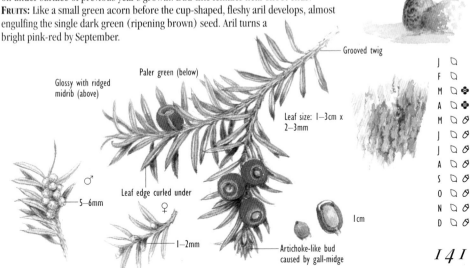

Grooved twig

Glossy with ridged midrib (above)

Paler green (below)

Leaf size: 1–3cm x 2–3mm

♂ 5–6mm

Leaf edge curled under

♀ 1–2mm

Artichoke-like bud caused by gall-midge

1cm

J
F
M
A
M
J
J
A
S
O
N
D

141

Golden Irish Yew –
T. baccata 'Fastigiata
Aureomarginata'
As 'Fastigiata' but with golden
needles. Male clone (no 'berries').

Irish Yew – *T. baccata* 'Fastigiata'
Planted in churchyards and formal gardens.
Differs in the needles being slightly twisted and
not 2-ranked. Upright branches produce a
columnar shape. A female clone.

Small-leaved Yew –
T. baccata 'Adpressa'
A large spreading shrub
with small (<1.5cm) oval
needles not in 2 ranks. A
female clone.

Yellow-berried Yew –
T. baccata 'Lutea'
With ripe aril a yellow-
orange colour. Unusual.

West Felton or **Weeping Yew** –
T. baccata 'Dovastoniana'
Stem has long horizontal branches
bearing hanging twigs. Mostly female.

A number of uncommon, introduced species include:

Plum-fruited or **Chilean Yew** – *Podocarpus andinus*
Shorter (<2cm), softer, blunt-tipped, blue-green needles. Unridged stem. Dark grey smooth bark. Flowers in
June, male in clusters, more elongated. Fruit like a small
green speckled plum, 2cm long in bunches of 2–6.

♀

Cone-like fruit

Prince Albert's Yew –
Saxegothaea conspicua
Bark flakes in large, circular
patches. Pendulous, whorled
branchlets. Needles in 2 untidy
ranks, matt, hard, curved and
sharply pointed. White bands
below. Grassy smell when
crushed.

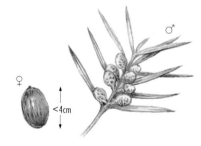

♀

<4cm

♂

California Nutmeg –
Torreya californica
Bark grey-brown, not peeling.
Long hard, widely spaced
needles (3–7cm), 2-ranked.
2 narrow white bands below.
Oily smell when crushed.
Green and purple fruit
Nutmeg-like seed.

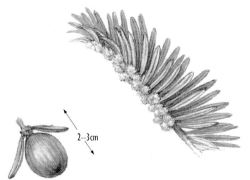

2–3cm

Cow's-tail Pine – *Cephalotaxus harringtonia*
An infrequent bush recognised by its foliage with the
longer, broader 5cm x 5mm needles in two ascending
ranks. Olive-like green fruits.

Other more common introductions with flat,
two-ranked needles include:

Coast Redwood –
Sequoia sempervirens – see p.146
Shorter needles at ends of shoots and
much paler green on younger shoots,
white bands on lower surface. Smell of
grapefruit when crushed. Fissured, not
scaly bark. Small woody cones at very
tip of shoot. Very tall, single-boled tree
with thick spongy bark.

Dawn Redwood – *Metasequoia
glyptostroboides* – see p.144
A recent introduction with deciduous needles which arise in opposite pairs. Buds are borne below
the branchlets. Soft round-ended
needles turn purple in autumn.
Fluted bole. Long stalked cone.

Long-stalked cone

Winter

Western Hemlock – *Tsuga heterophylla* – see p.148
A large tree with yew-like leaves of variable lengths
which smell of Hemlock or Ground Elder. Fruits are
small, stalkless, few-scaled woody cones.

143

Dawn Redwood

Metasequoia glyptostroboides

Known only from fossils until living specimens were found in S.W. China in 1941. Initial growth very rapid, does best in light shade on damp soil. Deciduous but in leaf for 8–9 months with attractive, feathery foliage which produces wonderful autumn colours. Opposite branchlets and needles help distinguish it from Swamp Cypress.

Uses:
Purely ornamental to date.
Used for coffins in China.

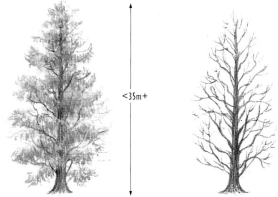

<35m+

Introduced to parks and gardens. Tapering bole often deeply fluted, with elongated pits beneath the lowest branches which start near ground level. Regular, ascending branches give a conic, open crown with a sharp apex.
Bark: Rich orange-brown with darker, stringy flakes; thin.
Timber: Scarce as trees not yet mature. Red-brown, soft.
Twig: Bears opposite pairs of deciduous, green, ribbed branchlets.
Buds: Opposite and unusual in being borne on or under the base of the branchlets.
Leaves: Up to 20–25 prs of soft, thin flat needles, slightly curving away from branchlet apex and in two flat ranks. Pale or grey-green. Yellow to brick red colours in autumn when whole branchlet falls. Some spirally arranged needles between the branchlets.
Flowers: Erect green, globular, fleshy female cones. Catkin like males (on the same plant, but rare) as many tiny paired yellow ovoids on long hanging stalks.
Fruit: Pendulous, ripening woody, dark brown with c.15 broad closed scales.

J
F
M 🌿
A 🌿 ✿
M 🌿 ✿
J 🌿 ✐
J 🌿 ✐
A 🌿 ✐
S 🌿 ✐
O 🌿 ✐
N 🌿 ✐
D

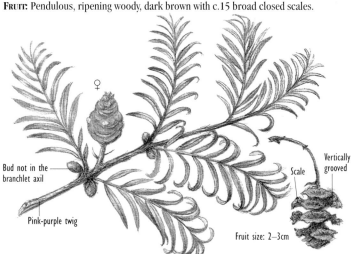

♀

Bud not in the
branchlet axil

Pink-purple twig

Scale

Vertically
grooved

Fruit size: 2–3cm

Cultivars, Closely Related and Confusable Species

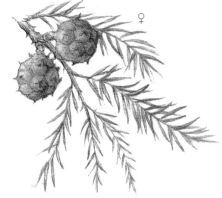

<15cm

Swamp Cypress – *Taxodium distichum*
From Florida; frequent in S. England parks especially near water where it produces knee-like above ground breathing roots. The buttressed bole has grey-brown bark. Like *Metasequoia* it is deciduous but comes into leaf much later in the spring. Darker main shoots (with alternate, normal axillary buds) bearing alternate, forward-pointing, very slender green branchlets with 80–100 short, narrow, alternately-borne needles. Young pale apple-green needles mature darker and turn rusty-brown in autumn. Short-stalked cones ripen purple-brown and have small, downturned spines in the centre of each diamond-shaped bract.

Other confusables include:

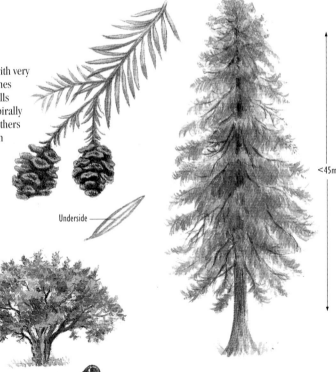

Underside

<45m

Coast or **Californian Redwood** –
Sequoia sempervirens – see p.146
Differs in its huge size, broad bole with very thick, spongy bark and lower branches descending. **Evergreen** foliage smells of grapefruit. Leading shoot bears spirally produced, twisted scale-leaves but others are needles in 2 rows. These differ in being stiff and dark green, with 2 white bands underneath. Similar sized cones but on branch tips; the broad scales have blunt ends, sunken centres and open far apart.

Yew – *Taxus baccata* –
see p.141
Evergreen foliage
with very dark green flat
needles on ribbed twigs.
Short, much divided bole
with jigsaw-like scaly
bark showing pink and
purple colours. Fleshy
fruit on female plants.

EVERGREEN
Taxodiaceae

Coast or *Californian Redwood*
Sequoia sempervirens

The world's tallest tree; over 100m in its native U.S.A. where it was named after the Cherokee Indian, Sequo-yah. There it may live over 2,000 years and rarely succumbs to attack by insects, fungi or fire – the latter thanks to its very thick bark which causes confusion with Giant Redwood (p.170) but this has very different foliage.

USES:
Good for estate fencing and gates. Foliage used in wreath making.

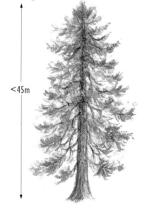

<45m

Thick and spongy

COMMON in parks and large gardens. Best in the west on deep, fertile soil away from cold, dry wind. Stout bole bears sparse, irregular whorls of long, down-pointing branches. Pointed, oblong, open, untidy crown. New trees from root suckers.

BARK: Ageing v. thick and spongy. Deeply furrowed with interweaving ridges. Flakes to reveal redder underbark.

TIMBER: Soft but durable; ruddy-brown colour.

TWIG: Green, ribbed 1st year and side branchlets. Older branches orange-brown.

BUDS: Slender, green and with scales.

LEAVES: Waxy/grapefruit smell on crushing. Leading and cone-bearing shoots bear spirally produced scale-like, narrowly triangular leaves. Drooping side branchlets bear broad, hard, sharp-pointed needles in two neat flat rows. Pale green then dark and shiny. Short at both ends of branchlet, longer in the middle.

FLOWERS: Monoecious. Males on the ends of side branchlets. Bud-like females on short shoots.

FRUIT: Small. Green. Brown in 2nd year. Remain on tree for some years.

♀

2cm

Scale leaves

15–20 scales

2 white bands on underside

♂

J	◌	◌
F	◌ ✦	◌
M	◌ ✦	◌
A	◌ ✦	◌
M	◌	◌ ◌
J	◌	◌ ◌
J	◌	◌ ◌
A	◌	◌ ◌
S	◌	◌ ◌
O	◌	◌ ◌
N	◌	◌ ◌
D	◌	◌ ◌

S. sempervirens 'Adpressa'
A much smaller, slow growing cultivar with cream-
coloured tips to the new shoots. Unusual.

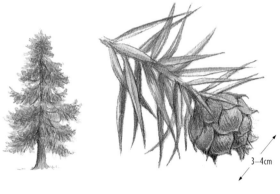

Chinese Fir – *Cunninghamia lanceolata*
Mostly in collections and large gardens in
S. England. Smaller, but with similar bark.
Sparsely, horizontally branched – like a
Monkey Puzzle. Dead needles retained as
brown patches in inner crown. Shiny green
shoot and leaves. Leaves very broad at base
(4mm), 3–7cm long, tapering to point.
Roughly parted but also curving over the
shoot. Thin cone scales end in a point.

3–4cm

Giant Redwood – *Sequoiadendron giganteum* – see p.170
Similar from afar but with denser crown with branches
sweeping down and then up. Larger bole with very spongy
bark. Differs in having all scale-like overlapping leaves
smelling of aniseed when crushed and larger
(6cm) cones.

Scale leaves

Dawn Redwood –
Metasequoia glyptostroboides – see p.144
Smaller, conical bole base, ascending branches, thin
bark. Side branches and needles on them opposite
and deciduous. Soft needles. Cone hangs from long,
slender stalk.

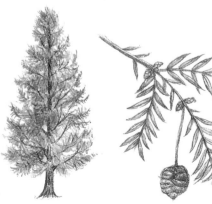

Yew – *Taxus baccata* – see p.141 (not illustrated here)
Small often bush-like tree with much branched trunk
but similar bark colour – though thin and flaking.
Similar looking foliage but the longer, very dark green
needles are yellow-green below. No scale-like leaves.
Fleshy fruit on female plants.

Western Hemlock
Tsuga heterophylla

A 19th-Century American introduction and now an important timber tree in the wetter West and North of Britain, not least because it tolerates shade and can be planted under existing trees. Also grown as a hedge. The unpleasant smelling crushed foliage (like Ground Elder or Hemlock) and the drooping leader shoot help distinguish it from other species with flattened needles in two ranks.

<50m

INTRODUCED and frequent in plantations and large gardens. Common in wetter areas e.g. N.W. Scotland. Single, undivided bole with branches set at 45°, the lower ones more down pointing. Narrow spire-like crown topped by a drooping leading shoot.

USES:
Mostly used for paper pulp. Good for wooden crates and shingles. Foliage used in floristry.

BARK: Red-brown becoming purple-brown and flaking from shallow fissures.
TIMBER: Pale brown, fine and uniform. Grain resists splitting.
TWIG: Slender, pale brown. 1st year curly brown hairs; later hairless, greyish, ribbed.
BUDS: Small, ovoid, grey-green.
LEAVES: Untidy mix of longer needles in 2 ranks at right-angles to the stem and shorter ones more upright and forward pointing. Inrolled entire margins and blunt, rounded tips; the base narrowing abruptly to a short appressed stalk. Shiny above. Two blue-white bands below. Unpleasant smell when crushed.
FLOWERS: Monoecious. Clusters of small (3mm), globular male catkins turn pale yellow when pollen is shed. Solitary female flower at shoot tip.
FRUIT: Stalkless but hanging under the foliage. Small (2–2.5cm) egg-shaped cones with relatively few, rounded, entire scales. Start a bronzy green, ripen brown by October when leathery scales peel open like a flower to release winged seeds.

J	◻	♂
F	◻	♂
M	◻	
A	◻	❖
M	◻	❖
J	◻	♂
J	◻	♂
A	◻	♂
S	◻	♂
O	◻	♂
N	◻	♂
D	◻	♂

Needle length 2cm

Orange-brown bumps where needles have dropped off

Needles very dark green

♂

Lower surface

Shorter needles 0.5cm long

♀

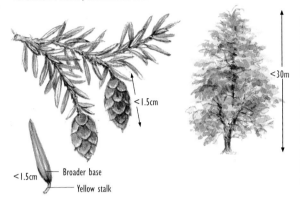

Eastern Hemlock – *Tsuga canadensis*
Bole (with grey ridged bark) divides v. low down giving multiple trunks. Heavy branches produce a domed, untidy tree (no drooping leader). The shorter 2-ranked needles have margins with occasional fine teeth (lens) and are more inrolled giving a narrow, silver-white band either side of the midrib on the lower surface. Stalks of upper needles twist so that needles lay flat on the top of the stem, pointing forwards and revealing the lower surface. Fruity smell. More pointed cones on short stalks.

Yew – *Taxus baccata* –
see p.141
'Tsuga' is Japanese for 'Yew-like'. Yew differs from *T. hetero-phylla* in its short broad domed crown from multiple stems with jigsaw flaking bark. The 2-ranked needles end in a short point and the lower surface lacks the paler stripes. Lacks the unpleasant smell. Berry-like fruits.

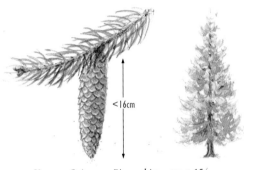

Norway Spruce – *Picea abies* – see p.154
More level branches, orange-brown twigs with woody, peg-like projections. Harder, less-flattened, spine-tipped needles. Much larger, tapering, pendulous cones

Silver Fir – *Abies alba* – see p.153
Similar foliage with mixed-length flat needles; shorter ones on upper surface, up-turned and almost in 2 ranks, longer ones from lower side of twig and 2-ranked. Leave small round depressions on being pulled (or falling from) twig. Very different large erect cones.

Douglas Fir – *Pseudotsuga menziesii* – see p.150
Tall, narrow tree with furrowed bark. Curved, fruity smelling needles are more parted than 2-ranked, well spaced on the twig, blunt tipped and not so distinctly stalked. Fallen needles leave raised oval scars. Pendulous cone with 3-pointed bract scales.

Douglas Fir

Pseudotsuga menziesii

EVERGREEN
Pinaceae

Discovered in America by Menzies in the 1790s; the seed was brought back by Douglas in 1827. Fast growing and producing high quality timber it is also a feature in large gardens though it does not thrive in smoky cities. Fallen needles leave a slightly raised, oval scar unlike the pegs of the closely related Spruces (see p.154).

Young bark

Old bark

USES:
Telegraph poles, building work, fencing, flagpoles railway sleepers and packing cases.

<60m

FREQUENT in plantations and large gardens, especially in Scotland. Best on moist, acid soil. Straight trunk with whorls of branches; upper ascending, lower more pendulous. Some heavy branches sweep down before turning sharply upwards. Slender crown.

BARK: Exudes a clear, pungent resin in young trees. Later deeply fissured.
TIMBER: Known as Oregon Pine. Red-brown with attractive grain. Often knotty.
TWIG: Grey-brown with raised, oval leaf scars.
BUDS: Long and tapered at both ends, red-brown with unfringed scales. Not resinous.
LEAVES: Soft. Fruity, resinous aroma when crushed. Densely set, loosely parted into ranks, the lower spreading, the upper raised and forward pointing. Upper side from bright to dark green, grooved. Pinched to a short stalk, angled to the stem.
FLOWERS: Monoecious. Males on previous year's growth, on undersurface, bud-like. 1–3 red-tinged females at shoot tip, spreading then drooping and turning green.
FRUIT: Egg-shaped, pendulous, becoming glossy as the rounded scales open.

J
F
M
A
M
J
J
A
S
O
N
D

Raised oval leaf scar

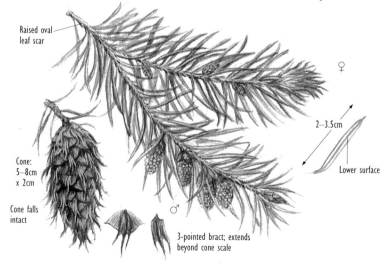

♀

2–3.5cm

Lower surface

Cone: 5–8cm x 2cm

Cone falls intact

♂

3-pointed bract; extends beyond cone scale

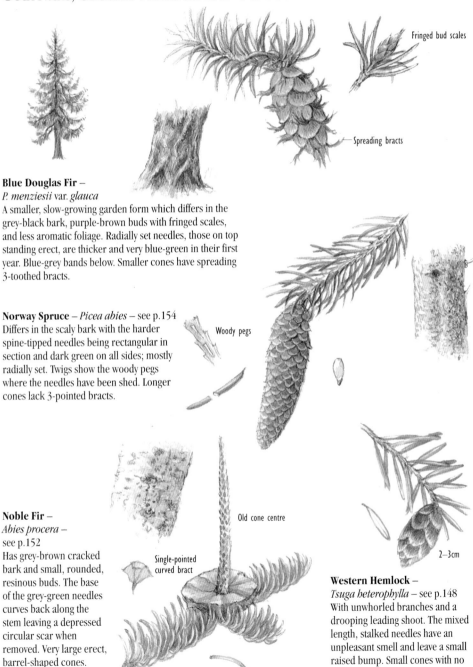

Fringed bud scales

Spreading bracts

Blue Douglas Fir –
P. menziesii var. *glauca*
A smaller, slow-growing garden form which differs in the grey-black bark, purple-brown buds with fringed scales, and less aromatic foliage. Radially set needles, those on top standing erect, are thicker and very blue-green in their first year. Blue-grey bands below. Smaller cones have spreading 3-toothed bracts.

Norway Spruce – *Picea abies* – see p.154
Differs in the scaly bark with the harder spine-tipped needles being rectangular in section and dark green on all sides; mostly radially set. Twigs show the woody pegs where the needles have been shed. Longer cones lack 3-pointed bracts.

Woody pegs

Old cone centre

Noble Fir –
Abies procera –
see p.152
Has grey-brown cracked bark and small, rounded, resinous buds. The base of the grey-green needles curves back along the stem leaving a depressed circular scar when removed. Very large erect, barrel-shaped cones.

Single-pointed
curved bract

2–3cm

Western Hemlock –
Tsuga heterophylla – see p.148
With unwhorled branches and a drooping leading shoot. The mixed length, stalked needles have an unpleasant smell and leave a small raised bump. Small cones with no visible bracts Between the scales.

Circular leaf scars

EVERGREEN
Pinaceae

Noble Fir

Abies procera

Introduced by Douglas from America in 1825 and like the other species of *Abies* (Silver Firs) is a tall, columnar tree with large erect cones which remain as a central 'candle' after seed dispersal. The needles leave a circular, depressed scar in contrast to Douglas Fir.

USES:
Kitchen furniture, joinery and pallet making. Saplings make good Christmas trees.

<55m

Tapered bole

PLANTATIONS, estates and large gardens. Commonest in Scotland. Stout bole and rings of horizontal branches.

BARK: Silver-grey with resin blisters. Later cracking to show red underbark.

TIMBER: V. pale brown, close-grained, similar to Spruce.

TWIG: Dark orange then red-brown. Circular leaf scars.

BUDS: Tiny, red-brown, tipped with white resin; hidden by leaves.

LEAVES: Like a toothbrush; those from below the shoot strongly parted, curving down then sweeping up. The basal 2–3mm of the upper surface needles is appressed to the stem before curving to stand erect. Flat needles have a rounded apex and are dark grey-green, grooved above and with two indistinct, narrow grey bands beneath.

FLOWERS: Monoecious. Males on most shoots, clustered on the undersurface. Females high on the crown, on upper surface, brush-like.

FRUIT: Very large erect, barrel-shaped cone (tapers to a flat top). Blunt scales almost hidden by the paler brown, downward-curving bracts which are abruptly pointed.

J

F

M

A

M ✿

J ✿

J ✇

A ✇

S ✇

O ✇

N ✇

D

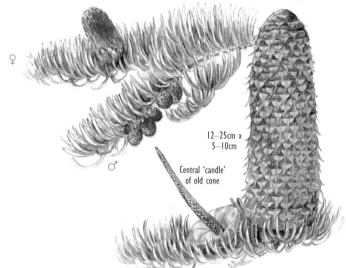

♀

♂

12–25cm x
5–10cm

Central 'candle'
of old cone

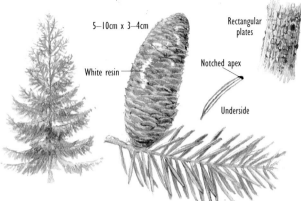

5–10cm x 3–4cm

Rectangular plates

White resin

Notched apex

Underside

Grand Fir – *Abies grandis*
Plantations and large gardens in wetter areas. Differs in more open branching and large resin blisters on a brown-grey bark. Needles are mostly longer and flatter, and arranged as if parted into two shallow 'V' ranks, at right angles to the stem which is not hidden. Bright mid-green and grooved above. Smells of orange when crushed. Male cones smaller. Smaller, red-brown cone stained with white resin. Very broad, shallow scales and no exposed bracts.

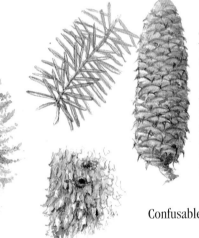

Pinker underbark

Common (European) Silver Fir – *Abies alba*
Widely planted in the 18th Century but many succumbed to aphid and pollution damage. More sparsely branched. Sinuous bole top frequently divides to give 'storks nest' appearance. Bud virtually resin free. Leaves less dense, lower ones in 2 flat ranks, upper ones as if parted like a 'V'; all slightly forward-pointing. Shiny dark-green above, 2 silvery white bands below. Fruit slightly shorter and slimmer with a more pointed apex. Only the points of the bracts protrude.

Confusables include:

Douglas Fir –
Pseudotsuga menziesii –
see p.150
Older bark red-brown and deeply cross fissured. Twig with raised, oval leaf scars and beech-like bud. Softer, greener needles pinched to a short stalk. Fruit egg-shaped and pendulous with 3-pointed bracts.

Coast Redwood – *Sequoia sempervirens* –
see p.146 (not illustrated here)
Similar lofty outline but with thick, spongy bark and broad flat leaves. Some leaves on leading and cone-bearing shoots are scale-like. Tiny, pendulous, few-scaled cones.

Spruces – *Picea* spp – see p.154 (not illustrated here)
4-sided needles are borne on small woody pegs which remain on twig when needle falls. Most have pendulous cones which fall in one piece.

Norway Spruce
Picea abies

EVERGREEN
Pinaceae

The most well-known Spruce, species of which have scaly bark, pendulous cones and hard needles borne on wooden 'pegs'. Spruces are important in forestry and some are grown as decorative garden species. Norway Spruce has been the traditional British Christmas Tree since Prince Albert introduced the custom from Germany in 1841.

<40m

USES:
House rafters, timber frames and flooring, pallets, packing cases, violin sounding boards and paper pulp.

J ▢
F ▢
M ▢
A ▢
M ▢ ✤
J ▢ ✤
J ▢ ✪
A ▢ ✪
S ▢ ✪
O ▢ ✪
N ▢ ✪
D ▢

INTRODUCED from Europe. Common in plantations (mostly in the S.E.). In shelter belts and as ex-Christmas Trees in gardens.
Regular whorls of horizontal branches (lowest swept down, upper ones ascending) bear small side branches giving a symmetrical, tall, conical crown.
BARK: Harsh to touch, dark brown. Breaking into small, thin scales.
TIMBER: 'White deal' is soft and light with hard knots.
TWIG: Orange-brown, grooved. Prickly with peg-like projections.
BUDS: Small, pointed, oval, glossy red-brown, no resin.
LEAVES: Spiral and close set on upright shoots but on lateral shoots the lower ones are parted, at right angles to the stem, the upper ones point forwards and overlap. 4-sided stiff pointed needles mature dark green on all surfaces.
FLOWERS: Monoecious. Males in erect clusters of crimson cones at the ends of the previous year's growth. Turning yellow with pollen. Females solitary, dark red; only on upper branches.
FRUIT: Stalkless, becoming pendulous. Green then purple; finally red-brown. Long, tapered at each end. Many, regular, overlapping, thin, leathery scales. Shed whole.

Needle size: 1.5–2cm

Pegs remain after needles fall

♀

2–3cm

<16cm

1cm

♂

CULTIVARS, CLOSELY RELATED AND CONFUSABLE SPECIES

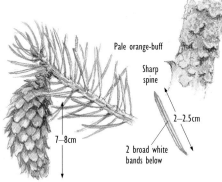

Pale orange-buff

Sharp spine

2–2.5cm

7–8cm

2 broad white bands below

Most cultivars are slow growing dwarf forms for rockeries and heather gardens e.g. *P. abies* 'Nidiformis' which produces a dense, spreading bush up to 1m high.

Sitka Spruce – *Picea sitchensis*
Introduced from N. America in 1831. Now the main plantation tree of western and upland Britain and common in large gardens. Taller, it also has greyer, peeling bark. Small, new branches often grow from the lower bole. Stiff flatter ridged needles, shiny dark-green above. Cone much shorter, less tapering, pale brown. Soft, springy feel to irregular-toothed, crinkle-edged scales.

The following are common in parks and larger gardens:

Oriental Spruce – *Picea orientalis*
Has v. short 4-sided shiny needles each with a short rounded tip, 4 fine pale lines above, 10–14 below. Densely foliated. On strong shoots needles are closely appressed to stem. Short-pointed, slightly curved cones. Smooth, rounded scales.

Serbian Spruce –
Picea omorika
Has a narrow spire-like crown. Flat, broad, blunt-tipped needles are blue-green above with 2 broad white bands below. Small cone on short, thick, curved stalk, ripens purple-brown with shallow, rounded scales.

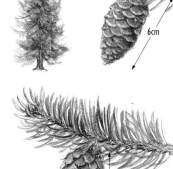

Needle length: 1–1.8cm

6cm

<1cm

6–10cm

White resin patches

Two species (not illustrated) are:

Morinda or **Himalayan Weeping Spruce** – *Picea smithiana*
<30m. Best in the N. and W. Horizontal branches sweep down then up and bear pendulous, hairless shoots with long (<4cm), slender, 4 angled, shiny dark-green pointed needles borne all round the stem, curving forwards and inwards. Large bright brown cone (<17cm x 4cm) with shiny, notched, round-ended scales.

Blue Spruce –
Picea pungens 'Glauca'
Slow growing, often only a bush. Stout, pale yellow-brown twigs. Most needles above the stem, upswept, those below curving forwards. Stiff, spine-tipped, 4-angled and varying (there are many different cultivars under the Glauca banner) but by 2nd year most are dark blue-green with 2 grey bands on each surface. Cone similar to *abies* but shorter and paler. Scales as *sitchensis*.

1.5–2cm

5–8cm

Brewer's Weeping Spruce –
Picea breweriana
Becoming more common. Differs from *smithiana* in the much longer (to 2m) pendulous, hairy shoots from upswept branches. Flatter, blunt-ended, blue-green needles (<3cm). Smaller (<12cm x 2.5cm) red-brown cone with paler resin stains and incurved scales.

Cedar of Lebanon
Cedrus libani

EVERGREEN
Pinaceae

True Cedars native to the Mediterranean and N. India have whorls of evergreen needles which, like the wood, smell strongly of balsam. Unrelated Cedars also have aromatic wood but come from the New World and Australasia. Of the true Cedars the young shoot tips are level in *libani,* ascending in *atlantica* and drooping in *deodar.*

USES:
Timber was used to construct King Solomon's Temple, now mostly for veneers or drawer linings. Cedar oil was used for embalming, now used in perfumery.

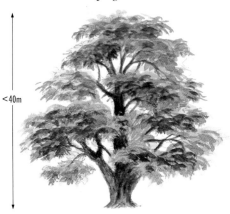

<40m

INTRODUCED c.1638. Frequent in churchyards and country house gardens/parks. Massive short bole. Lower branches arch to near ground, upper ones are level, shelf-like; easily damaged. Foliage densely packed. Crown often flat-topped.
BARK: Red-brown, finely fissured between shallow ridges.
TIMBER: Brown, wavy-ringed, aromatic. Soft but durable.
TWIG: Soon becoming glabrous, grey-brown. Fallen needles leave flat peg-like projections. Short (3–4mm) ribbed spur shoots.
BUD: Tiny (2–3mm), pale brown.
LEAVES: Spirally, singly on a woody base on long shoots; forward pointing, spreading. Upright tufts on spur shoots of 10–20 stiff, blue-green needles with short sharp translucent points. Shallowly triangular in cross section
FLOWERS: Monoecious on spur shoots. Many soft finger-like ♂ cones from mid-summer; yellow with pollen by autumn. Fewer smaller, more rounded ♀ cones; bright green, purple tinge.

FRUIT: Erect barrel-shaped cone of thin, broad, rounded scales. Apex depressed or shallowly domed. Ripens over 2 years to grey or pinky-brown. Scales fall leaving central 'candle'.

White resin patches

Long single needles on new shoot

Cone: 8–15cm long

Needle length: 2.5cm

5cm ♂

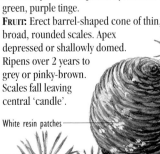

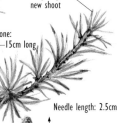

J	⌀	∅
F	⌀	∅
M	⌀	∅
A	⌀	∅
M	⌀	∅
J	⌀	∅
J	⌀	∅
A	⌀	❀ ∅
S	⌀	❀ ∅
O	⌀	❀ ∅
N	⌀	❀ ∅
D	⌀	∅ ∅

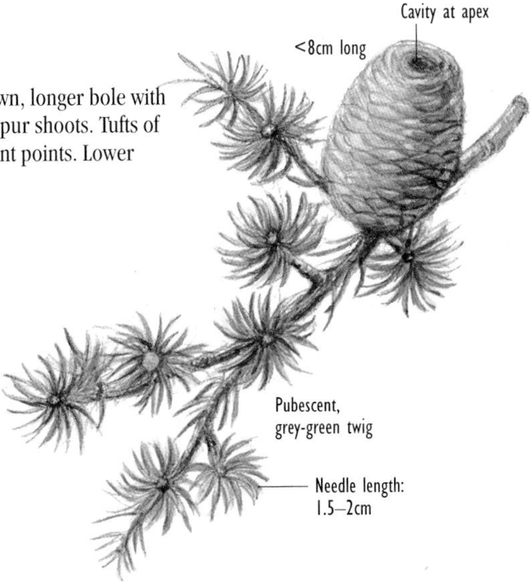

Cavity at apex

<8cm long

Atlas Cedar – *Cedrus atlantica*

Frequent; best specimens in E. Anglia. More conic crown, longer bole with widely-spaced ascending branches. Longer (1–2cm) spur shoots. Tufts of 30–45 shorter, dark green needles with long translucent points. Lower surface round-keeled. Cone smaller.

Pubescent, grey-green twig

Blue Cedar –
C. atlantica 'Glauca'
The most commonly planted cultivar. Usually single-boled with a neat crown, the needles are blue-white.

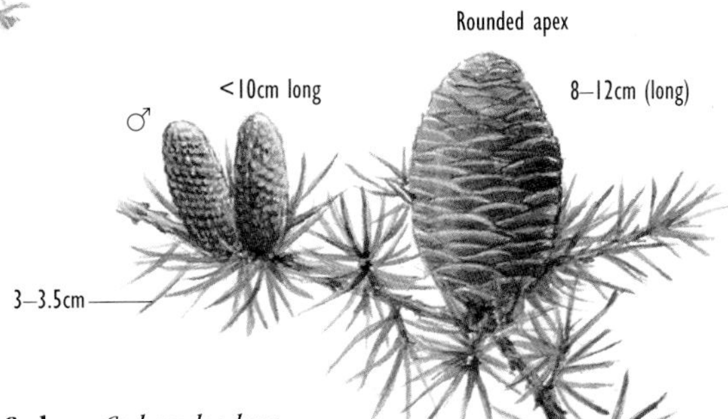

Needle length: 1.5–2cm

Rounded apex

<10cm long ♂ **8–12cm (long)**

3–3.5cm

Deodar Cedar – *Cedrus deodara*

With a narrower crown from a single bole or a number of near vertical branches. Weeping habit when young. Densely pubescent young twigs. Pendulous lead shoot (and new growth) with long (<5cm) pale-green, singly borne needles. 1cm spur shoots bear tufts of 10–25, mid-green, flexible long (3–3.5cm) needles. Longer male flowers often curving. Females less common. Cone purple-brown.

Larches – *Larix* spp (not illustrated – see p.158)

The only other common Conifers with tufts of needles on short shoots. Shorter, soft, paler green, unpointed needles are deciduous. Ridged twigs; slimmer bole. Smaller more open cones persist on tree intact.

European Larch
Larix decidua

DECIDUOUS
Pinaceae

Larches, with fresh green spring growth and beautiful golden autumn tints, are the only common deciduous conifers and are often used to screen less attractive plantations. A 17th Century introduction, *decidua* is often confused with the more recently introduced *L. kaemferi* and the hybrid between the two species.

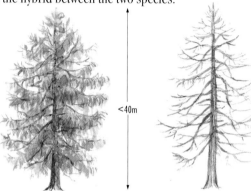

<40m

USES:
Fences, gates, staircases, fishing boats and vats.

INTRODUCED from central Europe. Plantations and parks. Tapering trunk. Whorled branches (irregular ones between) sweep down then up bearing pendulous shoots. Conical crown becomes broader and more untidy with age.

BARK: Grey-brown, later longitudinally cracked and scaly.

TIMBER: Strong, durable when wet, golden-brown.

TWIG: Markedly ridged from the leaf bases, straw yellow. Old shoots with knobbly short shoots which on younger twigs bear needle tufts and flowers.

BUDS: 3mm, golden brown, pointed, not resinous.

LEAVES: Long, spirally borne single needles appressed to lead shoots. Most as tufts on short shoots, 30–40 together. Flat, slender and soft with blunt or short-pointed apex. Emerge emerald green, later darker and yellow/gold before falling in autumn. 2 indistinct paler green bands below.

FLOWERS: Together on side shoots. Males as small pendulous globular clusters. Erect females purple-red (or green-white) with young leaf tuft below.

FRUIT: Small, egg-shaped, cones. 40–50 smooth, rounded erect scales. Bract-scales just visible. Persist; ripen in 2nd year.

J			♂
F	❀		♂
M	◗	❀	♂
A	◗	♂	♂
M	◗	♂	♂
J	◗	♂	♂
J	◗	♂	♂
A	◗	♂	♂
S	◗	♂	♂
O	◗	♂	♂
N	◗	♂	♂
D		♂	♂

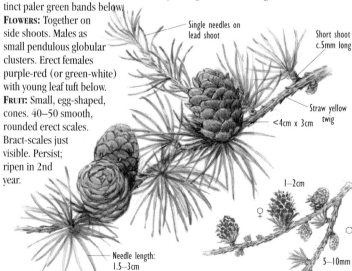

Single needles on lead shoot

Short shoot c.5mm long

Straw yellow twig

<4cm x 3cm

1–2cm

♀

♂

5–10mm

Needle length: 1.5–3cm

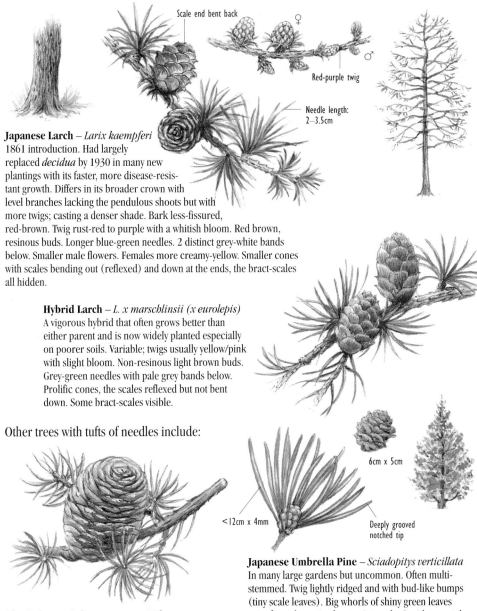

Scale end bent back

♀

Red-purple twig

♂

Needle length:
2–3.5cm

Japanese Larch – *Larix kaempferi*
1861 introduction. Had largely
replaced *decidua* by 1930 in many new
plantings with its faster, more disease-resis-
tant growth. Differs in its broader crown with
level branches lacking the pendulous shoots but with
more twigs; casting a denser shade. Bark less-fissured,
red-brown. Twig rust-red to purple with a whitish bloom. Red brown,
resinous buds. Longer blue-green needles. 2 distinct grey-white bands
below. Smaller male flowers. Females more creamy-yellow. Smaller cones
with scales bending out (reflexed) and down at the ends, the bract-scales
all hidden.

> **Hybrid Larch** – *L. x marschlinsii (x eurolepis)*
> A vigorous hybrid that often grows better than
> either parent and is now widely planted especially
> on poorer soils. Variable; twigs usually yellow/pink
> with slight bloom. Non-resinous light brown buds.
> Grey-green needles with pale grey bands below.
> Prolific cones, the scales reflexed but not bent
> down. Some bract-scales visible.

Other trees with tufts of needles include:

6cm x 5cm

<12cm x 4mm

Deeply grooved
notched tip

The Cedars – *Cedrus* spp – see p.156
Evergreen with unridged twigs and pointed needles.
Only Deodar Cedar has soft, pliable needles. Large bole
with grey bark. Large, barrel-shaped, erect cones take 2
years to ripen and then break up leaving a central spike.

Japanese Umbrella Pine – *Sciadopitys verticillata*
In many large gardens but uncommon. Often multi-
stemmed. Twig lightly ridged and with bud-like bumps
(tiny scale leaves). Big whorls of shiny green leaves
arise from the main shoot at intervals. Ovoid cones take
2 years to ripen. Loose, flexible, grooved scales.

In winter the deciduous **Gingko** (see p.36)
can also be mistaken for a Larch.

159

Scots Pine
Pinus sylvestris

EVERGREEN
Pinaceae

Of about 100 species of Pine, all having clusters of 2, 3 or 5 needles from a single basal sheath, Scots Pine is our only native species. Of the many introduced species some have replaced *sylvestris* in forestry and others are popular in parks and gardens. Scots Pine is most easily confused with other Pines bearing needles in pairs.

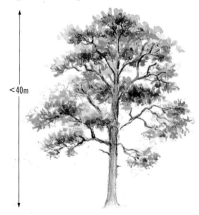

<40m

USES:
House joists, rafters and floors, ship building, telegraph poles, furniture, chipboard, turpentine.

NATIVE but only truly wild in the Scottish Highlands. Common and planted in plantations and gardens across Britain. Naturalised on heathland. Trunk forks near apex. Crown becomes untidy and flat-topped as short branches are shed.

BARK: Brown at the base; developing deep, crocodile-like fissures. Upper third of trunk more orange-red.

TIMBER: 'Redwood'. Orange-brown heartwood with prominent rings and clusters of knots. Strongest when slow-grown.

TWIG: Green-brown in 1st year then grey-brown. Rough to the touch from the short shoots where denuded of needles.

BUDS: Resinous, pointed, red-brown.

LEAVES: Paired on tiny wooden short shoots; as dense tufts near the twig ends. Brown sheathing base. Mostly <5cm but longer on young growth. Blue/grey-green, stiff, slightly twisted and short-pointed. Diverge from shoot.

FLOWERS: Females at apex of leading shoots; males, clustered on side shoots. Open early summer.

FRUIT: Small, pendant, short-stalked glossy green cones over-winter and do not ripen brown until the following autumn. Broad, diamond-shaped scales end in a raised peak.

♀

♂

Juvenile single needles

Needle length: <5cm

3–7cm long

J	🜆	♂
F	🜆	♂
M	🜆	♂
A	🜆	♂
M	🜆 ✿	♂
J	🜆 ✿	♂
J	🜆	♂
A	🜆	♂
S	🜆	♂
O	🜆	♂
N	🜆	♂
D	🜆	♂

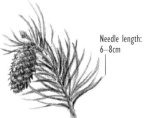

Needle length:
6–8cm

Shore or **Coastal Pine** –
Pinus contorta var. *contorta*
American introduction.
Common in western planta-
tions. Square-scaled bark and
purple-brown, twisted buds.
Slender, yellow-green twisted needles
are appressed to the shoot. Smaller
sessile cones hug the shoot and persist
for many years. Scale centres have
small, spreading or upturned prickles.

5cm

Lodgepole Pine –
Pinus contorta var. *latifolia*
From the Rockies. Grown on
inland peat soils. Has more-
spreading, longer, broader needles and shorter, bright-brown
cones with scales bearing longer
(3mm), spreading spines.

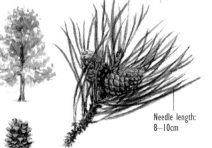

Needle length:
8–10cm

Austrian Pine – *Pinus nigra* ssp. *nigra*
A 19th-century introduction to parks, shelterbelts and large
gardens. Grey-black, deeply ridged bark, wide crown and
long, heavy branches. Resin-stained long buds and dense tufts
of foliage. Long, dark green, curved needles. Pale brown
spreading cones. Less rigid scales
end in a transverse ridge.

Corsican Pine – *Pinus nigra* spp *laricio (maritima)*
From S. Europe. Grown for forestry in the South and East.
Widely-spaced, shorter branches; paler, less-rough bark,
more open foliage. Long wavy, less rigid lighter green
needles. Cones slightly curved.

Needle length:
<25cm

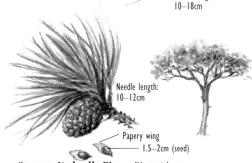

Needle length:
10–18cm

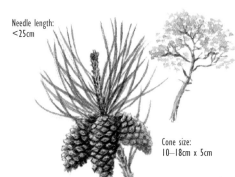

Cone size:
10–18cm x 5cm

Needle length:
10–12cm

Papery wing
1.5–2cm (seed)

Maritime Pine – *Pinus pinaster*
Mediterranean tree. Local on our south coast. Open
crown. Leaning bole sheds lower branches. Purple-red
scaly bark. Buds with reflexed scales. V. long rigid,
spaced glossy green needles. Sessile clusters of large
taper-pointed, glossy cones remain unopened for years.

Stone or **Umbrella Pine** – *Pinus pinea*
Large gardens in S. England. Umbrella-like crown from
much-forked upper trunk. Grey-green needles. Solitary,
glossy, globular cones contain large edible seeds.

161

Monterey Pine
Pinus radiata

EVERGREEN
Pinaceae

Native to S. California; fast growing and tolerant of salt spray. Unopened cones stay on the tree up to 30 years; in its native land, heat from forest fires opens the scales enabling seed dispersal. Needles are borne in groups of **three**; a feature shared by only two other commonly-found introductions.

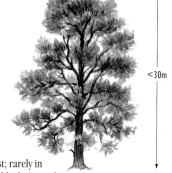

<30m

Uses:
Important timber tree in many countries. In Britain mostly used in shelter belts by S.W. coasts.

Introduced in 1833 and frequent in the West; rarely in plantations. Broad, rounded crown appears black. Spaced trees retain lower, heavy, spreading branches which may descend to the ground.
Bark: Grey, thick. Deep vertical fissures between flaking ridges.
Timber: Soft, light and brittle.
Twig: Initially grey-green, matures pale brown. Knobbly.
Bud: Grey-purple, resinous.
Leaves: Crowded, on short shoots in groups of 3. Long, v. slender, untwisted, sharp-pointed, flexible. Triangular in cross-section. Grass-green; orange-brown when old or if stressed.
Flowers: On same tree; males crowded at base of new side shoots, short-stalked erect females in clusters of 3–5 near the apex of leading shoots.
Fruit: Clustered round shoot. Downward-pointing from curved stalk which presses near side with flat scales to stem while the woody, rounded, outer-side scales protrude giving an asymmetric base to the cone. Retained unopened for many years, even on main trunk.

J
F
M
A
M
J
J
A
S
O
N
D

♂

♀

7–15cm x 9cm

Needle length:
av. 15cm

Knobbly short shoots
of discarded needles

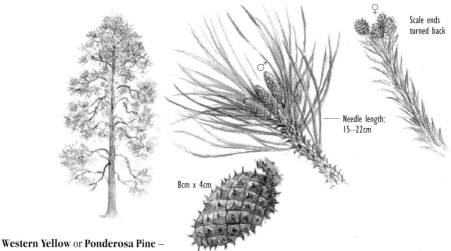

Scale ends turned back

♂

Needle length: 15–22cm

8cm x 4cm

Western Yellow or **Ponderosa Pine** –
Pinus ponderosa

Mostly in large gardens, especially in Scotland; rarely in plantations. An important timber tree in its native America. More conic; upper branches ascend. Old trees have drooping branches with foliage restricted to tufts at raised ends. Jigsaw-like bark with large pink/red-brown plates and wide shallow fissures. Mature shoot shiny brown. V. long crowded, stiff, dull grey-green needles. Smaller egg-shaped, grey-brown cones are sessile, symmetrical and more spreading. Each diamond-shaped woody scale bears a horizontal ridge with a short, spreading prickle. Cone base remains on tree after rest is shed.

Cone size:
20cm long x <15cm broad

Jeffrey's Pine – *Pinus jeffreyi*

Widespread but less frequent than *ponderosa* with which it is confused. Older trees retain columnar shape. The smoother black bark has less frequent narrow fissures. Cut branches emit a lemon scent. New shoots show a blue-grey bloom. Blue-green needles. Large broad, dark purple-brown cone. Scales bear down-curved prickles. Cones fall leaving basal region on tree.

Weymouth Pine
Pinus strobus

A Pine with needles grouped in fives. Widely planted in country estates (e.g. by Lord Weymouth at Longleat) following its introduction from N. America. Many older trees have succumbed to blister rust (a fungus) and it is now less widely planted than the similar Bhutan Pine.

USES:
An important timber tree in N. America. Previously used for small boxes, musical instruments and mouldings.

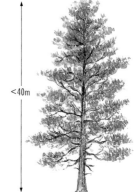

<40m

Stump of dead branch

INTRODUCED in 1705. Old trees are still frequent in estates and graveyards. Straight trunk. Conical crown with horizontal branches. Becomes flat-topped from vertical twigs on upper branches.

BARK: Purple-brown with deep furrows; not scaly.

TIMBER: Even grained; workable in all directions.

TWIG: Green-brown; hairless except below needle clusters.

BUD: Pointed. Orange-brown scales with dark-red tips.

LEAVES: In fives. Initially forward-pointing and tightly bundled, later spreading. Medium length. Slender, soft, blue-green below, paler above.

FLOWERS: Monoecious. Males as pale-yellow clusters on side shoots. Single or paired, erect, stalked, green-pink females at new shoot tips.

FRUITS: Pendulous, short-stalked, banana-shaped green cones ripen brown over two years. Sparse, convex scales curve up at maturity.

J	◠	◈	♂
F	◠	◈	♂
M	◠	◈	♂
A	◠	◈	♂
M	◠	◈	♂
J	◠	✿ ◈	♂
J	◠	✿ ◈	♂
A	◠	◈	♂
S	◠	◈	♂
O	◠	◈	♂
N	◠	◈	♂
D	◠	◈	♂

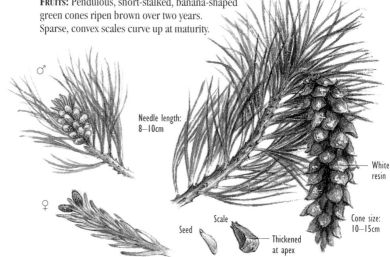

♂

♀

Needle length: 8–10cm

White resin

Seed

Scale

Thickened at apex

Cone size: 10–15cm

Needle length:
18–20cm

<35m

Cone size: 20–30cm

Bhutan Pine –
Pinus wallichiana
Common in parks and large
gardens; also in plantations.
More open, strongly whorled
branches; the lowest heavy
and descending before arching up. Orange-brown bark
has wide, shallow fissures
and resin blisters. Young
shoot hairless and with a lilac
bloom. Needles in fives, slender, drooping, very long and
crinkled/bent. Inner surface
white banded. Very long
cones mature yellow-brown.

Mexican White Pine –
Pinus ayacahuite
Mostly in large gardens in
the West; less common.
Retains conic crown with
short, horizontal branches.
Young shoot with pale-
brown pubescent hairs.
Shorter needles (5s) not
crinkled/bent. Very long,
taper-pointed cones.

Bottom scales
reflexed

Cone size: <35cm

Needle length:
13–15cm

Cone size:
5–8cm

Needle length: 5–8cm

<20m

Arolla or **Swiss Pine** – *Pinus cembra*
Smaller; slow growing and densely
foliated. Gardens on well-drained soil.
Level branches with upturned ends are
retained even at base. Furry orange
young shoots. Crowded needles (5s)
much shorter as are erect, broadly egg-
shaped cones which ripen over three
years from blue through purple to red-
brown. Scales remain closed.

165

Common Juniper
Juniperus communis

One of only three native 'Conifers'; the others are Scots Pine, and Yew which like Juniper, has a fleshy fruit. Very widely distributed throughout the N. hemisphere, including Britain; it is frequently overlooked due to its small, shrubby habit. Some cultivars and introduced Juniper species are more like trees such as Lawson's Cypress but this bears only scale leaves.

USES:
Oil from fruit used to flavour gin and in cooking. Smoke from wood used for curing hams and cheeses.

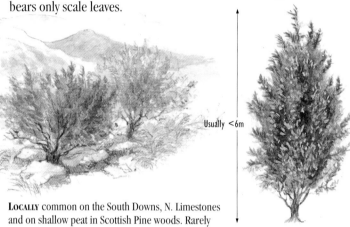

Usually <6m

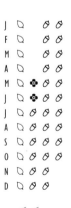

LOCALLY common on the South Downs, N. Limestones and on shallow peat in Scottish Pine woods. Rarely above 6m. Twisted, divided bole gives many-topped outline. Variable in size and shape.

BARK: Red-brown, paper-like sheets peel away.

TIMBER: Red-brown. Resinous smell when newly cut.

TWIG: Green then pale brown. Lower branches retain dead, brown needles.

BUDS: Tiny, hidden within foliage.

LEAVES: Flattened, needle-like but awl shaped; tapering from broader, swollen base to prickly, sharp-pointed apex. In whorls of three, almost at right-angles to the stem. Upper (inner) surface concave, blue-green with a broad waxy white band. Lower (outer) surface bluntly keeled and light grey green. Crushed foliage smells of apple or gin.

FLOWERS: Usually on separate plants. Small, oval, yellow male cones are set in the leaf axils as are the bud-like green females.

FRUIT: Gobular, fleshy, stalkless, 3-seeded, berry-like cone. Takes 2–3 years to ripen from green via bloomed blue to black.

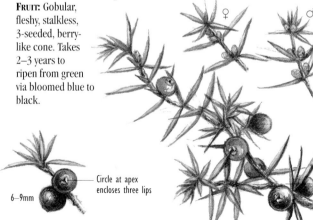

♀   ♂

Circle at apex encloses three lips

6–9mm

Needle len 5–20mm

J	◻	∂ ∂	
F	◻	∂ ∂	
M	◻	∂ ∂	
A	◻	∂ ∂	
M	◻ ✿	∂ ∂	
J	◻ ✿	∂ ∂	
J	◻	∂ ∂ ∂	
A	◻	∂ ∂ ∂	
S	◻	∂ ∂ ∂	
O	◻	∂ ∂ ∂	
N	◻	∂ ∂	
D	◻	∂ ∂	

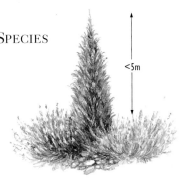

<5m

Dwarf Juniper – *J. communis* ssp. *alpina*
A prostrate, creeping form with dark green leaves. Native in parts of N. England, Wales, Scotland and W. Ireland.

Irish Juniper – *J. communis* 'Hibernica'
Common in gardens. <8m forming a narrow, pointed columnar crown with ascending branches (tips turn out) and upright, dense blue-grey foliage.

Chinese Juniper – *Juniperus chinensis*
Common in parks, gardens and churchyards. Deeply fluted bole produces a tall (18m) narrow crown. Can be multi-stemmed and broader. Retains dense foliage almost to ground. Juvenile pointed needles in whorls of 3 (2), on young shoots and at base of older growth. V. small adult, 3-ranked, over-lapping scale leaves tightly appressed to stem and with pale margins. Sour, catty smell. Dioecious. Fruit shows scale out-lines. 'Aurea' has golden foliage.

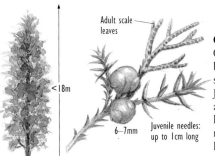

Adult scale leaves

<18m

6–7mm

Juvenile needles: up to 1cm long

Pencil Cedar – *Juniperus virginiana*
Used in America to make pencils; infrequently planted. Untidy columnar crown. More slender leaves; adult spread-pointed, 4-ranked scale leaves topped at branchlet ends by paired juvenile needles. Smooth fruit ripen violet-brown. Some cultivars produce only juvenile, needle-like foliage.

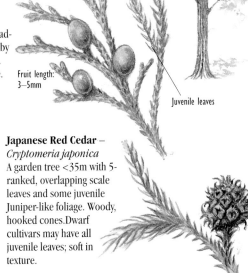

Fruit length: 3–5mm

Juvenile leaves

Japanese Red Cedar –
Cryptomeria japonica
A garden tree <35m with 5-ranked, overlapping scale leaves and some juvenile Juniper-like foliage. Woody, hooked cones. Dwarf cultivars may have all juvenile leaves; soft in texture.

6–7mm

15m

Alerce or **Patagonian Cypress** –
Fitzroya cupressoides
Differs in its deeply ridged red-brown bark and vase-shaped crown. Upswept branches bear pendulous foliage. Leaves all scale-like in threes with boat-shaped end curling out from shoot. Woody cones of 9 opening scales remain on tree.

Species of Cypress, *Thuja* and *Chamaecyparis* may have a similar outline to the Junipers but they have only appressed, scale leaves and small **woody** cones.

Monkey Puzzle or *Chile Pine*

Araucaria araucana

The only frost-hardy member of an important Southern Hemisphere family. Introduced (1795) by Archibald Menzies who was offered the seeds as a dessert while dining with the Governor of Chile! The trees featured in many larger Victorian gardens. Recognised by its whorls of branches and very broad, thick, overlapping spine-tipped leaves.

USES:
Much used in S. America but British grown timber is too knotty.

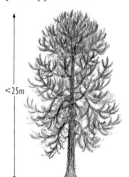

<25m

FREQUENT in parks and gardens but best away from dry winds and pollution. Straight, single trunk with regular whorls of spreading branches (lowest pendulous), tips upturned. Healthy trees maintain branches to near the ground, others lose all but those at the top.

BARK: Initially composed of small green plates each bearing a pointed leaf. Later grey/black with horizontal leaf scars.

Branch scars exuding resin

TIMBER: Aromatic. With regular knots from side branches.

TWIG: Hidden by the overlapping leaves.

BUD: At shoot tip, hidden within overlapping leaves.

LEAVES: Spiral, thick, stiff, glossy and narrowly triangular (bases overlap). Brown dead leaves persist.

FLOWERS: Dioecious. 1–5 egg-shaped, papery, brown male catkins from below the shoot tip. Remain for < a year. Solitary, erect globular female at shoot tip.

FRUIT: Pineapple-like. Overlapping green bracts end in yellow spines. Ripens brown over 2 years. Chestnut-tasting edible seeds.

Wrinkled like an elephant's foot

J		
F		
M		
A		
M		
J	❖	
J	❖	
A	❖	
S		
O		
N		
D		

Fruit size: <20cm

♂ Catkins: 10cm long

Scale

Seed

4cm

Brown spine at apex

♀

Leaves: 3–5cm x 1–2cm

Norfolk Island Pine – *Araucaria heterophylla*
Another S. Hemisphere species but this one is not
frost hardy and the only British example to reach
maturity outdoors is on the Isles of Scilly. It is however grown as a large pot plant. Its very regular
whorls of branches carry vertical upswept shoots
giving a palm-like appearance. The leaves are much
softer and smaller (1cm long); spaced on young
shoots but overlapping on older ones.

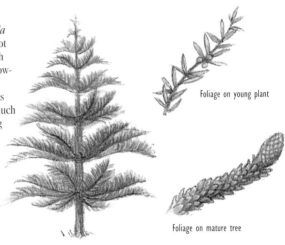

Foliage on young plant

Foliage on mature tree

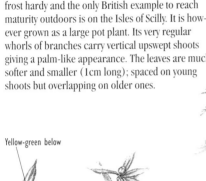

Yellow-green below

Grey-green above

Leaves: 2cm x 0.4cm

Totara – *Podocarpus totara*
This frost-sensitive New Zealand species rarely reaches tree size
away from Cornwall and Ireland. It differs from *Araucaria* in having
a peeling brown-grey bark and a narrower, less tidy crown. Smaller,
narrow, spreading, non-overlapping leaves end in a short spine.

Cone size: 3cm x 3cm

Spine-tipped scales

Chinese Fir –
Cunninghamia lanceolata
An introduced Redwood, largely
confined to Southern England.
Thick red-brown bark and
branches with most foliage at
the apices. Smaller, much
narrower, tapering, shiny green
leaves. Appressed base but
much of the blade spreads at
right-angles to stem. Small
green cones ripen brown.

Leaves: 3–7cm
x 0.4cm

In 1994 a previously unknown member of the
Araucariaceae was discovered not far from Sydney.
Wollemi Pine – *Wollemia nobilis* has fern-like foliage.
Saplings have been sent to Kew Gardens as a tree for the
new millennium.

Giant Redwood or Wellingtonia

Sequoiadendron giganteum

The largest tree in the world; individuals in its native area of Sierra Nevada can grow for 3,000 years, reach 80 metres and weigh 2,000 tons. Deep roots and thick, tannin-containing bark protect it from windthrow, fire, insects and fungi. Introduced the year the Duke of Wellington died (1853), rapidly becoming popular as an avenue tree.

USES:
Timber is used for estate gates and fences. Foliage used for wreaths.

<60m

Hole left by fallen branch

Fluted and tapering

INTRODUCED and common in estates, parks and churchyards. Narrowly conical. Pointed apex prone to lightening damage. Short level branches but upper ascend and lowest sweep down. Up-turned ends bear majority of foliage. Broad bole.
BARK: Thick (<50cm), rufous-brown, soft and spongy.
TIMBER: Heartwood ruddy-brown but brittle.
TWIG: Curving, much-branched. Covered by green scale leaves, later brown.
BUD: Small, hidden. No scales.
LEAVES: 3-ranked; overlapping, sharp-pointed, elongated scales. Appressed in young shoots, later spreading with incurved tip. Grey-green ageing darker. Harsh texture; strong aniseed smell when crushed.
FLOWERS: Monoecious. Females at stem tips. Males at tips of minor shoots from October. Pollen shed in spring.
FRUIT: Pendent cone (stalk bears smaller scale leaves) with broad, diamond-shaped, tightly packed corky green scales.

J
F
M
A
M
J
J
A
S
O
N
D

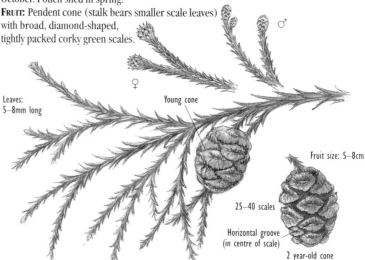

♂

♀

Leaves:
5–8mm long

Young cone

Fruit size: 5–8cm

25–40 scales

Horizontal groove
(in centre of scale)

2 year-old cone

Coast (or Californian) Redwood – *Sequoia sempervirens* – see p.146
Also has thick, spongy brown bark. Its similar size and shape differs in the more open, untidy crown. Most branchlets bear Yew-like needles in two ranks though leading and cone-bearing shoots produce spirally ranked, short scale-like leaves. Foliage smells of grapefruit. The much smaller ovate cones have fewer scales.

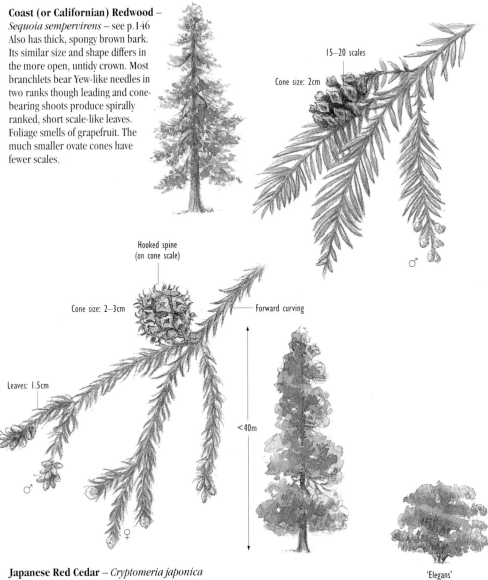

15–20 scales

Cone size: 2cm

♂

Hooked spine (on cone scale)

Cone size: 2–3cm

Forward curving

Leaves: 1.5cm

<40m

♂

♀

'Elegans'

Japanese Red Cedar – *Cryptomeria japonica*
A mid-19th Century introduction most frequent in western gardens. Less tall, paler green and with a more rounded, billowing crown. Slimmer bole. Thinner bark peels in long vertical strips. Pendulous branchlets bear longer, narrower, bright green spreading scale leaves. Small globular cone at the apex of a turned-up stalk.

C. japonica 'Elegans'
A smaller, slow-growing, multi-stemmed, shrubby cultivar with much longer, Juniper-like, spreading leaves which turn bronzy-purple in winter. Suitable for small gardens.

Western Red Cedar

Thuja plicata

EVERGREEN
Cupressaceae

Not a true Cedar (p.156) but a member of the Cypress family and often confused with Lawson Cypress (p.176). A well-shaped tall tree in its native western states of N. America. Here frequently grown as a hedge or nurse crop at the edge of young broad-leaved plantations.

USES:
Garden sheds, green-houses and fences. Weather boarding, window frames, ladders and rugby posts.

Cultivar 'Zebrina'

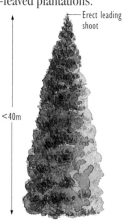

Erect leading shoot

<40m

INTRODUCED in 1853. Abundant in parks, gardens and churchyards. Best in the damper North and West. Very narrow, dense conical shape; bole hidden by lowest branches which sweep down then up and appear layered.
BARK: Red-purple, soft and thick. Peeling in strips.
TIMBER: Aromatic and red-brown, weathers silver-grey.
TWIG: Green ageing red to purple-brown. Flat-sprayed foliage feels thicker at tips.
BUDS: Tiny, hidden among foliage.
LEAVES: Scale-like, 4-ranked. Side pr larger, overlapping other pr. 6–8mm on main shoots with a long incurled tip. Others 2–3mm, appressed, short-pointed. Deep, shiny green above, paler below with grey/white margins. Fruity scent on bruising.
FLOWERS: Minute red males from January, later yellow with pollen. Yellow-green, short-stalked females near branch ends.
FRUIT: Small, erect, flask-shaped green cones. 5–6 prs of leathery scales ripen brown and open flower-like.

Fluted or buttressed

J
F
M ❖
A ❖
M ⬠
J ⬠
J ⬠
A ⬠
S ⬠
O ⬠
N ⬠
D

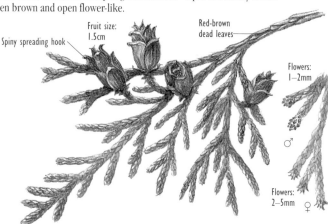

Fruit size:
1.5cm

Spiny spreading hook

Red-brown
dead leaves

Flowers:
1–2mm

♂

Flowers:
2–5mm ♀

Resin glands on leaves

Thuja plicata 'Zebrina'
A popular cultivar with bands of creamy-yellow foliage
(see illustration on p.172).

Northern White Cedar – *Thuja occidentalis*
Less common, mostly as hedging. Untidy, often leaning
and multi-stemmed. Spicy cooked apple aroma of
crushed foliage. Green leaves bronze in winter. Many
small pendent cones. Most dwarf garden cultivars have
golden foliage.

— No hook on scale

Cone size: 1cm

Chinese Thuja – *Thuja orientalis* (right)
Commonest in West Midland and East Anglian towns. Vertical
branches end in vertically-sprayed foliage. Small blunt-ended
scentless leaves. 6-scaled blue-green cones ripen brown.

Lawson Cypress –
Chamaecyparis lawsoniana – see p.176
Drooping leader. Parsley smell to less-flattened
foliage. Smaller narrow leaves, white-lined at
junctions below. Tiny (7mm) globular woody
cones. Bark not peeling.

Curved hooked tip
Cone size: 2cm
<15m

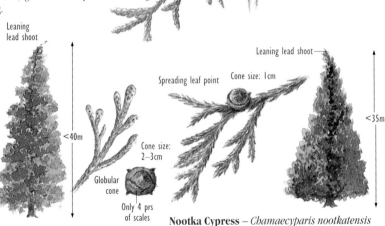

Leaning
lead shoot

Leaning lead shoot

Spreading leaf point   Cone size: 1cm

Leyland Cypress –
*x Cupressocyparis
leylandii* – see p.174
Non-peeling bark.
Almost vertical,
sparsely-foliated
branches. Smaller
appressed leaves.
Grey-green, bright
green and gold
cultivars; most do
not bear cones.

<40m

Globular
cone

Cone size:
2–3cm

Only 4 prs
of scales

<35m

Nootka Cypress – *Chamaecyparis nootkatensis*
Broader conical shape. Drooping foliage smells of
turpentine and feels rough (stroked inwards).
Dull-green ridged leaves. Blue-green globular
cones ripen brown.

<20m

Fleshy berry-
like fruit

Chinese Juniper – *Juniperus chinensis*
Deeply fluted bark, foliage smells of cat. Juvenile 3-ranked
spreading needles at base of branchlets; tightly appressed
small scale-leaves elsewhere. Golden and other cultivars.

Leyland Cypress
x Cupressocyparis leylandii

EVERGREEN
Cupressaceae

A hybrid of Monterey Cypress and Nootka Cypress. Fast growing and popular as a garden hedge. Most earlier plantings were cuttings of the 1888 'Haggleston Grey' and 1911 'Leighton Green' crosses. Since 1970 golden-leaved cultivars have been widely planted. Confusable with both parents and other scale-leaved species.

USES:
Garden hedging and screening buildings. Timber used for estate work.

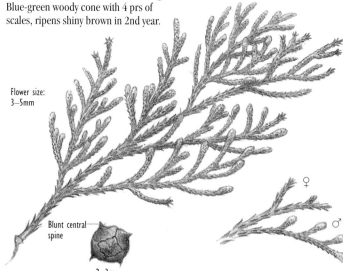

<40m

GARDEN ORIGIN. Abundant. Narrow conical crown. Crowded, almost vertical branches hide the single (or forked) bole. Sparsely foliated, leaning leader.
BARK: Red-brown with shallow vertical fissures.
TIMBER: Creamy white and even-textured.
TWIG: Green, later orange-brown. 'Leighton Green' bears dense sprays of flattened, fern-like foliage; 'Haggerston Grey' has sparser branchlets in 3 dimensions. Mild smell.
BUD: Tiny and hidden among leaves.
LEAVES: Small (0.5–2.0mm) overlapping green/grey/yellow scales in 4 ranks (like braided cord). Closely appressed with pointed tips. Oval cross-section to branchlet.
FLOWERS: Monoecious. Commonest on 'Leighton Green'. Yellow males and inconspicuous green females.
FRUIT: Unusual. Most common on 'Leighton Green'. Blue-green woody cone with 4 prs of scales, ripens shiny brown in 2nd year.

Flower size:
3–5mm

Blunt central
spine

2–3cm

♀

♂

J	◻	𝄢
F	◻	𝄢
M	◻	𝄢
A	◻	𝄢
M	◻	𝄢
J	◻ ✦	𝄢
J	◻ ✦	𝄢
A	◻ 𝄢 𝄢	
S	◻ 𝄢 𝄢	
O	◻ 𝄢	
N	◻ 𝄢	
D	◻ 𝄢	

All plants belong to one of about 15 named cultivars and are propagated from cuttings. Those with golden-yellow young and bronzy-green older leaves include 'Castlewellan Gold' and 'Robinson's Gold'.

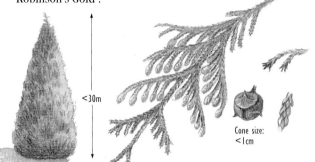

<30m

Cone size: <1cm

Nootka Cypress – *Chamaecyparis nootkatensis* A parent of *leylandii*. More broadly based. The less compact, pendulous dull green foliage feels rougher when stroked inwards as the ridged leaves end in a sharp spreading point. Turpentine smell to crushed foliage. Flowers frequent. Frequent smaller cones ripen in 2nd year.

Similar trees, frequently grown as hedges include:

Monterey Cypress – *Cupressus macrocarpa* The other parent of *leylandii*. Mostly in S.W. England and by coasts as it is frost sensitive. Trunk often divides near ground. Older trees may become flat-topped with horizontal branches. Erect lead shoot. Foliage in erect/spreading 3-D sprays. Tiny appressed leaves, lateral pair with blunt, swollen tip giving rounded cross-section to branchlet. Lemon smell when crushed. Larger cones with 7–8 prs of scales.

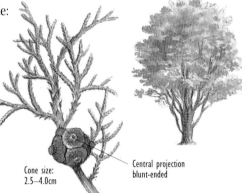

Cone size: 2.5–4.0cm

Central projection blunt-ended

Cone size: 5–8mm

Lawson Cypress – *Chamaecyparis lawsonii* – see p.176
Differs in the drooping lead shoot; flatter, softer foliage which smells of resin or parsley when crushed and the white 'X' between the leaves on the lower surface. The much smaller cones are frequent.

Western Red Cedar – *Thuja plicata* – see p.172
Differs in the fluted bole with peeling rufous bark. The larger shiny green leaves have long incurled points on main shoots and smell of fruit when crushed. Erect flask-shaped cones have 5–6 prs of spreading leathery scales.

EVERGREEN
Cupressaceae

Lawson Cypress
Chamaecyparis lawsonii

Seed sent from the Sacramento Valley in 1854 was first raised by the Lawson nursery at Edinburgh. There are now c.200 cultivars and it is the most planted of all the garden conifers. The fern-like foliage is easily confused with other species; its aroma, together with the cone size and shape are important diagnostic features.

USES:
Hedging. Timber for fencing and estate work. Wardrobe lining (U.S.A.). Foliage used by florists.

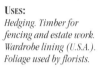

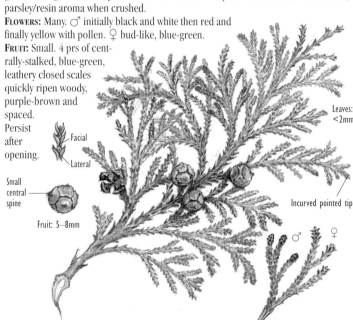

<40m>

ABUNDANT in gardens, parks and churchyards. Yet to reach full size. Lead shoot and branch tips droop. Foliated to the ground. Small branches become layered in old trees.
BARK: Initially grey-green, later red-brown with vertical fissures.
TIMBER: 'Port Orford Cedar' – creamy-yellow, durable and aromatic.
TWIG: Green. Red-brown older shoots. Bears flattened, slightly pendulous foliage.
BUDS: Tiny and hidden among foliage.
LEAVES: Small overlapping scales cover the shoot in 4 ranks; the paired facials are shorter than the paired laterals. Elongated diamond shape with a central translucent gland. Dark green above, paler below with a white waxy x between the leaves. Soft feel; parsley/resin aroma when crushed.
FLOWERS: Many. ♂ initially black and white then red and finally yellow with pollen. ♀ bud-like, blue-green.
FRUIT: Small. 4 prs of centrally-stalked, blue-green, leathery closed scales quickly ripen woody, purple-brown and spaced. Persist after opening.

Facial

Lateral

Small central spine

Fruit: 5–8mm

Leaves: <2mm

Incurved pointed tip

♂   ♀

J	◻	◊
F	◻	◊
M	◻ ✿	◊
A	◻ ✿	◊
M	◻ ◊	◊
J	◻ ◊	◊
J	◻ ◊	◊
A	◻ ◊	◊
S	◻ ◊	◊
O	◻ ◊	◊
N	◻ ◊	◊
D	◻ ◊	◊

Of the many common garden cultivars of *lawsonii* some are dwarf forms grown in rockeries, others are grown for their colours which range from blue-green to gold. Examples include 'Lutea' with a narrow columnar shape and outer golden foliage and the erect branching 'Erecta' with a flame-like outline.

'Erecta'   'Lutea'

Hinoki Cypress –
Chamaecyparis obtusa
Japanese introduction. Large gardens in the south and west. Broader base to crown with more rounded apex. Red-brown peeling bark. Lead shoots unbranched, side branchlets curve backwards. Also dwarf cultivars. Bright, glossy green leaves lack glands. Blunt-tipped leaves (laterals longest) smell of Eucalyptus when crushed. Larger cone of 8 scales.

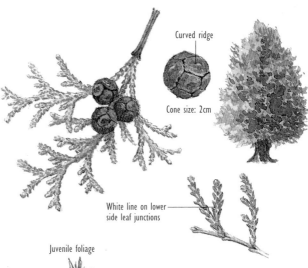

Curved ridge

Cone size: 2cm

White line on lower side leaf junctions

Juvenile foliage

Sawara Cypress – *Chamaecyparis pisifera*
Uncommon as the type tree when it has an open crown and looks like *lawsonii*. Mostly fine scale leaves with a sharp, spreading point and an acrid resinous smell. Pea-like, 6-scaled cones ripen dark brown. Much commoner cultivars e.g. 'Squarrosa' and 'Plumosa' have only juvenile, Juniper-like foliage giving a mossy appearance.

Nootka Cypress – *Chamaecyparis nootkatensis*
Parks and large gardens. Very neat conical shape with drooping, dull green foliage which is rough when stroked due to the sharp, spreading point on each ridged scale leaf. When crushed smells of turpentine. Cones ripen brown in 2nd year. Sharp, conical spike at centre of each scale. ♂ and ♀ on same tree.

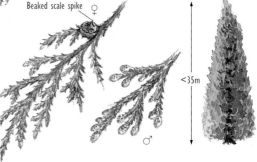

Beaked scale spike ♀

<35m

♂

177

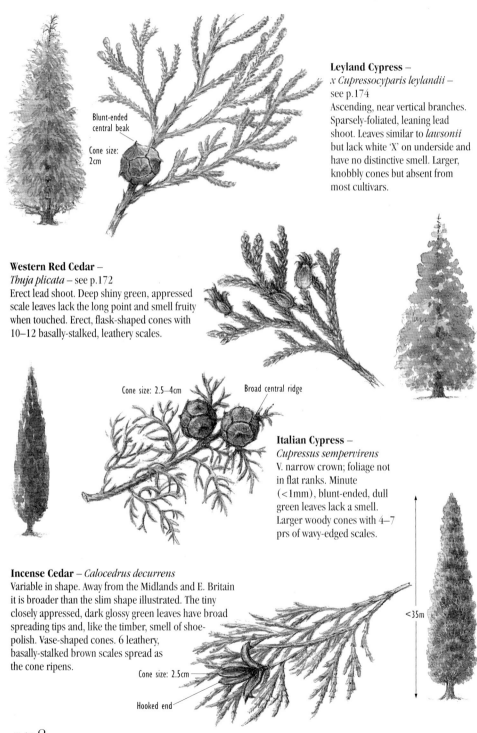

Leyland Cypress –
x Cupressocyparis leylandii –
see p.174
Ascending, near vertical branches.
Sparsely-foliated, leaning lead
shoot. Leaves similar to *lawsonii*
but lack white 'X' on underside and
have no distinctive smell. Larger,
knobbly cones but absent from
most cultivars.

Blunt-ended
central beak

Cone size:
2cm

Western Red Cedar –
Thuja plicata – see p.172
Erect lead shoot. Deep shiny green, appressed
scale leaves lack the long point and smell fruity
when touched. Erect, flask-shaped cones with
10–12 basally-stalked, leathery scales.

Cone size: 2.5–4cm

Broad central ridge

Italian Cypress –
Cupressus sempervirens
V. narrow crown; foliage not
in flat ranks. Minute
(<1mm), blunt-ended, dull
green leaves lack a smell.
Larger woody cones with 4–7
prs of wavy-edged scales.

Incense Cedar – *Calocedrus decurrens*
Variable in shape. Away from the Midlands and E. Britain
it is broader than the slim shape illustrated. The tiny
closely appressed, dark glossy green leaves have broad
spreading tips and, like the timber, smell of shoe-
polish. Vase-shaped cones. 6 leathery,
basally-stalked brown scales spread as
the cone ripens.

<35m

Cone size: 2.5cm

Hooked end

Classification of Trees

TREE TAXONOMISTS STUDY DIFFERENT WAYS OF CLASSIFYING SPECIES. Most modern classification schemes attempt to take account of the evolutionary relationships between species. As exact evolutionary links are seldom clear cut and are open to interpretation there is no universally accepted scheme. As with other organisms trees are divided into a small number of orders; each order contains a number of different families; each family is divided into different genera and each genus contains closely related species.

Trees in the same genus are likely to have very similar leaf arrangement, flower and fruit structure while those in different genera but of the same family will still have some features in common. Many tree books are arranged in order of family and all the members of a genus will be described on consecutive pages. In this book the running order is based on leaf characteristics and hence it does not follow a rigid taxonomic scheme. Numbers references below indicate page numbers in this book.

Trees are given a Latin binomial name and as with other plants the first name (always starting with a capital) is that of the genus and may be shared by other trees in the same genus; the second is the species name: e.g.
Acer pseudoplatanus = Sycamore
Acer campestre = Maple
Trees which belong to the **ANGIOSPERMS** or Flowering Plants (class Angiospermae) have seeds enclosed in an ovary and are divided into two subclasses:
1. **Dicotyledons** (subclass Dicotyledoneae) (seedlings with two cotyledons, leaves typically broad and with net veins, flower parts in multiples of 4 or 5)
2. **Monocotyledons** (Subclass Monocotyledoneae) (seedlings with one cotyledon, leaves typically narrow and with parallel veins, flower parts in multiples of 3)

DICOTYLEDONS

The principle Orders, Families and Genera which include tree species mentioned in this book are listed below and follow the scheme of Heywood V.H. (*Flowering Plants of the World*).

ORDER MAGNOLIALES

Family Magnoliaceae
A family of trees and shrubs from America and Asia. Leaves alternate with stipules which fall as the leaf opens. Flowers large, showy, bisexual and often solitary. Free petals in whorls as are the numerous stamens.

Genus *Liriodendron* (Tulip Trees) 68
Genus *Magnolia* (Magnolias) 106

ORDER HAMAMELIDALES

Family Platanaceae
A small family of trees with flaking bark; many from N. America. Most have palmately lobed leaves with a swollen base to the petiole. Separate long-stalked male and female catkins on the same tree; fruit spherical.

Genus *Platanus* (Planes) 70

ORDER FAGALES

Family Betulaceae
A family of mostly north temperate deciduous trees and shrubs. Alternate leaves, separate male and female flowers on the same tree, males as drooping cylindrical catkins. Nut-like fruit often winged. Some taxonomists now put Hornbeams and Hazels into their own families.

Genus *Betula* (Birches) 38
Genus *Corylus* (Hazels) 82
Genus *Alnus* (Alders) 84
Genus *Carpinus* (Hornbeams) 86

Family Fagaceae
Mostly trees of temperate and tropical regions. Deciduous or evergreen alternate leaves often with

lobed margins. Unisexual flowers usually in separate catkins on the same tree (Spanish Chestnut has some mixed flower-heads). Nuts partly or completely surrounded by a cup-shaped sheath.

Genus *Quercus* (Oaks) 50, 66
Genus *Castanea* (Spanish Chestnut) 52
Genus *Fagus* (Beeches) 88

ORDER MALVALES

Family Tiliaceae
A family of temperate and tropical trees and shrubs. Deciduous alternate hairy leaves. Flowers bisexual with 5 sepals and petals; scented nectar not uncommon. Fruits usually spherical.

Genus *Tilia* (Limes) 130

Family Ulmaceae
A family of tropical and temperate trees and shrubs. Alternate leaves. Flowers without petals, bisexual or unisexual, often in inconspicuous clusters. Single seeded fruit often winged.

Genus *Ulmus* (Elms) 77

Family Moraceae
A family of tropical and sub-tropical plants which also includes Hop and Cannabis. Leaves alternate or opposite, lobed or unlobed with latex usually evident in the cut petiole. Unisexual flowers; male and female on same or separate plants. Fruit often fleshy (and edible).

Genus *Morus* (Mulberries) 42
Genus *Ficus* (Figs) 62

ORDER SALICALES

Family Salicaceae
A family of north temperate trees and shrubs. Most have alternate, deciduous leaves. Unisexual catkin flower-heads on separate male and female plants with or before the leaves open. Fruit many-seeded, each seed having cottony hairs to aid dispersal.

Genus *Populus* (Poplars and Aspen) 40, 72
Genus *Salix* (Willows) 90, 92, 122

Family Ericaceae
Worldwide; many are shrubs (e.g. Heathers and most Rhododendrons). Mostly alternate, often evergreen leaves. Flowers often bisexual with 4/5 fused sepals and 4/5 petals. Fruit usually a capsule.

Genus *Rhododendron* (Rhododendrons) 104
Genus *Arbutus* (Strawberry Trees) 108

ORDER ROSALES

Family Rosaceae
A worldwide family of trees, shrubs and herbs. Leaves deciduous or evergreen, alternate and often stipulate. Flowers bisexual and showy with usually 5 sepals and petals and many whorls of stamens. Most British species have fleshy fruits.

Genus *Sorbus* (Rowan, Service Tree) 55, 74
(Whitebeam) 80
Genus *Crataegus* (Hawthorns) 64
Genus *Malus* (Apples) 94
Genus *Pyrus* (Pears) 96
Genus *Prunus* (Cherries, Plums, Almond) 98, 100, 100 (Cherry Laurel, Portugal Laurel) 102, 103

ORDER FABALES

Family Fabaceae (Leguminosae)
Worldwide; include trees, shrubs and herbs. Leaves alternate, compound and with stipules. Raceme flower-head. Flowers in the main subfamily (Papilionoideae) like the pea and with 10 stamens. Fruit a pod, often constricted between the seeds.

Genus *Laburnum* (Laburnums) 60

ORDER MYRTALES

Family Myrtaceae
Australian and American trees and shrubs. Aromatic leaves usually opposite but can be alternate; evergreen, leathery and entire. Flowers bisexual with 4/5 petals and numerous stamens. Fruit a dry capsule or fleshy berry.

Genus *Eucalyptus* (Gum Trees) 110

ORDER CORNALES

Family Cornaceae

Most are north temperate trees and shrubs with opposite leaves (some are evergreen). Umbel-like flower-heads often with showy bracts surrounding the small 4/5-petalled flowers. Fruit berry-like, fleshy.

Genus *Cornus* (Dogwoods) 132

ORDER CELASTRALES

Family Celastraceae

A family of trees and climbing shrubs. Leaves opposite or alternate. Flowers small, often greenish-white in cymes and usually with 3-5 petals. Fruit a capsule or berry-like; seeds often covered with a coloured fleshy layer.

Genus *Euonymus* (Spindles) 136

Family Aquifoliaceae

Trees and shrubs most of which are species of Holly. Leaves leathery, usually alternate and often evergreen. Green-white 4-petalled small flowers are bisexual or if unisexual there are separate sex plants. Fruit a berry.

Genus *Ilex* (Hollies) 47

ORDER EUPHORBIALES

Family Buxaceae

Consists of a small number of species, most are evergreen shrubs. Temperate, subtropical and tropical. Leaves opposite or alternate, leathery. Flowers unisexual, small, petalless. Fruit usually a capsule; seeds black and shiny.

Genus *Buxus* (Boxes) 138

ORDER RHAMNALES

Family Rhamnaceae

Worldwide family of trees, shrubs and climbers. Leaves opposite or alternate. Small, bisexual flowers with 4/5 incurved petals (or none). Fruits mostly fleshy.

Genus *Rhamnus* (Buckthorns) 134

ORDER SAPINDALES

Family Hippocastanaceae

A family of only 2 genera; most are north temperate trees. Opposite, palmate leaves emerge from large sticky winter buds. Irregular flowers of 4/5 petals borne in cymes. Fruit a leathery capsule enclosing a large, usually single seed.

Genus *Aesculus* (Horse Chestnuts, Buckeyes) 120

Family Aceraceae

Contains 2 genera of mostly north temperate trees. Leaves (and branches) opposite, usually deciduous; some compound others simple (often palmately lobed). Flowers with 5 sepals and 5 (or 0) petals. Winged, paired fruits.

Genus *Acer* (Maples, Sycamore) 122, 125

ORDER JUGLANDALES

Family Juglandaceae

Most are north temperate and subtropical deciduous trees. Leaves alternate, compound (pinnate) without stipules. Winter buds brown and hairy. Flowers unisexual, males usually in hanging catkins. Fruit a nut or drupe.

Genus *Juglans* (Walnuts) 58

ORDER GENTIANALES

Family Oleaceae

Temperate and tropical trees and shrubs including Olive. Opposite leaves may be compound or simple and along with the twigs are often covered in short grey hairs. Flowers normally bisexual, petals 4 (or none) and a range of fruit types.

Genus *Fraxinus* (Ashes) 115
Genus *Ligustrum* (Privets) 128

ORDER DIPSACALES

Family Caprifoliaceae

Mostly small trees, shrubs and climbers (including Honeysuckles). Leaves usually opposite, simple but compound in Elder. Bisexual flowers. Fruit a berry.

Genus *Sambucus* (Elders) 118
Genus *Viburnum* (Wayfaring Tree) 130
(Guelder Rose) 131

MONOCOTYLEDONS

ORDER ARECALES

Family Palmae
A large, mainly tropical family. Species are typically unbranched (the stem has no secondary thickening) and the leaves are grouped at the apex. Blades are folded and split to form either feather or fan palms. Flower-heads vary greatly but flower parts are in threes. Fruits are either berries or drupes.

If the single apical bud of a palm is killed by frost the tree dies and most introduced palms in Britain are found near the sea or in greenhouses.

Conifers belong to the **GYMNOSPERMS** and produce flowers but the seeds are not protected by an ovary.

ORDER GINKGOALES
This ancient order is now represented by only one family with one genus and one living species:

Family Ginkgoaceae
Differs from all other trees with its deciduous wedge-shaped leaves with forked veins like fan ribs. Separate male and female trees, male catkins producing swimming cells, females producing small green plum-like fruit. Native to China.

Genus *Ginkgo* (Maidenhair Tree) 36

ORDER CONIFERALES

Family Taxaceae
Some authors put this group in a separate Order as the single seeds are not borne laterally in cones but terminally, surrounded by a fleshy aril. Evergreen separate sex trees or shrubs with needle-like leaves, mostly from the northern hemisphere.

Genus *Taxus* (Yews) 141

Family Taxodiaceae
Contains both evergreen and deciduous species; mostly from the northern hemisphere. Leaves needle or scale-like, spirally arranged except in Dawn Redwood (opposite). Separate male and female flowers on the same tree. Cones with fused bract and ovuliferous scales.

Members of the family lack resin ducts.

Genus *Metasequoia* (Dawn Redwood) 144
Genus *Sequoia* (Coast Redwood) 146
Genus *Sequoiadendron* (Giant Redwood) 170

Family Pinaceae
A large family widespread in the northern hemisphere. The members contain resin ducts. Most are evergreen (Larch is deciduous) trees and shrubs with spirally arranged needle-like leaves. Male and female flowers on the same plant. Female cones with separate bract and ovuliferous scales bearing winged seeds.

Genus *Tsuga* (Hemlocks) 148
Genus *Pseudotsuga* (Douglas Firs) 150
Genus *Abies* (Noble Fir) 152
Genus *Picea* (Spruces) 154
Genus *Cedrus* (Cedars) 156
Genus *Larix* (Larches) 158
Genus *Pinus* (Pines) 160, 162, 164

Family Cupressaceae
Evergreen trees and shrubs from Europe, Asia and the Americas. With the exception of some Junipers which have needle-like leaves the adult leaves of this group are small and scale-like, usually in opposite pairs or whorls of three. Separate male and female flowers either on the same or on different trees. Cones mostly small, globose and woody but berry-like in the Junipers.

Genus *Juniperus* (Junipers) 166
Genus *Thuja* (incl. Western Red Cedar) 172
Genus *Chamaecyparis* (incl. Lawson Cypress) 176
Genus *Cupressus* (Monterey Cypress, Italian Cypress) 175, 178
Hybrid *x Cupressocyparis* (Leyland Cypress) 174

Family Araucariaceae
A small group of evergreen trees mostly from the southern hemisphere. Leaves up to 2cm wide in Monkey Puzzle. Separate sex plants, the male cones unusually large.

Genus *Araucaria* (Monkey Puzzle) 168

Organisations involved with the Growing or Conservation of Trees

Arboricultural Advisory and Information Service, Alice Holt Lodge, Wrecclesham, Farnham, Surrey GU10 4LH

Brogdale Horticultural Trust, Brogdale Road, Faversham, Kent ME13 8XZ

British Trust For Conservation Volunteers, 36 St Mary Street, Wallingford, Oxfordshire, OX10 0EU

Common Ground, Seven Dials Warehouse, 44 Earlham Street, London WC2H 9LA

Community Forest Unit, Care of Countryside Commission (see below)

Council for the Protection of Rural England, Warwick House, 25 Buckingham Palace Road, London SW1W 0PP

Countryside Commission, John Dower House, Crescent Place, Cheltenham, Gloucestershire GL50 3RA

Countryside Council for Wales, Plas Penrhos Ffordd Penrhos, Bangor, Gwynedd LL57 2LQ

English Nature, Northminster House, Peterborough, Cambridgeshire PE1 1UA

Farming and Wildlife Advisory Group, National Agricultural Centre, Stoneleigh, Warwickshire CV8 2LZ

Forest Education Initiative, Great Eastern House, Tenison Road, Cambridge CB1 2DU

Forestry Commission (Head Office), 231 Costorphine Road, Edinburgh EH12 7AT

Green Wood Trust, Station Road, Coalbrookdale, Telford, Shropshire TF8 7DR

Sir Harold Hillier Gardens and Arboretum, Jermyn's Lane, Ampfield, Hampshire SO51 0QA

International Tree Foundation, Sandy Lane, Crawley Down, Crawley, West Sussex RH10 4HS

National Trust, 36 Queen Anne's Gate, London SW1H 9AS

Royal Botanic Gardens, Kew, Richmond, Surrey

Royal Botanic Gardens Edinburgh, 20A Inverleith Row, Edinburgh EH3 5LR

Royal Forestry Society, 102 High Street, Tring, Hertfordshire, HP23 4AF

Royal Scottish Forestry Society, The Stables, Dalkeith Country Park, Dalkeith, Middlothian EH22 2NA

Scottish National Heritage, 12 Hope Terrace, Edinburgh EH9 2AS

Tree Council, 51 Catherine Place, London SW1E 6DY

Veteran Trees Initiative, English Nature, Northminster House, Peterborough, Cambridgeshire PE1 1UA

Wildlife Trusts, The Green, Witham Park, Waterside South, Lincoln LN5 7RJ

Woodland Trust, Autumn Park, Dysart Road, Grantham, Lincolnshire NG31 6LL

Woodland Trust (Scotland), Glenruthuen Mill, Abbey Road, Auchterarder, Perth PH3 1DP

Woodland Trust (Wales), Pantyronnen, Pencarreg, Llanybydder, Dyfed SA40 9XG

Further Reading

1. BOOKS ABOUT TREE IDENTIFICATION

Those seeking information about a wider range of non-native trees in Britain are referred to:

Bean, W.J. (1970) (8th Edition) *Trees and Shrubs Hardy in the British Isles.* John Murray

Hillier Nurseries (1991) (6th edition) *The Hillier Manual of Trees and Shrubs.* David & Charles

Mitchell, A.F. and Wilkinson, J. (1988) *The Trees of Britain and Northern Europe.* HarperCollins

Mitchell, A.F. (1974) *A Field Guide to the Trees of Britain and Northern Europe.* HarperCollins

Mitchell, A.F. (1972) *Conifers in the British Isles.* Forestry Commission Booklet No 33. HMSO

Mitchell, A.F. (1981) *The Gardener's Book of Trees.* Dent

2. BOOKS ABOUT TREES

Milner, J. (1992) *The Tree Book* (guide to tree facts, crafts and lore). Acacia – Channel 4

Mitchell, A. (1996) *Alan Mitchell's Trees of Britain.* HarperCollins

White, J. (1995) *Forest and Woodland Trees in Britain.* Oxford University Press

Various Forestry Commission Handbooks. HMSO

3. WOODLAND ECOLOGY

Packham, J.R., Harding D.J.L. *et al* (1992, 1996 reprint) *Functional Ecology of Woodlands and Forests.* Chapman & Hall

Peterken, G.F. (1993 rev. ed.) *Woodland Conservation and Management.* Chapman & Hall

Peterken, G.F. (1996) *Natural Woodland: Ecology and Conservation in Northern Temperate Regions.* Cambridge University Press

4. HISTORY

Ingrouille, M. (1995) *Historical Ecology of the British Flora.* Chapman & Hall

Rackham, O. (1986) *The History of the Countryside.* Dent

Wilkinson, G. (1981) *A History of Britain's Trees.* Hutchinson

5. FOLKLORE AND TREE USAGE

Aaron, J. and Richards, E. (1990) *British Woodland Produce.* Stobart Davies

Edlin, H.L. (1949) *Woodland Crafts in Britain.* Batsford. (David & Charles 1973)

Edlin, H.L. (1969) (1994 reprint) *What Wood is That?* Thames & Hudson (reprint Stobart Davies)

Mabey, R. (1996) *Flora Britannica.* Sinclair-Stevenson

Wilks, J. (1972) *Trees of the British Isles in History and Legend.* Muller

6. TREES IN LITERATURE

Cotter, G. (1988) *Natural History Verse – An Anthology.* Christopher Helm

James, N.D.G. (1973) *A Book of Trees – An Anthology of Trees and Woodlands.* The Royal Forestry Society

King, A. and Clifford, S. (Ed) (1989) *Trees be Company (An Anthology of Poetry).* Bristol Press

Llewellyn-Williams, H. (1987) *The Tree Calendar.* Poetry Wales Press

Glossary

Acute at a narrow angle; pointed

Alternate (e.g. leaves) placed successively on each side (e.g. of a stem)

Ancient Woodland that dating from before AD 1700

Angiosperm flowering plant with ovules (later seeds) enclosed in ovary

Annual ring yearly increment of wood (in tree stem)

Apical (e.g. of buds) at or near the tip

Appressed (e.g. buds to a twig) pressed close to

Aril succulent covering around seed in Yew

Axil upper angle between petiole and stem, also between side vein and midrib

Bark external protective layer of woody stem and old root

Basal leaf part or flower nearest the stem

Berry many-seeded succulent fruit

Blade flat region of leaf or leaflet

Bloom blue-grey powdery deposit

Bole lower unbranched region of tree trunk

Bract small leaf beneath a flower, stalk or scale

Branchlet small branch

Broad-leaved tree angiosperm tree, typically with wide-bladed leaves

Burr knobbly outgrowth near bole base

Cambium region of actively dividing cells which produce new tissue

Carpel ovary together with style, at the tip of which is the stigma (receives the pollen)

Catkin a dense, often pendulous spike of tiny (usually single-sexed) flowers and bracts

Clone vegetative descendants of a single plant

Compound leaf one with a blade of two or more distinct leaflets

Cone single-sex flower-head and woody fruit in Conifers

Conifers gymnosperm trees with needle or scale-like leaves; most bear woody cones

Coppice to cut back to a low stump from which many new stems grow

Crown tree shape; influenced by upper trunk region and branches

Cultivar cultivated variety e.g. dwarf or cut-leaved form

Cyme (flower-head) forking cluster with flowers at stalk ends

Deciduous tree one with annual leaf drop (during Autumn in temperate regions)

Decussate successive pairs (e.g. of leaves on a stem) at right-angles to those preceding them

Dioecious with male and female flowers on separate plants

Drupe fleshy fruit usually with only one, stoney-coated seed

Entire (e.g. leaf) margin that is not toothed or lobed

Evergreen tree one with leaves retained all year

Fastigiate columnar crown from near vertical branches

Fluted (e.g. bole) with deep rounded, vertical grooves

Fruit tissue bearing and enclosing seed(s)

Gall abnormal tissue growth resulting from reaction to insect, fungal or bacterial activity

Glabrous smooth; lacking hairs

Gland small secretory organ

Glaucous blue-grey colour

Graft artificial fusion of aerial part (bud or stem) of one species on to rooted stem of another

Gymnosperm flowering plant with seeds unprotected by an ovary e.g. Coniferous trees

Hardwood alternate term for Broad-leaved tree

Heartwood central supportive core in trunk or branch

Hybrid offspring of parents of different species

Inflorescence flowering shoot or flower-head

Juvenile leaves grow on young trees or shoots and may differ in size and/or shape from leaves on older parts

Lanceolate spear-shaped, pointed at each end; broadest near the base

Latex milky fluid found in some plants

Leading shoot (leader) dominant central shoot in young tree

Leaflet a division of a compound leaf; lacks a bud at its base

Leaf scar mark left on stem when leaf falls off

Lenticel small pore in bark, often elliptical

Lobe segment (often rounded) of leaf or petal

Long shoot one extending each year from terminal bud growth

Midrib central main leaf vein

Monoecious with separate male and female flowers on the same plant

Needle narrow, pointed leaves of many Conifers

Opposite facing each other; paired (e.g. of leaves)

Ovate broadest near rounded base; pointed apex

Palmate of leaflets or lobes radiating from a central point

Panicle a much-branched inflorescence

Pendulous drooping; e.g. of catkins

Persistent remaining attached; e.g. of fruits

Petiole leaf stalk

Phloem vascular tissue responsible for sugar transport

Pinnate of a compound leaf in which the leaflets are borne either side of a central stalk (rachis)

Pistil female parts of a flower; one or more carpels

Pith central core of soft tissue in stems and some roots

Pollard to cut back branches to bole (at least 2m high) from which new stems grow

Prostrate growing close to the ground

Pubescent covered with soft, short hairs

Raceme inflorescence with stalked flowers; oldest at base

Rachis axis of compound leaf to which leaflets attach

Reflexed bent back (e.g. cone scale)

Resin sticky, often aromatic fluid found in most Conifers

Sapwood outer, water-conducting wood in trunk or branch

Scale modified leaf e.g. on bud surface or in cones

Sessile not stalked

Short shoot one with very limited annual extension

Shrub woody perennial much branched from near ground level

Softwood alternate term for Coniferous tree

Spike inflorescence with unstalked flowers; oldest at base

Stamen male flower part; filament and pollen-producing anther

Stipule leaf-like outgrowth at petiole base, usually paired

Stigma apex of female flower part which receives pollen

Sucker new shoot arising from the roots or stem base

Terminal at or near the apex

Timber large diameter trunks suitable for sawing into planks

Tree typically single-stemmed woody perennial capable of attaining at least 6m in height

Trifoliate compound leaf with 3 leaflets

Turnery wooden articles made on a lathe

Umbel flower-head with stalks like umbrella spokes

Vascular tissue cells of xylem and phloem responsible for the transport of water and food stuff

Vein conducting tissue visible in leaves, usually branched

Veneer thin sheet of timber cut from revolving log

Wildwood woodland resulting from natural colonisation following the last ice-age

Wood small diameter stems, especially those resulting from coppicing or pollarding

Wood(land) area of dense tree growth

Xylem (also known as wood) water conducting tissue which also provides mechanical support

Index